Socialist China, Capitalist China

China is currently encountering increasing social problems, together with the rise of mass discontent and public protest, despite having achieved enormous economic growth after nearly 30 years of market socialism and embracing globalization. The future of China thus depends not only on the economic progress the nation has achieved – and will achieve – but also on how the government addresses growing social tensions. Focusing on why social tensions have arisen despite economic prosperity and how the state is responding, this book presents rich, original data about many of the social challenges facing China, including rural–urban migration, unemployment, the healthcare crisis, the rise of religion, the desire for increased individualism, and new mass movements. It investigates governmental responses to deal with the problems including legal and political reforms and local governance innovations, throughout setting the discussion in the context of how far a traditionally "socialist" nation can be integrated into global capitalism. Overall, the book provides a timely, up-to-date, and down-to-earth examination of and reflection on China's continuing socio-economic and political transition.

Guoguang Wu holds a chair in China and Asia-Pacific Relations at the University of Victoria, Canada, where he also teaches in both departments of political science and history. The author of numerous books, he and Helen Lansdowne have co-edited two other volumes, also published by Routledge: *Zhao Ziyang and China's Political Future* and *China Turns to Multilateralism: Foreign Policy and Regional Security*. **Helen Lansdowne** is the Assistant Director at the Centre for Asia-Pacific Initiatives, University of Victoria, Canada. She also lectures in the department of Pacific and Asian Studies at the University of Victoria and in the department of Social Sciences at Camosun College.

China policy series
Series Editor: Zheng Yongnian
China Policy Institute, University of Nottingham, UK

1 **China and the New International Order**
Edited by Wang Gungwu and Zheng Yongnian

2 **China's Opening Society**
The non-state sector and governance
Edited by Zheng Yongnian and Joseph Fewsmith

3 **Zhao Ziyang and China's Political Future**
Edited by Guoguang Wu and Helen Lansdowne

4 **Hainan – State, Society, and Business in a Chinese Province**
Kjeld Erik Brodsgaard

5 **Non-Governmental Organizations in China**
The rise of dependent autonomy
Yiyi Lu

6 **Power and Sustainability of the Chinese State**
Edited by Keun Lee, Joon-Han Kim and Wing Thye Woo

7 **China's Information and Communications Technology Revolution**
Social changes and state responses
Edited by Xiaoling Zhang and Yongnian Zheng

8 **Socialist China, Capitalist China**
Social tension and political adaptation under economic globalization
Edited by Guoguang Wu and Helen Lansdowne

Socialist China, Capitalist China

Social tension and political adaptation under economic globalization

Edited by Guoguang Wu and Helen Lansdowne

Routledge
Taylor & Francis Group
LONDON AND NEW YORK

First published 2009
by Routledge
2 Park Square, Milton Park, Abingdon, Oxon OX14 4RN

Simultaneously published in the USA and Canada
by Routledge
270 Madison Ave, New York, NY 10016

Routledge is an imprint of the Taylor & Francis Group, an informa business

Typeset in Times by Wearset Ltd, Boldon, Tyne and Wear
Printed and bound in Great Britain by TJI Digital, Padstow, Cornwall

British Library Cataloguing in Publication Data
A catalogue record for this book is available from the British Library

Library of Congress Cataloging in Publication Data
Socialist China, capitalist China: social tension and political transition under economic globalization/edited by Guoguang Wu and Helen Lansdowne.
p. cm. – (China policy series)
Includes bibliographical references and index.

1. China–Politics and government–2002– 2. China–Social conditions–2000–
3. China–Economic conditions–2000– 4. Capitalism–China.
5. Socialism–China. I. Wu, Guoguang. II. Lansdowne, Helen, 1958–

JQ1510.S63 2009
320.951–dc22
2008041680

ISBN10: 0-415-48226-7 (hbk)
ISBN10: 0-203-88011-0 (ebk)

ISBN13: 978-0-415-48226-4 (hbk)
ISBN13: 978-0-203-88011-1 (ebk)

Contents

Figures

Tables

Contributors

Chih-jou Jay Chen received his Ph.D. from Duke University in 1997. He is Associate Research Fellow at the Institute of Sociology of Academia Sinica, a jointly appointed Associate Professor at the Institute of Sociology, National Tsing Hua University, and Associate Director of the Center for Contemporary China, National Tsing Hua University. He is the author of *Transforming Rural China: How Local Institutions Shape Property Rights in China* (London and New York: RoutledgeCurzon, 2004).

Carol Lee Hamrin is a Chinese affairs consultant, Research Professor at George Mason University, and Senior Associate with the Global China Center in Charlottesville, Virginia. With a Ph.D. in Chinese and comparative world history, and 25 years as a senior Research Specialist at the US Department of State, Carol Hamrin provides a long-term perspective on China's transformation. Her research focuses on how the dynamics that drive market reforms spill over into social and cultural arenas, with implications for China's ambitions as a great power and for the many aspects of US–China relations, from societal ties to government to business. Dr. Hamrin advises nonprofit organizations supporting social services and training projects for the development of China's Third Sector, works on human rights and religious rights policy issues, and writes on culture and religion. She earned the Secretary of State's Career Achievement Award in 2000, and received the Center for Public Justice Leadership Award for outstanding public service in 2003. Her books include *God and Caesar in China: Policy Implications of Church–State Tensions, Decision Making in Deng's China*, and *China and the Challenge of the Future*.

Yanzhong Huang received his Ph.D. from the University of Chicago, is Assistant Professor and Director of the Center for Global Health Studies at the John C. Whitehead School of Diplomacy and International Relations, Seton Hall University. In addition to his research interest in global health governance and health security, he has written extensively on Chinese politics in general, and health politics in particular. He has testified before Congressional Committees and is frequently consulted by major media outlets, pharmaceutical firms, and governmental and non-governmental organizations on global health issues. He was a visiting fellow at the Center for Strategic and International Studies (CSIS) in Washington, DC and a consultant of the Department of Foreign Affairs Canada (FAC). He is a Term Member of the Council on Foreign Relations, a member of the National Committee on US–China Relations, and a member of the Security Experts Council of the Gerson Lehrman Group.

Pierre F. Landry is Assistant Professor of political science at Yale University and the Director of Undergraduate Studies for the International Studies major. He is a member of the International Affairs Council and the Council on East Asian Studies at the MacMillan Center. Pierre Landry received his Ph.D. from the University of Michigan in 2000, and has been a research fellow with the Research Center for Contemporary China at Peking University since 1997. His research interests focus on Chinese politics, comparative local government, and quantitative comparative political analysis. He is the author of a book *Controlling Decentralization: The Party and Local Elites in Post-Deng China* (forthcoming at Cambridge University Press) as well as articles on various aspects of local governance and survey research methodology.

Helen Lansdowne has a B.A. and M.A. in Pacific and Asian Studies, University of Victoria and has been with the Centre for Asia-Pacific Initiatives (CAPI) as Associate Director since 1998. Her areas of expertise include rural China state–society relations and development and gender-related issues in mainland southeast Asia. She participated in and managed the Cambodia–Canada Legislative Support Project and the Vietnam Legislative Assistance Support Project, both CIDA funded and CAPI-administered. Ms Lansdowne also teaches courses including Southeast Asia and Developmental Theory in the Department of Pacific and Asian Studies, University of Victoria, and in the Department of Social Sciences, Camosun College. She is co-editor of *China Turns to Multilateralism: Foreign Policy and Regional Security* (Routledge, 2008).

Barrett McCormick is a professor in the Political Science Department at Marquette University. He completed his Ph.D. at the University of Wisconsin in 1985. McCormick has been at Marquette since 1984, except for two years, beginning in 1991, spent at the Australian National University. His current research project is about media markets and the transformation of China's public sphere. Previous projects include edited volumes and articles on US–China relations [with Edward Friedman, *What If China Doesn't Democratize?* (M. E. Sharpe, 2000)] and comparing China to Eastern Europe and East Asia [with Jonathan Unger, *The Future of Chinese Socialism* (M. E. Sharpe, 1996)]. McCormick's other publications also include *Political Reform in Post-Mao China* (California, 1990) and articles in journals such as *The China Journal*, *Journal of Asian Studies*, *Pacific Affairs*, *Issues and Studies*, and *Twenty-First Century*.

Yan Sun is a professor of political science at City University of New York, Graduate Center and Queens College. She was educated at Nanjing University,

Beijing School of Foreign Affairs and the Johns Hopkins University. She is the author of *Corruption and Market in Contemporary China* (Cornell, 2004) and *The Chinese Reassessment of Socialism* (Princeton, 1995). Her numerous professional articles on China's transitional politics and economy and on comparative Chinese/Russian transitions have appeared in *Comparative Politics, Communist and Post-Communist Studies, Asian Survey, Current History, Crime*, and *Law and Social Change*, among others.

Guoguang Wu is Chair in China and Asia-Pacific Relations, University of Victoria, where he also teaches at Departments of Political Science and History. He has a B.A. from Beijing University and a M.A. from the Graduate School of the Chinese Academy of Social Sciences. In the 1980s he worked as an editor of *People Daily* in Beijing, and participated in the policy advisory group on political reform to the national leadership. He later earned a Ph.D. in political science from Princeton University. With research interests on China's domestic politics and foreign relations, he is author, co-author, and editor of 16 books, including *The Anatomy of Political Power in China* (Marshall Cavendish Academic, 2005) and *China Turns to Multilateralism* (Routledge, 2008), and a contributor to journals including *Comparative Political Studies, The Pacific Review, Social Research*, and *Third World Quarterly.*

Xiaogang Wu is Assistant Professor in the Social Science Division, Hong Kong University of Science and Technology. He received a M.A. and Ph.D. from UCLA, a M.A. from Beijing University, and a B.A. from Renmin University, China. Dr. Wu's research interests include internal migration from rural to urban areas in China; social stratification and mobility in state socialist and post-socialist societies; labour markets issues in transition economies; education and social inequality; and the change of residential patterns in Shanghai. His recent publications include articles in *American Sociological Review, Demography*, and *Social Forces*.

Feng Xu has a Ph.D. in Political Science from York University, Canada (1998), is Assistant Professor in the Department of Political Science, University of Victoria. Her research interests include political economy and development in China, gender politics in China, migration in China and the Pacific Rim, global migration issues, globalization and governance, and transnational identities. Dr. Xu is author of *Women Migrant Workers in China's Economic Reform* (Macmillan and St. Martin's Press, 2000), and author/co-author of forthcoming articles in *Women's Studies International Forum, Governance*, and *Asian Survey.*

Keyuan Zou is Harris Professor of International Law at the Law School of the University of Central Lancashire (UCLan), UK. His specialty is international law and Chinese law. He obtained a LLD in 1989 from Peking University. Before joining UCLan in 2007, he worked in the Department of Political Science of Dalhousie University, Law School of Peking University, Institute of Geography of the University of Hannover, and East Asian Institute of

National University of Singapore. He has published over 50 refereed articles in more than 20 international journals. His latest publications include *Law of the Sea in East Asia: Issues and Prospects* (Routledge, 2005), *China's Marine Legal System and the Law of the Sea* (Martinus Nijhoff, 2005), *China's Legal Reform: Towards the Rule of Law* (Martinus Nijhoff, 2006), and, co-edited, *China-ASEAN Relations: Economic and Legal Dimensions* (World Scientific, 2006).

Acknowledgements

First and foremost, we would like to acknowledge the generous sponsorship we have received from the Foundation of International and Cross-Strait Studies (FICS), without which this volume and the preceding conference could not have come into being. In particular, we thank Jonathan Chen of FICS for his assistance with the conference grant application.

We should like to thank all participants to the conference held in October 2006 at the Centre for Asia-Pacific Initiatives, University of Victoria, from which this volume draws the papers as chapters.

We also thank our editor, Peter Sowden, for his professional handling of the manuscript.

Our deep gratitude should go to our colleagues at the Centre for Asia-Pacific Initiatives, University of Victoria, particularly to Stella Chan, Richard King, and Heidi Tyedmers for their immeasurable support in organizing the conference and formatting this collection. As well, a special thank you to the late Fenwick Lansdowne for his numerous hours of copy editing. This book is for him.

Guoguang Wu and Helen Lansdowne

1 Introduction

Helen Lansdowne and Guoguang Wu

It is a widely-held belief that the growth of material wealth yields increasing social tranquillity, but studies of modernization have long revealed that certain stages of economic development are often accompanied by social instability and political conflict.[1] Now, in the twenty-first century, after three decades of post-Mao economic reform, China is seemingly entering such a stage, with the ever building economic prosperity constantly intensifying, rather than ameliorating, social discrepancies, and provoking, rather than diminishing, public protests. The experience of China, however, is much different from that of other countries, which have been subject to the scrutiny of modernization theory and its up-to-date offspring, because, as this volume attempts to collectively demonstrate, it emerges in peculiar international and domestic institutional circumstances hallmarked by the embracing of globalization by an authoritarian state yet without apparent ideological confrontations.

In this "harmonious" combination of capitalist development and sustained communist-state apparatus, as it pertains in the case of China, who must pay the cost of the dizzying growth of the economy? Who are they who pay and, if they suffer, why do they suffer? Is it simply because economic development takes time to reach the level at which everybody benefits? Are there peculiar institutional arrangements which deny to those on whom the burden of payment falls the resources and opportunities for economic advancement, and even channels to express their discontent? How much have market reforms, and in particular, globalization, changed China in the social and political spheres? How and why do various social conflicts take place during the process of marketization and globalization? How are the efforts to remedy social problems in China constrained by the country's authoritarian politics? For the average citizen, life has changed drastically. What have been the responses to the changes that are currently being experienced? These are some of the questions that are the focus of contributors to this volume. Their aim is to explore in depth the new China, a hybrid China, a capitalist China but, at the same time, a socialist China.

Though many items have been published to examine China's reforms and globalization, the social and political implications for China under globalization are still insufficiently explored, especially regarding three points. First, globalization is fundamentally a capitalist phenomenon, while China still claims to be "socialist". Questions thus arise concerning what are the contradictions of China under globalization and what are their implications for a transitional China. This way of questioning the institutional "nature" of the economic–social–political systems still matters because in China the regime exploits both the capitalist economy and the communist ideology to support its legitimacy, while largely abandoning the merits of socialism. In other words, China under globalization is a unique case. In it scholars may find some significant clues to help them ponder the fundamental direction of human development and the balance between economic prosperity, social welfare, and political liberty.

Second, though economic marketization and globalization are widely applauded both within China and abroad, the social problems that have arisen in the process of their development have not been well examined in their context of the unique Chinese institutional arrangements that combine global capitalism and domestic communist dictatorship. In this volume, seen through a social lens, rather than only from the point of view of profit-making, China will show us a different landscape.

Third, the problem of this interwoven process of globalizing China with the dictatorship's strength dependent on the globalization is manifested in widespread political conflict. The Chinese political institutions that draw power from globalization at the same time refuse to countenance other aspects of globalization lying beyond the economy, and this refusal has formed the fundamental political obstacle to settling the social problems facing China today.

To address these three themes in China's globalization, namely, the institutional conflicts between socialism and capitalism, the social problems arising from globalization, and the political constraints China faces in resolving the problems, this volume explores how globalization has transformed China, as reflected in the social and political spheres. With the focus on the rise of social discontent in parallel with successful economic development and the attempts of the state to deal with social tensions within the political framework of authoritarianism, this volume joins the ongoing scholarly discussions of the social impacts of globalization and the future of China's rise, while aiming to contribute to both the examination of China under authoritarian marketizing transition and, in general, to the comprehension of political economy and political sociology of modernization in developing nations.

"Market socialism", or "Leninist capitalism"? China's economic reforms under a social lens

Three decades have passed since the historic year of 1978, the year marked by Deng Xiaoping's throwing open China's doors to the world and ushering in what would become known as "market socialism". The aftermath left China watchers breathless and flummoxed; breathless because of the pace of change being witnessed and flummoxed because of the political about-face this change represents. It was tempting for many scholars, as market socialism quickly turned to market capitalism, to pose the question of whether the world would see

China assume a democratic face.[2] However, such a modernist-driven question now seems outdated, an anachronism from the pre-Tiananmen years; political changes have indeed taken place in today's China, but not in a way that had been anticipated. A new kind of authoritarian state has emerged, one that exploits both the capitalist economy and communist ideology to support its legitimacy, while the benefits of socialism are nowhere to be seen. With the Chinese Communist Party still firmly in control, the aim of the state continues to be one of ensuring stability, not for the average citizen, but rather, for itself, as well as for those players such as foreign investors and local entrepreneurs who have a direct stake in the international marketplace.

Over the past 30 years, China's socialist state has pursued a decidedly capitalist path of development. It moved from a command economy to one that initially advocated the household responsibility system of farming, the formation of rural township-village enterprises, the encouraging of foreign trade and investment under the guise of joint ventures and special economic zones, the relaxing of state controls over select prices, investment in industrial production and, in the workforce, education and training programmes, to one whose policies endorse an open global market system. The result has been a stunning rate of economic growth. Double-digit figures marked the 1980s and 1990s with real growth rates of more than 9 per cent of the average with several peak years of economic growth higher than 13 per cent.[3] By the twenty-first century, China had become globally engaged, both economically and politically,[4] and could boast a dramatic rise in comprehensive national power.

However, economic gains have come at considerable cost. With per capita income having more than tripled in the last 15 years, the increased standard of living has not been universally enjoyed throughout China, and economic growth and structural demands placed on the state as part and parcel of "market socialism" have created new challenges. Farmers, farmer migrant workers in urban areas, and urban working classes are prominent among those who shoulder the burden of the social cost of economic development, as Chapters 2, 3, and 4 of this volume demonstrate. The new industrial economy of China has led to the country's shifting away from its agrarian roots and moving towards an urbanized society. In 2003, urban per capita income was more than three times the rural average, up from twice the rural average during the 1980s.[5] This change over the past 25 years has translated into roughly 12 to 13 million people per annum leaving their farms to take up non-agricultural employment. For many, a "hand-to-mouth" existence is their reality, but the dream of being part of the growing urban middle class sends these workers far from their families and homes as they gravitate to the cities. This hope of improving their economic situation is what the state depends on to ensure a steady stream of workers; it is this flexible labour force that has become the lynchpin to China's economic success, and the major attraction for foreign direct investment to China, which in turn has led to the expansion of the export production sector, initially organized in the tightly-controlled Special Economic Zones.

For most of the rural migrant labour force the gap between themselves and their urban counterparts is wide. The 150 million rural workers, the ever-growing "floating population", must often take any type of job to survive, jobs such as short-term employment on construction sites, in factories, or in the service sector. Their precarious position is further complicated by the ever-present urban household registration system or *hukou* that continues to favour permanent urban residents over temporary ones. The *hukou*, a hold-over of the Mao years, was originally created to ensure that rural people stayed put in the communes in the countryside rather than making their way to the cities to seek employment in the privileged State-Owned Enterprises. Now, as Xiaogang Wu (Chapter 3) points out, "the system continues to play a critical role in drawing a social boundary in China's emerging labour markets and stratification system". Regardless of the location of employment there remains a persistent double standard, which helps to ensure that a vulnerable/flexible labour force continues to be available.

The shift from a planned, command economy to a state-regulated market economy has not been accompanied by a fundamental shift from a Leninist political system, though a new form of authoritarianism is emerging in the sense that it now incorporates not only the market mechanism but also some neo-liberal practices to its governance similar to those of states in the West, as Feng Xu (Chapter 4) points out in her chapter. This approach gives the Chinese state an appearance of adopting international norms and standards of employment like those found in the West. Chinese workers are now free to work outside the previous system of the *danwei* but their options are severely limited. This sleight-of-hand arrangement provides the state with a convenient mechanism for having not to provide social welfare, while at the same time it ensures the existence of a vulnerable/flexible labour force to supply the export production and service sectors in the ever-growing economy.

As with the changes of class relations, the imbalance between the profit-making and social welfare sectors is notable in conjunction with economic development, as the latter is being eroded by a market transition without a corresponding increase of citizens' power to influence public finance. For example, during the height of socialism, basic healthcare was provided under the "barefoot doctor" system throughout the country. With "market socialism" a new approach to healthcare was undertaken, with drastic consequences. Hospitals for profit now exist in China and both public and private hospitals are allowed to charge for drugs, often at inflated prices. The major share of healthcare support goes to the urban areas where larger hospitals tend to attract more funding. Public hospitals are being sold off to the private sector with the profits being pocketed by local government officials. As Yanzhong Huang points out in his chapter (Chapter 5) on the political forces behind the changes to China's healthcare system, the ability of government officials to shirk their responsibility to provide universal, affordable, healthcare has led to healthcare becoming prohibitive for the majority of the people in China. Of course, healthcare is not the only sector of Chinese society that is rife with opportunistic cadres. They are everywhere, and the result is that China in its new guise as a capitalist economy has lost many of the benefits of socialism previously enjoyed by its citizens.

Properly, the term, "Leninist capitalism", therefore, should be used for conceptualizing the China that has experienced three decades of economic reforms, and where, as viewed through the lens of social equality, justice, and welfare, the merits provided by either market or socialism are virtually absent. This label emphasizes how the Leninist political institutions, either residual or continuously open to different interpretations, employ the capital-dominating markets to shape the new political economy of China. This combination doubtlessly has its advantages for promoting economic development, because monopolized political power aids powerful capital, and vice versa, to their mutual benefit. It is socially unjust, however; it utilizes both political and economic control to block the public decision-making and market opportunities of ordinary citizens, or at the very least, puts them at an extreme disadvantage in both regards. It is "extreme" in comparison with the market without political authoritarianism, where free labour can use the power of numbers to gain benefits; it is also extreme in contrast with socialism, under which the working classes are entitled to social rights and social welfare, and may even enjoy some of them in practice. China in its new guise as a capitalist economy has lost many of the previous hard-won benefits of socialism, while state control of resources together with authoritarian deprivation of civic freedoms have reduced the opportunities that a free market may provide for the well-being of ordinary citizens.

Who gets what through China's globalizing? The politics of authoritarian–capitalist integration

This is the politics of the involvement of the authoritarian China with market-driven globalization, in the classic sense of the politics of who gets what. In the material world, the Chinese state helps international capital gain cheap labour through its institutional "advantages" that actualize the monopoly of resources and opportunities, apportioning as small a share as possible to the majority of this populous nation, while the regime and its elite supporters gain every benefit, ranging from political legitimacy to daily luxury consumption through both institutional and illegal methods. In the spiritual world, however, globalization tends to empower Chinese citizens in terms of information access, belief alternatives, and the like, and here the state turns its power to the reducing of such a trend, using every possible means to circumscribe the growth of individual and societal autonomy. In other words, the Chinese authoritarian regime frowns upon and chooses to repress the spiritual effects of globalization, while it accepts and enjoys the wealth created by Chinese workers responsible for its success.

Religion in China is a case in point. The opening-up of China to the global market economy has led to the opening-up of other sectors in society, including religion. In principle, the state has endorsed religious freedom, as suggested in its signing of a number of multilateral agreements, including the UN's International Covenant on Political and Civil Rights in 1998.[6] In addition, faith-based organizations have been permitted to provide some social services that in the past had been provided by the state, thereby allowing the state to abdicate its responsibilities. However, the confines of operating in China are restrictive. As Carol Lee Hamrin (Chapter 6) shows, Christian groups are allowed to operate only under the auspices of state-sanctioned official churches, which must comply with restrictive rules and regulations.

Mass communication is another field in which the state manages to control citizen access to the information flow provided by globalization. As Barrett McCormick argues in his chapter (Chapter 7) on the examination of mechanisms of state control in mass media, the open-ended ability of the state to intervene and set restrictions on the content of mass media without being held accountable has led to its continued use of domination rather than hegemony to maintain stability. Whenever the state is able to openly dominate without suffering political repercussions, it will do so.

The double-edged influence of globalization on China often brings about an illusion that fools observers of China's change. There are plenty of instances in which the state makes use of the façade of a freer society that globalization appears to bring to various aspects of Chinese life, while in reality it employs underlying authoritarian mechanisms that ensure state control. It should be highlighted, therefore, that, as China embraces globalization, it is the authoritarian state, rather than any other power or body, that decides who gets what of the pie provided by China's globalizing. Furthermore, the state is to a great degree hijacked by self-serving elites, while the majority of people have almost no influence on the decisions concerning fiscal policy. They, as demonstrated in this volume, particularly in Chapters 8 and 2, contributed by Keyuan Zou and Jay Chen, respectively, must resort to personal petitions or collective demonstrations to draw the attention of government to their sufferings, ways of expressing discontents that are often ineffective. Those who are involved in such demonstrations are also often regarded as enemies by the local Party-state cadres, if not by the whole regime. Yes, globalization is stimulating changes in and challenges to many aspects of China, but, as we look at what political facilities Chinese institutions provide for settling the social problems, and at their failure to do so, we find that these political institutions are concerned mainly with defending and maintaining authoritarianism and with little else.

For example, the flood of protests by Chinese citizens in recent years has led to the state's revising its system of *xinfang*, a system of petitioning to air grievances that dates back to Mao's era, in the tradition of "following the mass line". But the new initiatives also put limits on the users of the *xinfang* system, with various restrictions for the petitioners, who are already at a great disadvantage. The system of *xinfang* may appear to provide another avenue of dispute resolution for the average citizen of China, and it most certainly helps to relieve pressure on the courts, but as Keyuan Zou points out in his chapter on the contradiction of the revised *xinfang* system, the system actually becomes a mechanism of social control, "a governing instrument of the ruling party in China".

The same contradiction can be found in China's legal system, another major institution for settling social conflicts. As Pierre Landry points out (Chapter 9), despite the state's attempting to create a legal climate that promotes a rule-of-law society, there is no independent judiciary, no proper judicial review of appeals, and court cases are often tainted with political bias, particularly if the petitioner is challenging the state. At present, the very fact of engagement with the institution helps to legitimize the Chinese state, despite case results. However, this rather hollow legitimacy will be hard to sustain if legal mechanisms prove to be empty avenues of recourse for the average citizen.

Court use might speak more to the increased number of disputes rather than to institutional legitimacy. As Chen (Chapter 2) reminds us in his chapter on the escalation of social protests, there has been an increase in the number of people and groups protesting and also a change in the types of issues being brought forward. Common problems include: property rights, cadre corruption, labour issues, environmental problems, and taxation. Among these, corruption is prominent and is one of the defining characteristics of post-Mao China. It is a problem that has grown over the past three decades and is now so rampant and widespread that it threatens to become endemic.[7] In a manner reminiscent of the "Anti-Corruption Struggle" of the mid-1990s when much effort on the part of the central government was put into offering the appearance of tackling the issue of corrupt officials, a "paste-over" approach is being taken today. President Hu Jintao, in January of 2008 publicly acknowledged the severity of the situation but offered only nebulous solutions while a token number of cadres was charged with corruption, so providing a smoke screen to conceal ineptitude.[8] Selective enforcement of China's anti-corruption laws provides the illusion of state remedy without truly addressing the problem.[9] What would be a better way to deal with China's corruption? In her contribution to this volume, Yan Sun (Chapter 10) argues that "at the very least, democracy alone, in the absence of attendant economic development and its social fallout, will not suffice to restrain corruption". This reservation about democracy is reasonable, but, as all the preceding chapters have demonstrated through their investigations of different aspects of Chinese development, the lack of government accountability and of citizens' civic rights are the two major institutional sources of social tensions in transitional China. In the Chinese politics of who is getting what, average citizens have no legal and effective way to voice their discontent, and feel deprived of material and spiritual sources and opportunities. Democracy cannot solve all social problems, of course; but it is unquestionable that a democracy that functions well can provide the populace with some basic and vital channels to join the game of who gets what in the nation. Citizens are not always right, and they are not saints, but the state leaders, either Communist, self-claimed omni-representative, or democratically elected, are also fallible in both public decision-making and personal morality. If government officials are corrupt, the nation's citizens should have the legal right to protest.

Organization of the volume

The substantive content of the volume opens with Chih-jou Jay Chen's chapter on "Growing social unrest, risings discontents and popular protest", an overview of protest movements in today's China. Setting the stage for the remaining chapters,

Chen provides an examination of the increased number of "mass incidents", the source of the protests, as well as who is protesting. Although not all protests are effective, Chen argues that through the act of protesting, various groups in society are coming together to challenge local authority, thereby fundamentally re-configuring state-society relations.

A particularly pressing issue that causes social tension is the disparity of the economic opportunities and social rights between rural and urban residents. Chapter 3, "Household registration, social exclusion, and rural migrants in cities", by Xiaogang Wu takes a close look at the rural–urban migrant labour, with an analysis of the institutional contribution to such disparity, particularly how the *hukou* system, created during the Mao years to restrict rural–urban migration and now somewhat relaxed, continues to be an effective tool to disadvantage rural population during China's urbanization.

The topic of limited employment opportunities is taken up by Feng Xu in Chapter 4, "Training the unemployed to become active job-seekers in post-Mao China". Through an examination of job training, employment, and community service centres, Xu offers an analysis of the new approach being taken by the state, and best thought of as a blend of authoritarianism and neo-liberalism, to deal with high rates of urban unemployment. The unemployed would-be-worker is given the task of creating or recreating him/herself for the new flexible job market, but freedom to do so is hampered by the state in its use of systems of control that are reminiscent of the "resident committee".

The next chapter moves to healthcare. In "An institutional analysis of China's failed healthcare reform", Yanzhong Huang argues that as a result of the administrative changes of fiscal decentralization experienced in the health sector during market reform a new political climate of "buck-passing" has emerged. Fiscal responsibilities are now shared with a number of central ministries as well as local government, thereby enabling state actors to simply pass the buck when dealing with healthcare. The result is a system of healthcare that is inaccessible, inequitable, of poor quality, and too expensive.

In Chapters 6 and 7 the volume turns to the non-material dimensions of social problems. In the work on "China, Christianity and the global market of belief systems", Carol Lee Hamrin examines the contradictions inherent in China's sanctioning of faith-based organizations. The opening of China to global market forces has led to a demand for the opening of other aspects of society, including religion, but the Chinese party-state denies its citizens spiritual freedom. Official Christian churches have been set up in China but they are expected to operate under tight rules and regulations set down by the state. Such restricted access to religion has led to the coming together of unofficial congregations and the employing of passive resistance.

Reluctance by the state to allow greater freedom of religion has its parallel in China's media, the subject of Chapter 7, contributed by Barrett McCormick under the title of "*Super Voice Girls* and *Freezing Point*: media, hegemony and domination in the new China". This chapter offers two examples of Chinese media, namely, *Super Voice Girls*, a Chinese version of the popular *American Idol* television series, and a newspaper weekly supplement, *Freezing Point*, to test whether China has moved to a phase of political control that is more hegemonic than dominating. Together, the examples show how the entertainment is sanitized by the state, while censorship remains arbitrary. The author argues that the open-ended ability of the state to intervene and set restrictions on content without being held accountable has led to its continued use of domination rather than hegemony.

The last three chapters before the Conclusion investigate the legal and political arrangements for accommodating social troubles. In Chapter 8, "Granting or refusing the right to petition: the dilemma of China's *xinfang* system", Keyuan Zou examines China's mass petition system, or *xinfang*, its recent reform, and the limitations for the system and the reform. Pierre Landry focuses on legal reform in the chapter on "The diffusion of legal institutions in China", and offers an examination of why some people make use of the courts and how successful adopters of the system help facilitate the dissemination of institutional legal reforms. Chapter 10 is Yan Sun's work, "Would democratization help remedy China's corruption problem? Comparative insights on China and India", in which the author poses the question through examining how the level of development and the type of regime interactively affect governmental corruption.

Notes

1 Samuel P. Huntington, *Political Order in Changing Societies*, New Haven, Connecticut: Yale University Press, 1968.
2 See Suzanne Ogden, *Inklings of Democracy in China*, Cambridge, Massachusetts: Harvard University Asia Center, 2002.
3 Zuliu Hu and Mohsin S. Khan, *Why Is China Growing So Fast*, Washington, D.C.: International Monetary Fund, *Economic Issues* (8), 1997.
4 See Guoguang Wu and Helen Lansdowne (eds), *China Turns to Multilateralism: Foreign Policy and Regional Security*, London: Routledge Contemporary China Series, 2008.
5 B. Zhao and S. P. Tong, "Unequal economic development in China: spatial disparities and regional policy reconsideration, 1985–1995", *Regional Studies* 34 (6), 2000, pp. 549–61.
6 It should be noted that so far the Chinese national legislation has chosen to take no action to approve China's joining of this Covenant, which simply means the Covenant has not taken effect in China.
7 Hilton Root, "Corruption in China: Has It Become Systemic?", *Asian Survey* 36(8), August 1996. For a thorough analysis of the connection between economic liberalization and corruption see Gordon White, "Corruption and the Transition from Socialism in China", *Journal of Law and Society* 23(1), March 1996, pp. 149–69.
8 "China in Anti-Corruption Struggle", BBC News, Wednesday, 16 January 2008, 08:17 GMT. Available online at: news.bbc.co.uk/2/hi/asia-pacific/7191021.stm.
9 See Flora Sapio, "Implementing Anticorruption in the PRC Patterns of Selectivity", Working Paper No. 10, Sweden: Centre for East and Southeast Asian Studies, Lund University, 2005.

2 Growing social unrest in China

Rising social discontents and popular protests

Chih-jou Jay Chen

Introduction

After nearly three decades of "reform and opening", China's burgeoning economy still shows relentless growth. But economic growth has been uneven, benefiting the elite rather than the workers and farmers, and promoting the development of the cities more than the countryside. Economic development has brought in its wake a host of social and political problems revolving around official corruption and malpractices, ambiguous and unjust property rights, and environmental pollution, which in turn have fuelled grievances. This situation has indeed raised the citizenship consciousness of ordinary citizens who have seen the failure of their expectation for redress of grievances through legal or political institutions. As a result, a baffling array of social protests has appeared. The increasing popular discontent and mass protests signal a new set of state–society relations. These relations appear to be developing into key factors that are challenging regime stability in the near future, and to a certain extent, are becoming primary incentives behind regime transformation.

This chapter describes incidents of mass protest in China over the past decade, identifying issues that the principal social groups have taken up. Highlighted as well are the emerging trends of recent incidents which illuminate the underlying causes of particular aspects of social unrest. Within this context the chapter assesses the potential impact of the social struggles on China's political economy.

As mass protests become an inextricable part of daily life in China, statistics released by the Chinese government documenting increasing collective protests are frequently cited by news analyses and academic studies. More specifically, public protests, officially labelled "mass incidents" (*quntixing shijian*), have escalated dramatically over the past few years, growing almost fourfold between 1993–99 (from 8,700 to 32,000), and concurrently tenfold between 1993–2005 (from 8,700 to 87,000). These incidents come in various forms, from peacefully petitioning small groups, to sit-ins, marches, rallies, labour or merchant strikes, student demonstrations, ethnic conflict, and even violent riots. In 2005, mass incidents that involved "disturbing social order" rose by 13 per cent, while those that "interfered with government business" showed an upward surge of 19 per cent.[1] In November 2006, Beijing reported that the number of "mass incidents" that the police "had dealt with" in the first three quarters of that year had dropped by 22 per cent compared with the statistics of the same period of the preceding year.[2] However, it is unclear whether these statistics indicate a real decline in protests or are simply figures engineered for political purposes.[3] Like many other official statistics in China, the figures for protests cannot be independently verified. Nevertheless, it is apparent that the alarming rise of mass protests over the past decade has provoked the government to pledge the building of a harmonious society.

This chapter highlights the various sources of social protest since the mid-1990s and the substantial changes of protest issues emerging in the mid-2000s. What becomes apparent in this analysis is not only the growth in frequency and scale of violence but also the involvement of various social groups, old and new which, in turn, signals the unleashing of new social forces and state-society relations.

Social groups and issues of mass protests

What are the sources of social tensions and "mass incidents" in current China? Who, indeed, are those disgruntled groups and what constitutes the basis of their contentious issues? Over the past decade, from the mid-1990s to mid-2000s, what (if any) are the significant changes in social contentions and the characteristics of disgruntled groups? How has social discontent and protest evolved coterminously with the rapid promulgation of reforms? Are the old disgruntled groups – namely, state-firm workers in cities and poor peasants in inland areas – protesting against new social injustices, or are they still engaged with old issues such as unpaid laid-off subsidies or rising taxes? Are there newly emerged discontented groups whose contested claims mark unique social tensions? What are the implications of the various upswings in protests on state-society relations and regime transformation in China?

It is against the background of these questions that this study has constructed a database by collecting as many reports as possible on China's mass protests in the press from 1997 to 2006, which identifies major sources of Chinese mass protests.[4] While by no means statistically representative of national conditions throughout China, this news database reflects the types of problems resulting from unregulated economic development and insufficient political reform. So far, no public quantitative data exists on the frequency, intensity, or types of popular protests in China, but sporadic media reports with remarkable patterns of anecdotal evidence still provide useful information that calls for further analysis.

An analysis of these reported mass protest incidents presents a frequency distribution of the participants and issues involved (Table 2.1 and Table 2.2). A listing of the major social groups and issues involved in mass protests in urban areas are:

1 State-owned enterprise (SOE) or collective-owned enterprise (COE) workers, laid-off, retired, or still employed, who are engaged in protesting for unpaid

(or insufficient) payments and/or for their status in the employment hierarchy while their firms were being privatized.

2 City dwellers protesting over the terms and inadequate compensation offered for their requisitioned (or to be requisitioned) homes for city redevelopment.

3 Students rioting over rising fees and the "downgraded" status of their diplomas from the higher status which the authorities had promised that these diplomas would have.

Table 2.1 The distribution of mass protest groups in China, 1997–2006 (number of reported incidents)

	1997	*1998*	*1999*	*2000*	*2001*	*2002*	*2003*	*2004*	*2005*	*2006*	*Total*
Urban											
SOE/COE workers	4	15	18	9	8	30	20	22	25	25	176
Displaced city residents		2	4	1	2	1	17	3	7	6	43
Ordinary citizens	4				1	1	4	7	14	14	45
Falung Gong			19	9	4	1	1				34
FDI workers	1					1	1	10	15	4	32
Taxi drivers	1	4	1		3	3	1	3	7	3	26
Students			2	2	1	3	3	2	3	9	25
Home owners/ city residents						2	4		5	10	21
Peasant workers							2	6	9	4	21
Merchants and vendors		1	1			1	1	1	6	3	14
Investors		5	3	1		1	1		1		12
Tricycle drivers	3	2		1	1		1	1		1	10
Retired state employees			1					1	3	1	6
Other occupational groups[a]		2	2	2		3	2	2	4	6	23
Others[b]		1		1	3	2	3	11	8	14	43
Rural											
Peasants/villagers	4	4	7	5	1	13	7	24	40	65	170
Ethnic minority	1	1		2				1	3	1	9
Investors		2	1				1				4
Others[c]							2	4	2	3	11
Total	18	39	59	33	23	63	71	98	152	169	725

Source: The author's database of mass protest news in China.

Notes

a "Other occupational groups" in urban areas includes teachers, bus drivers, motorcycle drivers, truck drivers, real estate developers, and other occupational groups.

b "Others" in urban areas includes Christians, consumers, foreigners, job seekers, ethnic minority groups, pet owners, relatives of patients/victims, student parents, sports fans, and the gathering of more than one group in a single event.

c "Others" in rural areas includes fishermen, patients, prisoners, teachers, and some events in which more than one group participate.

Table 2.2 The distribution of mass protest issues in China, 1997–2006 (number of reported incidents)

	1997	*1998*	*1999*	*2000*	*2001*	*2002*	*2003*	*2004*	*2005*	*2006*	*Total*
Urban											
SOE/COE wage or pension disputes	3	10	16	9	6	27	11	3	14	2	101
Anti-privatization/ anti-marketization	1	5	2		2	3	9	13	10	21	66
Urban relocation/ forced evictions		2	4	1	2	1	17	3	12	6	48
Falun Gong			19	9	4	1	1				34
Wage or layoff disputes in non-state firms	1					1	3	10	17	6	38
Fees or Tolls		5	2		5	1	1	1	4	1	20
Worker rights in non-state firms						1		7	8	3	19
Anti-Japan/US/ Taiwan-Independent			2			2	2	1	9		16
Students' rights						1	1	1	1	7	11
Rural											0
Rural land seizures	3	2	3	1	1	5	1	19	18	44	97
Election disputes/ cadre corruption		1	2	1		2	1	3	4	4	18
Tax and fees		1	2	2		1	1		2		9
Urban and Rural											0
Law enforcement/ police misconduct	2			2	1	2	3	8	6	11	35
Income rights of occupational groups	3	4	2	1				7	7	9	33
Specific policy/ regulation	1	1		2		3	3	2	7	8	27
Environmental/ community safety						4	2		10	11	27
Incidental conflict	3					1	1	5	9	6	25
Property rights						2	3	1	2	11	19
Investment		6	4	2		1	2		1		16
SARS							5	6			11
Income rights of state employees			1	2		1	1	1	3	2	11
Others[a]	1	2	0	1	2	3	3	7	8	17	44
Total	18	39	59	33	23	63	71	98	152	169	725

Source: The author's database of mass protest news in China.

Note

a The "Others" includes events associated with ineffective administration, ethnic minority conflict, medical malpractice, consumer complaints, regional price inflation, religious oppression, gatherings of petitioners, and some unspecified reasons.

4 Private homeowners organizing for better service delivery by property managers, for transfers of the usage of public amenities, for access to which is included in the sales contract for an apartment, and a variety of property rights relations with the developers and local governments.
5 Occupational groups, particularly taxi drivers, teachers, tricycle drivers, and merchants struggling for their respective work rights or complaining about specific regulations harmful to their benefits or income rights.
6 Peasant workers in foreign-funded firms protesting against anomalies in their wage remuneration, and their working environment.
7 Falun Gong members and other political dissidents confronting and challenging the Communist Party's monopoly of power.

Among the abovementioned protest groups, the Falun Gong and pro-democracy movements arose from specific political contexts and have been acting mostly on their own terms and initiatives. Falun Gong's confrontation with the state which culminated in 1999 sparked off world-wide criticism of the Chinese government. Falun Gong and pro-democracy dissidents are relatively well-organized across the country, although they are not powerful enough to pose a great threat to the stability of the regime. Since they have drawn vast media and scholarly attention, this chapter excludes them from the discussion of mass protests in China.[5]

In the rural areas various specific issues single out the peasants as the principal participants of mass protest. The most important issue that emerged in the late 1990s and which grew to serious proportions after 2003 was linked to land seizures in suburban rural areas where local cadres underpaid or embezzled the compensation due to peasants for the seizure of their lands. The second confrontational rural issue relates to village elections and cadres' corruption, followed by the other important issue of pollution and environmental protection. Mass protests regarding taxes and fees mostly occurred in the late 1990s, but faded out in the mid-2000s, presumably due to China's decision to reduce and gradually cancel agricultural taxes.

Urban unrest of workers' protests

The first and biggest category of mass protests in China involves the SOE or COE workers (or former workers), who launched mass protests against unemployment, cuts and/or suspension in pay and benefits, loss of pensions, and managerial corruption. China's market-oriented reform measures on SOEs were introduced in the early 1990s, and exacerbated in the late 1990s and early 2000s when further privatization measures were implemented. Since the mid-1990s, the SOE sector has been downgrading, with employees declining from 112 million in 1996, to 81 million in 2000, and finally to 62 million in 2004 (China Statistical Yearbook 2000, 2005). Casting off such a massive army of employees from the Chinese state's productive sector would necessarily have dictated the existence of policies and programmes for re-deployment of the unemployed masses. But the government's re-employment programmes have hardly improved the situation of the massive lay-offs (Gu 1999). Every step along the path of market reform has amounted to a setback for the social status and livelihood of SOE and COE workers who were not only deprived of their jobs but also of various social welfare provisions and other benefits. Once the pride of Mao's China, they felt betrayed, hopeless, and desperate. As a result, not surprisingly, incidents of contentious collective action by displaced workers protesting against late pay-cheques and unreasonable layoffs have erupted in various parts of the country, particularly in the traditionally heavy industrial-oriented northeast provinces. This has led to backtracking in further SOE reforms (Lee 1999, 2000; Weston 2004).

Although no public statistics on the frequency and types of workers' protests is available, figures in labour disputes provide a clue as to the extent of contentious labour issues in China. The number of labour disputes increased from 47,951 cases in 1996, to 135,206 in 2000, and skyrocketed to 313,773 in 2005. This represents an average annual dispute growth rate of 24 per cent. Among others, the number of *collective* labour disputes grew from 3,150 in 1996, to 8,247 in 2000, and again jumped to 19,387 in 2005, with a sixfold increase in the period of 1996–2005. Furthermore, in terms of the number of cases or of workers involved, labour disputes occurring in SOEs and COEs have remained significantly large compared with those in the non-state sector. In 1996, 32,706 SOE and COE workers were involved in collective labour disputes. This was a massive 35 per cent of the total work-force involved in collective labour disputes. In 2003, the number increased more than tenfold to 342,590 and accounted for 67 per cent of the total work-force involved in collective labour disputes (Table 2.3). After more than a decade of reforms in the SOE and COE sectors, labour dispute statistics show a steady annual deterioration of workers' satisfaction.

The fast-increasing number of workers involved in collective labour disputes since 2002 corresponds with this study's news dataset of mass protests in China. From the news reports in 1997–2006, among various social groups involved in mass protests, the number of the protests launched by SOE or COE workers jumped nearly fourfold from 8 to 30 in 2001–02, and then remained at the height until 2006 (Table 2.1). Insofar as labour protests were concerned, the number of protest incidents fighting for laid-off stipends or pensions amounted to 27 and 11 in 2002 and 2003, respectively, which were leading other contentious issues in urban China in 1997–2006 (Table 2.2).

Many of the strikes and workers' protests that were endemic in urban China in the early 2000s narrowly focused on economic compensation and revolved around such income-related issues as unpaid or underpaid wages and laid-off compensations or pensions (Hurst and O'Brien, 2002). The strikers' demands were individual and firm-oriented. Nevertheless, as the unrest moved into the mid-2000s, issues and certain component aspects of workers' mass protests gradually expanded. Workers' protests took root and were driven by their anti-privatization actions in state firms and the burning issues of workers' rights in foreign-funded firms.

Table 2.3 Labour disputes in China, 1992–2005

Year	*Total number of labour disputes*	*Number of collective labour disputes*	*Total number of workers involved in labour disputes*	*Number of workers involved in collective disputes*	*SOE and COE enterprises (%)*	*State organs and institutions (%)*	*FDI enterprises (%)*	*Private sector enterprises (%)*	*Others (%)*
1992	8,150	548	17,417	9,100	–	–	–	–	–
1993	12,368	684	35,683	19,468	–	–	–	–	–
1994	19,098	1,482	77,794	52,637	–	–	–	–	–
1995	33,030	2,588	122,512	77,340	–	–	–	–	–
1996	47,951	3,150	189,120	92,203	35	1	58	5	0
1997	71,524	4,109	221,115	132,647	41	1	45	12	1
1998	93,649	6,767	358,531	251,268	47	0	34	17	0
1999	120,191	9,043	473,957	319,241	41	0	4	21	1
2000	135,206	8,247	422,617	259,445	46	1	24	24	5
2001	154,621	9,847	467,150	286,680	55	1	18	25	0
2002	184,116	11,024	608,396	374,956	53	1	13	31	1
2003	226,391	10,823	801,042	514,573	67	1	9	23	1
2004	260,471	19,241	764,981	477,992	–	–	–	–	–
2005	313,773	19,387	744,195	409,819					

Source: China Statistical Yearbook, various years.

Note

Private sector enterprises include private enterprises, share-holding, joint ownership enterprises and limited liability corporations.

For example, among the 25 reports on SOE/COE worker protests in 2006, 21 of such protests, rather than fighting for particular income rights issues such as unpaid or underpaid wages, targeted the privatization or sell-out of firms for which they had spent their entire lives working. In the meantime, white-collar workers from the state sector joined the struggles of their blue-collar comrades. Since 1998, a restructuring and downsizing of administrative agencies was launched with a more rigorous civil-service code aimed at constraining the number of officials. Such a downsizing "institute reform" targeted its once-highly cosseted state work force and thus led to discontent and tensions not only in the SOEs but also in the state organs and other public institutions.

A closer look at the mass protest news in 2006 highlights two kinds of newly-emerging protest: the anti-privatization of state firm workers and the participation of the white-collar workers. All but four of the 25 SOE/COE mass protests reported in 2006 involved workers united by a common grievance – i.e. the selling-off of their lifetime work enterprises. Also, there had been a significant increase of mass protests by white-collar urbanites, including home-owners of private housing, and specific occupational groups including civilian aircraft pilots, journalists in a Shenzhen government-endorsed newspaper, and ex-employees of state banks, all of whom protested against unfair labour relations and illegal dismissals.

To illustrate, on 16 January 2006, hundreds of military police clashed with protesting workers from a bankrupt state-owned arms factory in Chengdu, Sichuan.[6] About 1,300 military police entered the factory and tried to save the factory boss, who was taken hostage by disgruntled employees, because he was planning to sell the 300-million-yuan factory at the discounted price of 80 million yuan. To compound matters, 200 million yuan promised to workers as compensation was not paid. The disgruntled workers held the factory boss captive as a bargaining chip in their negotiations to buy up the facilities and continue operations. No. 354 Factory, which had been undergoing liquidation since September 2005, had been operating for about 40 years, employed about 3,000 workers, and provided support such as education and medical benefits to their 8,000 family members. A substantial number of workers agreed to pool their payouts to fund the re-purchase of the factory. The boss, however, disagreed. Many state-owned arms factories in China have faced similar privatization fates.

The second case by former state bank clerks rather than traditional blue-collar workers took place in 2006.[7] The discontented demonstrators, numbering about 500 or 600, gathered from 14 provinces of China, were former employees in China Construction Bank, the country's third largest bank. On 13 April 2006, they converged on the bank's main entrance in the financial street business district chanting slogans and demanding to meet representatives from the bank. Their spokeswoman said they had come to the capital "spontaneously" to protest against being forced to quit their jobs between 2002 and 2004 and accept inadequate compensation. Many of them were retrenched during the bank's restructuring to prepare for its listing on the Hong Kong stock exchange in October 2005. They were told that they would not be paid anything if they did not sign away their rights to social welfare support. The contracts they signed included a clause prohibiting them from working at any other bank for two years and many claimed that they were unable to find work. Most of the protesters demanded their old jobs back. The bank fired nearly a quarter of its staff between December 2002 and June 2005, reducing the number of its total employees from 398,843 to 304,434. This case illustrates a new round of SOE privatization, which, through the retrenching of staff, sought a better financial outlook to achieve stock listings abroad to attract international mergers. The incentive to lay off employees was not due to bankruptcy or closure, but for the intended purpose of reshaping its manpower so as to secure better chances for liquidation and mergers.

Urban anti-relocation protests

Equally, along with workers' protests on the streets, the number of protests triggered by urban redevelopment has risen since the early 2000s. China's major cities, particularly Beijing, Shanghai, and Nanjing, witnessed a spate of anti-relocation protests in the mid-1990s, which escalated in intensity qualitatively and quantitatively in 2003 before easing off in 2005–06. The resistance and protests triggered by "forced demolition and eviction" (*qiangzhi chaiqian*) escalated rapidly in 2000–03, as frenzied investment in construction poured into urban infrastructure and redevelopment projects. In 2001, the central government received 8,516 petitions complaining about forced relocation. The petitions increased to 13,513 in 2002, a rise of 59 per cent over the year before. Meanwhile, in 2001–02, the number of petitioners involved surged by 65 per cent with each petition involving a greater number of petitioners than before. In 2003, the petitions about forced relocation amounted to 11,641 for the first eight months – a rise of 50 per cent over the same period of the preceding year.[8] In Guangzhou, in 2003–04, forcible evictions constituted nearly one-fourth of protest activities – the largest source of social unrest in the city (Tanner 2005). Shanghai has been relocating people at a rate of 80,000 a year since 2000 and plans to move another 400,000 by 2007 because the city wants a new look for the 2010 World Fair.[9] In preparation for the 2008 Olympic games, Beijing evicted 300,000 people from their homes up to 2004, and an enforced relocation scheme was expected to cover more than 1 million residents in total.[10]

Previously, in socialist China, in keeping with socialist ideology, city residents could not own private housing but mostly had to live in work-unit accommodations. Housing was the most important non-monetary income and welfare provided by one's work unit. At that time, residents more than welcomed relocation because in most cases they could move into newer and better-equipped apartments. Since the late-1990s however, the state, overturning socialist principles, commercially reformed its housing strategy, terminating welfare housing and transforming publicly-owned homes into private homes. This has opened the doors to a booming real-estate market and an increased scale of urban renewals due to the increasing demand for private home ownership and the strong incentives of local governments for infrastructural construction.

True, urban relocation does not necessarily provoke mass protests. Then why did some residents desperately resist relocation? The sources of conflict were varied. Low compensation, poor resettlement, short notice and poor information, rude or violent evictions, and frustration with arbitration and legal remedies were readily identifiable causes (Human Rights Watch 2004).

According to law, the government cannot rescind residents' land-use rights except where public-welfare projects supersede such rights. In practice, however, local governments were frequently charged with rent-seeking in the housing market; local officials often colluded with developers and sold land-use rights without consulting the occupants of buildings already on the land. The residents would perhaps secure newer housing, but more often than not they would be relocated to areas far removed from the city. Citizens who saw their homes being demolished to make way for new development projects without being consulted or properly compensated went from petitioning to airing their grievances before local governments, marching onto the streets, pouring petrol over themselves and over offending officers and even in some cases actually immolating themselves. Local governments responded by using increasingly violent eviction methods, and were accused of sending "stick-team" gangsters to violently evict unwilling residents from their homes.

The news dataset reveals that protests against forced relocation slowed down by 2004, probably due to an edict from the central government to adhere to strict methods of control over demolition and relocation in an attempt to stem the mounting tide of social unrest and protests linked to relocations. This edict, issued by the State Council in June 2004, stated that some local governments had "blindly enlarged the scope of demolition", "failed to implement adequate measures for housing demolition compensation and resettlement and artificially reduced standards for compensation and resettlement"; and "some have even abused official power and illegally engaged in forced demolitions". The directive further asked government at various levels in the hierarchy to ensure that the total area demolished nationwide in 2004 was less than that of the year before. It also banned the common practice of forcible eviction of residents through the termination of essential services like water, electricity, and heating.[11] Further, Beijing took aggressive measures in 2005 to cool the country's red-hot economy through the exercise of controls over urban construction and infrastructural projects. At the same time, the state media was given more leeway to report illegal demolitions.

However, it is doubtful whether the conflict and grievance over demolition will really pass away because city redevelopment and investments in construction have been an elixir for political credit and economic performance. This research also shows that despite a low occurrence of three reported protests on evictions in 2004, the number of reported protests over evictions reached 12 and six in 2005 and 2006, respectively. Apparently the crackdown on urban redevelopment and illegal evictions in 2004 was only effective for a short time. In 2006, the Ministry of Land and Resources had launched investigations into 90,340 cases of irregularities related to transfers of land titles, a 20 per cent rise from 2005. The amount of land involved was 84,000 hectares, a 95.5 per cent rise over the average for 2005. About half of the land involved in irregularities is arable land in rural areas. The report further revealed that 1,051 officials had received "administrative punishment" in relation to such cases.[12]

In March 2007, China's National People's Congress passed the long-awaited Property Law, which had been under discussion for the last several years. This law is expected to provide the legal ground enshrining private property rights for China's swelling ranks of urban middle-class homeowners. But in practice, there is a lack of real checks-and-balances to curb the unlawful behaviour of local authorities. Thus, access to justice remains tightly constrained with courts still controlled by the bureaucratic system and lawyers involved in litigation against local state agencies remain highly vulnerable to retaliation by state and non-state officials. On the other hand, the law indirectly consolidates the concept of private property for Chinese urbanites who are more sensitive about their vested rights and interests and more sophisticated with regard to recourse to strategies for addressing grievances. Thus, they resorted to street demonstrations and collective petitions against arbitrary unchecked forced evictions for urban redevelopment

Rural turmoil and resistance of the peasantry

In the countryside, mass protests concentrated on issues of land seizures, followed by those of excessive taxes and fees, the corruption of cadres and the abuse of power (Table 2.2). Looking at the frequency of various kinds of mass protests in rural areas, an obvious turning point occurred in 2004 when protests against taxes and fees declined but protests against land seizures escalated. During the period between the 1980s and early 1990s, mass villager protests tended to focus on concrete issues such as excessive fees and rigged elections in their own village (O'Brien and Li 2005). Rural land expropriation and excessive taxation were important issues of social conflict into the early 2000s (Guo 2001; Bernstein and Lu 2003), but later indicators showed that changes in central government policy had ameliorated the problem. As a result, the peasant protests triggered by the burdens of taxes and fees declined after 2003.

As China's urban and suburban economy continued its growth from the early 2000s, local governments began selling villagers' farmlands to commercial developers and construction companies. Conflicts deriving from rural land seizure for commercial development became widespread and relentless. In 2005, a high-ranking state official reported that more than 65 per cent of rural mass protests in China were due to government land requisitions.[13] Also, protests against land seizures often correlated with complaints about corrupt cadres and illegal land appropriations.

Why did land seizures provoke mass rural protests and why did the peasantry vociferously protest against land requisitions? The crux of the matter was that local governments rarely consulted the villagers about the terms of requisitions, and more perniciously, withheld most of the earnings without letting the villagers have their fair share. Further, the villagers' protest activities turned violent most probably because they had exhausted all tried and tested legal measures, including appeals, petitions, reports to the media, and lawsuits, but achieved little. It is perhaps true to say that once farmers realized that, *inter alia*, their rights would not be maintained, fair compensation would not be delivered, and that corrupt local cadres ruled the roost, they felt exploited, angry, and inclined to seek every means possible to protect their interests.

Contrary to the "privileges" accorded to the peasantry, urban dwellers in China can now buy and sell their apartments while rural land remains under collective communal ownership and cannot be traded, bought, or sold by individual farmers. The collective communal ownership of rural land is controlled by local cadres who make decisions on the property rights transfer and manipulate the information flow and compensation deals. This demarcates the nature of property rights for city dwellers and the peasantry and provides wider room for rural cadres to manipulate land takings and to bypass the state's regulations. As a result, local officials can make huge profits by getting hold of rural lands and having them re-zoned for industrial use, thus facilitating their selling these lands to developers for housing or commercial projects. The farmers who were the victims of the forcible requisition of their lands faced severe limitations because the law gave little room for their ownership claims and actually allowed for legitimate requisitioning of farmland for "common interests". In most cases, farmers were not averse to the transference of arable land for the purposes of urban and industrial development. The tension and trenchant resentment was mostly due to unfair and inadequate compensation packages that the peasants received.

In many land-taking disputes, compensation for land requisitions is largely minimal and not nearly enough in a rural society where collective welfare mechanisms no longer exist in the post-reform era. A recent survey found that allocation of earnings from land expropriations were distributed in the following ways: 20–30 per cent went to local government, 40–50 per cent went to the developer, 30 per cent went to village government, and only 5–10 per cent went to the villagers whose lands were requisitioned.[14] Dissatisfied with such meagre compensation for land requisitions, villagers petitioned and fought with the government. However, at local levels, officials, courts, and enterprises involved in developing the land often collaborated to block challenges to their authority by the public. With nowhere to turn, some villager-petitioners took to more radical measures to find solutions to their problems.

The social tensions triggered by questionable land seizures and the scandal attached to low compensations are widespread in China. From January to April 2004, the country witnessed an accelerated scale of mass protests against land seizures that numbered 4,030 – an increase of 67 per cent against the same period over the preceding year (Zhang 2005). There are statistics for such protests occurring in the Danxi District of Zhenjiang City in southern Jiangsu. With a population of 370,000, this city district witnessed 129 mass protests in 2004, of which 51 (40 per cent) involved controversies pertaining to land seizures (Tang 2005).

In 2005–06, it was widely reported that in southern China several violent protests concerning land seizures turned into bloody clashes with the police. The incident in Dongzhou, Guangdong, which occurred in December 2005, was when police opened fire, killing some of the villagers protesting the seizure of their land for a power plant. This clash between paramilitary police and villagers protesting a land grab was unusual only because real live bullets were turned on demonstrators. The incident was the latest of many violent clashes over the past year, including one in Guangdong in which police roughed up and detained scores of villagers and activists over a land dispute in Taishi village. In another major incident in June, six villagers were killed and 51 wounded when the local government sent hundreds of thugs into Dingzhou village in the northern Hebei province to beat up locals who refused to make way for a power plant.

With regard to rural land requisitions and compensation fights, most peasant protests were aimed at defending rights recognized by the law and by the central government. There is a wide gap between what the central government promises and what local officials deliver. The central state may have shifted its loyalties to disadvantaged villagers from corrupt cadres, but the latter continue to regard protests as harmful to social order and political stability. Villagers still remain frustrated by the local bureaucracy's indifference to their claims and by the ineffectiveness of top-down measures to ban local officials who do not heed the peasantry's grievances. Considering that what are perceived as just verdicts are neither realized nor forthcoming, villagers will still adopt extra-legal forms of resistance and collective protest (Zweig 2003). Unless overall policies are altered and substantial property rights reforms carried out, the needs of China's vulnerable rural majority cannot be addressed and China will surely face more extended and violent challenges to the victims of the country's development and "redevelopment".

In the spring of 2006, the government, faced with increasing peasant unrest, formally announced a plan to build a "new socialist countryside" vowing to "give more and take less". The goals of this programme for the rural population included the abolition of agricultural taxes, the rebuilding of the cooperative healthcare system, freeing rural education, and improving drinking water and basic services for farmers. However, the fundamental source of rural unrest has been concentrating on land property rights, including individual peasants' housing allotments (*zhaijidi*) and the transfer of the villagers' collective land property. As long as problematic property rights arrangements and rural political institutions remain intact, rural unrest is hardly likely to abate.

Peasant workers in FDI firms

Peasants protesting over land seizures mostly reside in the suburban areas of big cities where local government officials covet the huge returns of transferring the farmland for commercial or industrial uses. Another group of peasants, mostly from poor inland provinces, flocked together in the factories in coastal cities, particularly in foreign-direct-investment (FDI) firms, and launched their protests early at the turn of the century. Since 2004, there has been an unprecedented surge of mass protests by disgruntled FDI workers, protesting against their foreign employers' underpayment of wages or bad working conditions. Recent significant developments indicate that this trend of FDI workers' protests will not decline, but most will likely accelerate and develop in intensity. Growing labour shortages, combined with relentless international competition, have shrunk the benefits of the FDI firms and have led to the creation of an unfavourable management environment for FDI owners. On the other hand, the workers have become extremely conscious of their rights and have learned to bargain and fight for their interests. At first, the Chinese government used to stand on the side of foreign capitalists, but of late it has altered its position and now leans towards a middle of the road stance to ensure its legitimacy and secure its political stability.

In the spring of 2006, President Hu Jintao explicitly ordered government organs to enhance building Party organizations and worker unions in FDI enterprises, implying that the government's intention was to empower workers in FDI firms. In Guangdong, all multinational companies, including the province's 300 companies which featured among *Fortune's* top 500 companies in the world, were ordered to set up labour unions by the end of 2007. China's union law bans workers from forming independent unions; all unions and their activities have to be under the lead of the state-run All China Federation of Trade Unions (ACFTU). It remains to be seen if such a policy of establishing labour unions in FDI firms may give rise to more frequent labour disputes, clashes, and protests between the FDI workers and the foreign capitalists. In most cases, union membership is very low and a cosy relationship is maintained between union leaders and the managerial ranks. This notwithstanding, empowering workers in FDI firms and setting up unions, is a progressive step though such unions affiliated with ACFTU do not automatically guarantee the enhancement of workers' collective bargaining power or interests. The ultimate analysis depends on how the unions are run and what their leaders do.

In any case, this empowerment of the working class should be contrasted with the period in the 1990s when peasant workers in FDI firms were virtually powerless to improve their lot. A survey reported that workers, particularly those in overseas Chinese-managed FDI firms, compared with their counterparts in SOEs, TVEs, and private enterprises, experienced extremely harsh management practices and rigid labour controls. For instance, strong monetary penalties were imposed on them for violating regulations, for lack of interest in overtime work, and there were even strict toilet restrictions (Chan and Zhu 2003). In the early 2000s, the Chinese government began to emphasize labour laws regulating industrial relations. This was to prevent unrest when international human rights groups started overseeing labour abuses and disputes in foreign-funded firms in China. The enforcement of such labour laws and regulations, however, depended on local governments, which in the run of things have to rely on foreign-funded firms for tax revenues, fees, and bribery. Since different regions compete with each other for foreign investment, local authorities were inclined not to enforce the law to the letter in order to attract foreign capital and technology for local growth.

Since 2004, China has faced manpower shortages, particularly for young workers in labour-intensive industries, particularly in the Pearl River Delta. The manufacturing capacity of the country has expanded so rapidly in the past several years that the stream of young workers from the underdeveloped agrarian sector is no longer large enough to fill the labour pool. For the first time, the labour shortage has given skilled peasant workers, particularly those employed in labour-intensive industries like shoe manufacturing, the textile industry, and the furniture industry, a morsel of bargaining power, particularly since factory owners cannot easily replace dissatisfied employees as they once could. Wildcat strikes can now cripple production for days or weeks on end. Thus, almost imperceptibly, workers are starting to win concessions. For example, as many as 3,000 employees at Shenzhen-based electronics manufacturer Haiyan, a Hong Kong-funded firm, staged a walkout in October 2005 to protest against anomalous salary structures that were below the minimum wage. They were enticed back to the factory floor by a raise and the promise of back pay.[15]

In the mid-2000s, the issue of union establishment in FDI firms signalled a tenuous change in the relationship between peasant workers, their foreign employers, and the state. This, in turn, may further affect workers' sense of rights and their collective behaviour. Take Wal-Mart as an illustrative case. In July 2006, Wal-Mart workers in Quanzhou, Fujian, formed a trade union, thus breaking the long-standing absence of unions in Wal-Mart's China stores. Since then, setting up union branches in Wal-Mart in China has snowballed, with a total of 17 union branches in cities around the country.[16]

Wal-Mart first entered China's domestic market in 1996 and in 2006 employed around 32,000 workers in some 60 retail stores nationwide. Since 2003, the company has been under sustained pressure from the ACFTU to allow the formation of ACFTU union branches in its China stores. In September 2004, ACFTU alleged that private and foreign companies were preventing workers from setting up trade unions. In the following months, several big multinationals, including Wal-Mart, Kodak, and Samsung were criticized in the Chinese press for neglecting China's law requiring trade unions to be formed in each firm.[17] Wal-Mart, Kodak, Dell, Samsung, and others, appeared on an ACFTU blacklist. The ACFTU also said that the government might take action against leading FDI firms because of their continued ban on trade union membership. As a result of criticism in the media, Wal-Mart announced in November 2004 that it was willing to let Chinese employees set up unions if its employees wanted to. The issue died down for nine months until the spring of 2005, when Hu Jintao issued instructions on a report titled, "A Situation Analysis on the Factors of Instability in Foreign-invested Enterprises in China's Coastal Area" and "Some Proposed Countermeasures". Hu Jintao issued an edict: "Do a better job of building Party organizations and trade unions in foreign-invested enterprises." This created a new and opportune moment for trade union building in FDI enterprises. On 16 March, the ACFTU instructed its staff to study Hu Jintao's comments. This prompted it to set targets for unionization in FDI enterprises: 60 per cent or more by the end of 2006, and 80 per cent or more by the end of 2007.[18] Now, the unions at Wal-Mart look set to influence what happens with unions in other FDI companies in China.

Concluding remarks

This study highlights China's most recent protest groups and issues, including SOE workers against unpaid payments and privatization, city dwellers against forced demolition and eviction, angry peasants fighting against land seizures and for fair compensations, and peasant workers in FDI firms struggling for better returns and better working conditions. These contentious issues and discontented social groups appear to persist and continue to act against the interest of those who hold the stakes. As a result, state–society relations in China are changing to a degree that the regime has to take due cognizance of these deleterious factors in order to maintain its legitimacy and effect good governance.

Reflecting on the day-by-day incidents, it is clear that each wave of social unrest can be traced to a particular government policy, economic or political context. The Chinese government's dilemma is that many of these protests emanate from the momentum of the enviable economic growth that China is keen to maintain. As the Chinese economy needs to keep growing, the rise of social protest and, consequently, confrontation between government and protestors seem inevitable.[19] The fundamental problems underlying social unrest are mainly collective property rights of rural land, unchecked power of local authorities, corruption and the weak rule of law. China's single authoritarian party regime is unable to resolve these problems without comprehensive political reforms.

China's current political system lacks effective channels for citizens to express genuine grievances and to seek redress from the misdemeanours of local officials, and therefore, social unrest is on the rise. Without any functional alternatives, discontented people tend to resort to collective action and to take extra-legal means such as demonstrations and violent mass protests. Given that violent incidents often occur after weeks or even months of simmering unrest, it appears that protesters resort to confrontation when alternative means of redress prove futile or unavailable. With some notable exceptions, most of the protests remain unreported, unknown, isolated, short-lived, and lack strong leadership. These factors make it easy for local governments to quell them since they are localized protests about specifics, not general attacks against the Chinese Communist Party. As such, at present they have not developed to a degree that will constitute an immediate threat to political stability and regime survival. After all, the vast majority of mass protests were not explicitly political but derive from economic grievances that are a product of the economic sphere, such as city redevelopment projects, land expropriation schemes, enterprise privatization programmes, and labour relations problems. For Beijing and China watchers, these are factors that have to be carefully watched. How long can unhappy protesters keep blaming local officials for their problems instead of placing the problem squarely at the central government's door and on the larger fundamental system? This is indicative of the level of threat that social protest poses to the politics of the Communist state.[20]

Notes

1 PRC Ministry of Public Security Press page and Xinhua News Agency; www.mps.gov.cn/webpage/showNews.asp?id=1810&biaoshi=bitGreatNews; www.-xinhuanet.org/index.php?categoryid=1&p2_articleid=42&s=& (accessed 1 October 2006). It should be noted that despite these alarming statistics that drew much media attention, the definition of the term "mass incidents" had been ambiguous and inconsistent, and varied across provincial governments that report their statistics upward. See Soong (2006) for a detailed report on the statistics of mass incidents in China.

2 Xinhua News Agency, 7 November 2006.

3 The number of declining mass incidents is at odds with the previous increasing "numbers" for mass incidents. One possible explanation is that declining figures like that for November 2006, represent only the protests that "police had dealt with". This can be interpreted to mean that the incidents that the police were not involved in were not included in the statistics. See Soong (2006) for more details and news sources.

4 Usually news of social unrest events in China, if known, is widely reported by news agencies, newspapers, and the Internet news in Hong Kong, Taiwan, and other Chinese information sources. This study mainly relies on the news archive of the Central News Agency in Taiwan, and the Internet news sources from the *China Labour Bulletin*, the *Epoch Times*, *Xinhua*, *BBC* and *VOA*. These sources have recorded all popular protest events in China between 1997 and 2006. The original news collections and indices are in this researcher's possession and can be acquired through this researcher.

5 For more studies on Falun Gong and pro-democracy movements in China, see, for example, Pei (2000), Shue (2004), Perry (2001), Wright (2004), Thornton (2002), and Dickson (2000).

6 The information was drawn from reports on *China Labour Bulletin* and Boxun.com. see http://big5.china-labour.org.hk/public/contents/news?revision%5fid=68267&item%5fid= 68266, and http://news.boxun.com/news/gb/china/2006/01/200601241241.shtml, accessed 10 May 2007. Also see *South China Morning Post*, 23 January 2006.

7 This story was drawn from *Mingpao*, Hong Kong *and VOA* news, 13 April 2006; and *South China Morning Post*, 14 April 2006.

8 *Xinhua News*, 10 September 2003, see http://news.xinhuanet.com/house/2003–09/10/content_1074578.htm, accessed 1 May 2007.

9 *South China Morning Post*, 30 November 2003.

10 "China kicking 1.1 million out of Beijing", 8 March 2004; www.worldnetdaily.com/news/article.asp?ARTICLE_ID=37470, accessed 1 May 2007.

11 Notice on Controlling the Scope of Housing Demolition and Relocation in Cities and Towns and Tightening Up Demolition and Relocation Management, www.mlr.gov.cn/pub/gtzyb/zwgk/zdgd/t20040625_52277.htm, accessed 1 May 2007.

12 See http://big5.xinhuanet.com/gate/big5/news.xinhuanet.com/politics/2007–03/20/content_ 5873474.htm, accessed 1 May 2007.

13 *Xinhua News*, http://big5.xinhuanet.com/gate/big5/news.xinhuanet.com/politics/2006–02/ 22/content_4213514.htm, accessed 1 May 2007.

14 The causes, characteristics, and measures for the mass group incidents caused by rural land expropriation, obtained from http://blog.chinacourt.org/wp-profile1.php?p=34974&author=5117, accessed 1 May 2007.

15 See http://finance.sina.com.cn/cjzh/20041014/13401079674.shtml, accessed 1 May 2007.

16 For detailed stories, see http://news.xinhuanet.com/employment/2006–08/24/content_5001352.htm, accessed 1 May 2007.

17 *People's Daily* (Overseas edition), 3 December 2004, see www.agri.cn/llzy/t20041203_281154.htm, accessed 1 May 2007.

18 *China Labour Bulletin*, www.china-labour.org.hk/public/contents/article? revision%5fid=39069&item%5fid=39060.

19 In August 2005, the Chinese government announced it was setting up special police units in 36 cities to put down riots and counter what the authorities say is the threat of terrorism.

20 See Tanner (2007) who provides six key questions to monitor for examining the future and implications of popular unrest in China.

Bibliography

Bernstein, Thomas P. and Xiaobo Lu, *Taxation without Representation in Contemporary China*, Cambridge University Press, 2003.

Chan, Anita and Xiaoyang Zhu, "Disciplinary Labour Regimes in Chinese Factories", *Critical Asian Studies* 35:4, 2003, pp. 559–84.

Dickson, Bruce J., "Political Instability at the Middle and Lower Levels: Signs of a Decaying CCP, Corruption, and Political Dissent", in David Shambaugh (ed.) *Is China Unstable? Assessing the Factors*, M. E. Sharpe, 2000, pp. 40–56.

Gu, Edward X., "From Permanent Employment to Massive Lay-Offs: The Political Economy of Transitional Unemployment in Urban China (1993–8)", *Economy and Society* 28:2, 1999, pp. 281–99.

Guo Xiaolin, "Land Expropriation and Rural Conflicts in China", *The China Quarterly* 166, 2001, pp. 422–39.

Human Rights Watch, 2004. Demolished: Forced Evictions and the Tenants' Rights Movement in China. Available online at: http://hrw.org/reports/2004/china0304/, accessed 1 May 2007.

Hurst, William and Kevin J. O'Brien, "China's Contentious Pensioners", *The China Quarterly* 170, 2002, pp. 345–60.

Lee, Ching Kwan, "From Organized Dependence to Disorganized Despotism: Changing Labour Regimes in Chinese Factories", *The China Quarterly* 157:157, 1999, pp. 44–71.

——, "Pathways of Labour Insurgency", in Elizabeth J. Perry and Mark Selden (eds) *Chinese Society: Change, Conflict and Resistance*, RoutledgeCurzon, 2000, pp. 71–92.

O'Brien, Kevin J. and Lianjiang Li, "Popular Contention and its Impact in Rural China", *Comparative Political Studies* 38:3, 2005, pp. 235–59.

Pei, Minxin, "Rights and Resistance: The Changing Contexts of the Dissident Movement", in Elizabeth J. Perry and Mark Selden (eds) *Chinese Society: Change, Conflict and Resistance*, RoutledgeCurzon, 2000, pp. 23–46.

Perry, Elizabeth J., "Challenging the Mandate of Heaven: Popular Protest in Modern China", *Critical Asian Studies* 33(2), 2001, pp. 163–80.

Shue, Vivienne, "Legitimacy Crisis in China?", in Peter Hays Gries and Stanley Rosen (eds) *State and Society in 21st Century China: Crisis, Contention, and Legitimation*, RoutledgeCurzon, 2004, pp. 24–49.

Soong, Roland, "China: Statistics of Mass Incidents", Friday, 24 November 2006. Available online at: http://my.opera.com/PRC/blog/show.dml/581789 (accessed 4 May 2007).

Tang, Suo Hong, "Qiantan quntixingshijian de tedian he yufangchuzhi duice" (A Preliminary Study on the Characteristics of Group Incidents and Tactics for Prevention and Management), *Gongan yanjiu (Public Security Research)* 2, 2005, pp. 17–20.

Tanner, Murray Scot, "Chinese Government Responses to Rising Social Unrest", Testimony presented to the US–China Economic and Security Review Commission on 14 April 2005, downloaded from www.rand.org/pubs/testimonies/CT240/index.html#.

——, "Can China Contain Unrest? Six Questions Seeking One Answer", Brookings Northeast Asia Commentary, 2007. Available online at: www.brookings.edu/fp/cnaps/commentary/tanner20070301.htm (accessed 1 May 2007).

Thornton, Patricia, "Framing Dissent in Contemporary China: Irony, Ambiguity and Metonymy", *The China Quarterly* 171, 2002, pp. 661–81.

Weston, Timothy B., "The Iron Man Weeps: Jobless and Political Legitimacy in the Chinese Rust Belt", in Peter Hays Gries and Stanley Rosen (eds) *State and Society in 21st Century China: Crisis, Contention, and Legitimation*, RoutledgeCurzon, 2004, pp. 67–86.

Wright, Teresa, "Contesting State Legitimacy in the 1990s: The China Democracy Party and the China Labour Bulletin", in Peter Hays Gries and Stanley Rosen (eds) *State and Society in 21st Century China: Crisis, Contention, and Legitimation*, Routledge-Curzon, 2004, pp. 123–40.

Zhang, Zhaorui, "Nongcun quntixing shijiang yu shehui hexiewending" (Rural Popular Group Incidents and Social Harmonious Stability), *Shandong jingchaxueyuan xuebao (Journal of Shandong Police College)* 5, 2005, pp. 5–18.

Zweig, David, "To the Courts or to the Barricades: Can New Political Institutions Manage Rural Conflict?", in Elizabeth J. Perry and Mark Selden (eds) *Chinese Society: Change, Conflict and Resistance*, Routledge, 2003, pp. 113–35.

3 Household registration, social exclusion, and rural migrants in cities*

Xiaogang Wu

The past quarter century has witnessed rapid economic growth and enormous social changes in the history of the People's Republic of China. China's total GDP has increased by 37 times, from 362.4 billion RMB yuan in 1978 to 13.7 trillion RMB yuan in 2004, and the GDP per capita has increased by 27 times, from 379 RMB yuan in 1978 to 10,561 RMB yuan in 2004 (NBS 2005). The economic reform has not only brought phenomenal growth in prosperity but also has unleashed dynamic forces that in many respects had been suppressed during the first three decades of communist rule. Government control on population migration has weakened and geographic mobility, particularly from rural to urban areas, has become much easier than before. The growing number of migrants without local household registration status (*hukou*) since the early 1980s reflects fundamental social and demographic changes in Chinese society. The 2000 population census data show that the number of inter-county migrants, predominantly rural farmers, has reached 79 million, a total greater than the population of either France or Britain (Liang and Ma 2004).[1]

Such a large fraction of the national population on the move has important implications for China's economic, social, and political, developments in the future (Murphy 2002). First, a sizable body of migrants continues to be denied the rights and benefits of citizenship on the basis of local household registration status. Although geographic mobility and employment change have become relatively easier, the social implications of *hukou* status remain largely intact. No matter how similar their jobs to those of urban workers, employees with rural *hukou* status are still classified as "peasant-workers" and are, thereby, not entitled to the many labour rights and benefits offered to employees with urban *hukou* (Solinger 1999). For example, certain occupations are reserved for local residents, pension and medical care are usually not available to migrants, and the children of such rural migrants are not allowed to enrol in local public schools (Liang and Chen 2005). Second, much of this migrating population results from a movement from rural to urban areas in response to the rising urban demand for cheap labour, particularly in the coastal regions where the export-oriented economy is to a large extent integrated into global capitalist productions (Pun 2005). The household registration system is employed as the means for social exclusion to maintain a large pool of cheap labour in the course of China's economic development, leading to the creation of a truly disadvantaged group in contemporary Chinese society.

The plight of rural migrant workers (*min-gong*) in cities has attracted increasing attention in academic journals, newspapers, and magazines in recent years. Their suffering and experiences also have raised a variety of issues related to government administrative controls, migration and urban policy, citizenship and human rights, and socioeconomic inequalities and poverty, which resulted from the interplay between the market-oriented reform and the socialist institutional legacy (*hukou* system). This chapter examines the origin and evolution of the household registration system since the 1950s and its adjustment in the late 1990s. We highlight the *hukou* as a socialist redistributive institution and how it is combined with contradictory forces such as market reform and economic globalization in shaping life chance and socioeconomic outcomes in China today. Our analysis is based mainly on the data from two national representative surveys conducted in 1996 and 2005.

Background: the *hukou* system as a socialist redistributive institution

In 1955, as one of its procedures for solidifying administrative control, the new Chinese communist government established the household registration (*hukou*) system, under which all households had to be registered in the locale where they resided and also were categorized as either "agricultural" or "non-agricultural" (synonymously, "rural" or "urban") households (Chan and Zhang 1999: 821–2).[2] The majority of the population was bottled up in the countryside and entitled to few of the rights and benefits that the socialist state conferred on urban residents, such as permanent employment, medical insurance, housing, pensions, and educational opportunities for children (Wu and Treiman 2004). The household registration system serves as an important mechanism in distributing resources and determining life chances in state socialist China.

The installation and subsequent tightening of the *hukou* system reflected an effort on the part of the government to cope with demographic pressures created by its rapid socialist-style industrialization. After the civil war and two ensuing years of economic rehabilitation (1950–52) millions of peasants were recruited by burgeoning state industrial enterprises established in urban areas as part of the first Five-Year Plan (1953–57), and many more moved without restriction into cities to look for urban jobs (Meisner 1999). To check this rapid influx into cities, the registration system made a distinction between agricultural and non-agricultural *hukou* that was used both to restrict further rural-to-urban migration and to return rural migrants to the countryside.

The use of this administrative means was especially prevalent in the aftermath of the Great Leap Forward (1958–60), which threw the newly established system into chaos. A dramatic increase in (nominal) industrial growth and urban inflow pushed China's urban population from 16.2 per cent in 1958 to 19.7 per cent in 1960, the all-time high in the pre-reform era (NBS 1999). The government soon realized that China's grain-production capacity was unable to sustain such a huge urban population, especially given the decline in agricultural production during the Great Leap Forward. Hence, beginning in 1959, the government expanded and rigorously enforced its use of the *hukou* system as a tool to control migration. About 18 million urban workers were sent back to their home villages between 1961 and 1963 (Chan 1994b:39), and more than 20 million university and middle-school students from urban areas were sent down to rural and border regions during the Cultural Revolution (1966–1976), to help reduce both urban unemployment and school crowding (Bernstein 1977; Zhou and Hou 1999).

The effectiveness of the *hukou* system in restricting internal migration relied on two other administrative systems, through which rationing was carried out. On the rural side, the commune system enabled local governments to bind peasants to the land. All adults had to participate in agricultural production to receive food rations for their households (Parish and Whyte 1978) and migration was generally prohibited except with the permission of the local government. On the urban side, the principal administrative unit for most urban residents was the workplace organization (*danwei*), which administered most social services for their employees (Bian 1994; Walder 1986, 1992; Naughton 1997). Without a work unit, it was very difficult to survive in a city because housing, food, and other social services were unavailable through the market. Moreover, because employment quotas in all urban work units were tightly controlled by the government labour administration (Li and Wang 1992; Walder 1986), even rural residents willing to risk losing food rations by leaving their home villages would have little chance of getting a job in a city.

Hence, the *hukou* system was built as a part of the socialist planned economy and intended to facilitate the redistributive process by tightly controlling labour force allocation. China's socialist industrialization programme was made possible by the *hukou* system and restricted migration, which allowed the government to exploit the agricultural sector and sacrifice the interests of rural residents to those of urban residents. For example, to ensure food grain needed for urban industrial growth, the government relied on a system of "unified purchase" (*tonggou*) to forcibly procure farm produce at low prices from the peasantry (Lin *et al.* 1994). At the same time, consumer products allocated free-of-charge or at low prices to urban residents as welfare benefits of their work units were sold at high prices in rural areas.[3] The government's discriminatory policy resulted in a substantial gap in income and living standards between rural and urban residents. Permanent urban residents also enjoyed many other welfare benefits delivered by the state, such as free or subsidized food grain, free or low-rent apartments, and retirement and medical insurance. The government also guaranteed every eligible urban resident a permanent job.

More crucially, children with urban *hukou* and rural *hukou* status did not enjoy equal opportunities to obtain education, especially higher education. Educational resources were unevenly distributed between rural and urban areas, with rural schools less widely available and generally of inferior quality. Further, local governments usually favoured students with urban *hukou* with respect to admission to vocational/technical schools and community colleges, levels of education that served as thresholds for changing *hukou* status. By setting admission standards higher for rural students, they were able to limit the rate of *hukou* conversion. Living in a city with an urban *hukou* was enormously advantageous (Wu and Treiman 2004).

In sum, when the socialist regime was installed in China, the low level of economic development and the large population meant that the new government could not afford to make socialist entitlements and benefits available to all citizens. The solution was to create a very pronounced and well-institutionalized distinction and to exclude the majority of the rural population from the socialist welfare system in favour of the 20–30 per cent of urban population. Rural residents were segregated on farms in poor rural areas and deprived of socio-economic opportunities in Maoist China. They were the truly disadvantaged.

Market reforms, economic globalization, and social exclusion of rural migrants

Economic reforms and labour migration

China's economic reform during the past two decades has substantially relaxed the administrative control of population migration and labour mobility via the *hukou* registration system (Cheng and Selden 1994; Chan and Zhang 1999). Starting from 1978, the household responsibility system has replaced the commune system as the major form of agricultural production. Peasants sign contracts with the local government to deliver a fixed quota of grain in exchange for farming on a household basis; as a result, they have gained freedom as to their labour and no longer need to report to the collective for daily work (Lin *et al.* 1994). The release of surplus labour tied to the land has helped create a rural labour market and drive the spectacular growth of rural non-agricultural sectors, largely constituted by local township and village-owned enterprises (TVEs) (Oi 1990), and later, by more private enterprises (Peng 2001). The employment size of rural industry reached 128,195,000 in 2000 (Cai 2002: 66). Most TVE employees were recruited from the local peasantry, who work as both part-time wage earners and part-time farmers (Parish *et al.* 1995; Yang 1997).

From its inception, the rural non-farm employment has been truly market-oriented. Wage determination in the rural public sector is found similar to that in the rural private sector, but quite different from that in the urban public sector (Peng 1992). Unlike urban workers, peasant-workers are not entitled to job security and welfare benefits such as housing, pension, and medicare plans, and thus provide sufficient cheaper labour to rural industrialization. During an economic recession, they can be easily let go to return to farming, regardless of whether they are employed in the public or the private sectors (de Brauw *et al.* 2002). Local governments have no responsibility to create jobs for them. They are not even counted in government unemployment statistics (Solinger 2001).

The initial development of labour markets in urban China was driven by labourers outside the urban formal employment system (Wu and Xie 2003). To enhance the development of the urban service sector, since 1983 the government had allowed peasants to enter cities and establish small urban businesses such as shoe-repair shops, barbershops, and restaurants (Li 1993). Furthermore, millions of young peasants from rural areas were hired in the growing urban private sector. Even the state-owned enterprises preferred to hire rural workers, either because there was no legal commitment to housing and other social benefits for these peasant-workers, or because the jobs were unattractive to urban workers (Cai 2002).

As a result, the release of surplus rural labourers from the land in rural reform and the emergence of a free social space in urban reform have triggered a massive labour migration in China. Geographic mobility is much easier than before. Since the late 1990s, out-migration to cities has prevailed over local employment in TVEs (Cai 2002; Rawski 2002). The government's bureaucratic control over population migration and labour mobility is waning rapidly (Liang 2001; Liang and Ma 2004; Zhao 2000).

Nevertheless, the household registration system still persists, though losing its effectiveness to some extent. This has led to a disparity between people's residence and registration place in the reform era. An estimate in the 2000 census put the figure of migration population at 144 million, more than 10 per cent of China's national population (Liang and Ma 2004: 475). The figure is even higher in the coastal cities. Inter-provincial migrants account for one-fifth to one-quarter of the total population in Beijing and Shanghai (NBS 2001).

The *hukou* continues to be used as the main criterion to allocate government subsidies, welfare, and employment opportunities to local urban permanent residents. Only temporary, undesirable, and menial jobs are open to migrants (Wang *et al.* 2001; Yang and Guo 1996). Most government services are not available to them: they need to pay extra fees to go to hospital, to rent an apartment, to have their children attend local schools (Cai 2002: 215). Moreover, many city governments have instituted a set of local regulations requiring migrants to have several documents (three certificates and one card) for their stay to be considered legal.[4] For those documents, on average, a migrant worker was charged about 223 yuan in 1995 (Zhao 1999: 777).

Since the *hukou* is employed as the main basis for social exclusion, employees with rural *hukou* status, regardless of their occupations, are classified as "*peasant*-workers" (*ming gong*), a synonym for underclass, who are not entitled to labour rights and benefits and are subject to severe discrimination (Solinger 1999). The large-scale migration from rural to urban areas in the reform-era has not dismantled the socialist segregation policy set by the household registration system. Instead, it has made the long-existing inequality and social injustice more visible.

As Chan (1994: 135) put it,

> Chinese reform socialism has created, structurally, a sizable 'second class' of urban citizens without permanent urban household registration status.

This informal segment of urban labour and population is an extension of the rural segment, which was largely bottled up in the countryside under Mao.

Economic globalization and the labour migrants in the "world factory"

China's decision to open its economy by promoting international trade and foreign direct investment (FDI) seems to have given it an edge and helped it integrate more thoroughly into the global economy. By 2003, FDI in China accounted for over 40 per cent of the GDP. China has become one of the largest destinations for international capital. Foreign companies now hold large shares in many sectors of China's economy, including its markets for automobiles and cellular telephones. They also account for half of China's exports – compared with 45 per cent for Malaysia, 38 per cent for Singapore, 31 per cent for Mexico, and 15 per cent for South Korea (Hale and Hale 2003).

China's rapid rise as an international production force, to a large extent, can be attributed to its low labour costs. In labour-intensive manufacturing companies, typically in the Pearl River Delta of Guangdong province, the majority of workers are rural migrants from inland provinces such as Sichuan, Hunan, and Jiangxi. China's 2000 census data show that there are over 11 million migrants in Guangdong province, nearly 70 per cent residing in cities and towns. Migrant workers account for one-third of all urban labour forces in the province. In Shenzhen, the pioneer city of Chinese capitalist experiment, there are 5.7 millions migrants which account for 82.1 per cent of the city's total residing population, and over 50 per cent work in the manufacturing sector. In the nearby Dongguan city, migrants are 5.8 million in contrast to 1.7 million local residents. Figures 3.1a and 3.1b show the scatterplots between FDI per capita and the ratio of migrants in the population, export per capita and the ratio of migrants in the population among the 31 provincial jurisdictions in China. Migration is clearly positively associated with China's economic globalization, measured by the FDI and export values.

In the capitalist global production chains, *hukou*, the institutional legacy from the state socialist redistributive economy, ironically has been used as the main means to maintain a large pool of low-wage labour. Most migrant workers work for long hours without adequate compensation and protection. Many injured workers are simply dismissed and sent back to their home villages. These peasant-workers are not entitled to medical insurance and pension plan, despite the fact that these are stipulated by the labour laws. They can be laid off easily without many dispute rights (Chan 2001; Pun 2005). The official trade unions do not treat them as eligible members. In the past 12 years, while the economy in the Pearl River Delta has grown exponentially, the monthly wages of migrant workers have increased by only 68 RMB yuan. (http://society.people.com.cn/BIG5/1063/4114454.html). The well-being of migrant workers has lagged far behind that of urban dwellers in China's economic prosperity.

It is in the interest of local government authorities to implement social exclusions and maintain a pool of flexible labour. Chinese rural migrants in the urban

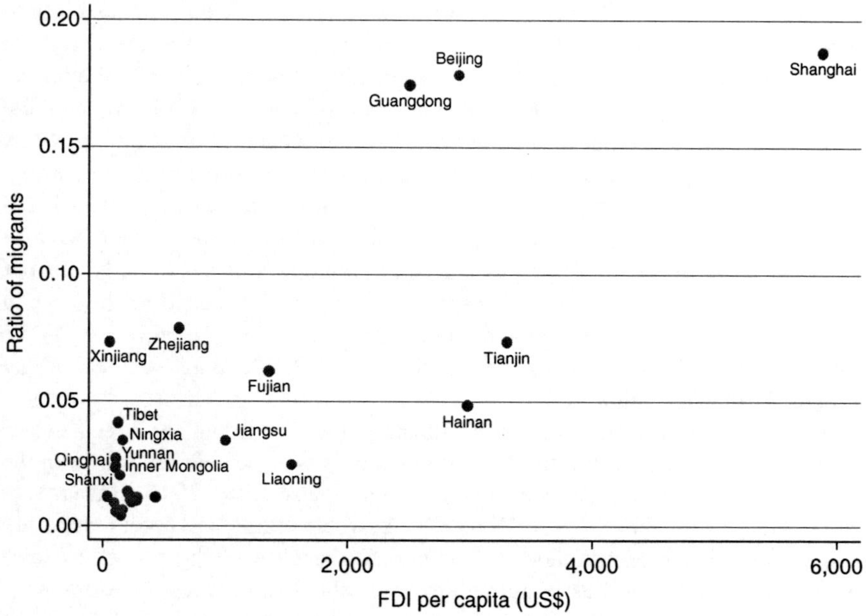

Figure 3.1a Scatterplot between FDI per capita and ratio of migrants.

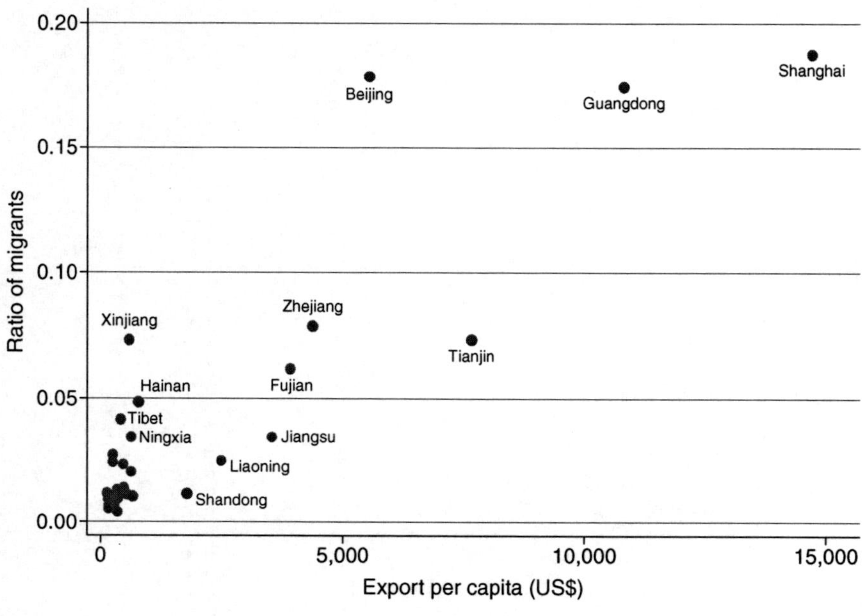

Figure 3.1b Scatterplot between export per capita and ratio of migrants.

economy serve a similar role to those illegal immigrants in western developed countries (Roberts 1997). First, the government does not have a responsibility to provide social service or public goods to rural migrants. When a labour dispute takes place, local governments are more aligned with the interests of the employers than with the protection of workers' rights, because local governments are competing with each other for FDI in order to boost local economic development, and serious implementation of the labour law would drive investors away. Second, a large pool of migrants not only contributes to the total GDP growth and generates extra revenue and surcharge fees for the local governments, but also helps to increase the GDP per capita, since migrant workers usually are not included in the calculation on a per capita basis. Figure 3.2 plots the difference in GDP per capita calculated with and without migrants in the denominator. As we can see, the GDP per capita in Shanghai is 7,800 RMB higher if migrants are excluded from calculation.

An interesting counter-example to illustrate the benefits of the social exclusion of rural migrants is the shortage of peasant-workers (*mingong huang*) in the Pearl River Delta, Fujian, and Zhejiang provinces since 2004. Because of competition from the Yangtze River Delta, where migrant workers' monthly wages are 8.5 per cent higher on average and because of the central government's increased subsidies to agriculture and inland rural areas, factories were drained of migrant workers. Some estimates put the shortage at 0.5 to one million in Guangdong province. The size of the shortage is particularly high in Dongguan, where the monthly salary is 16.8 per cent lower than the average

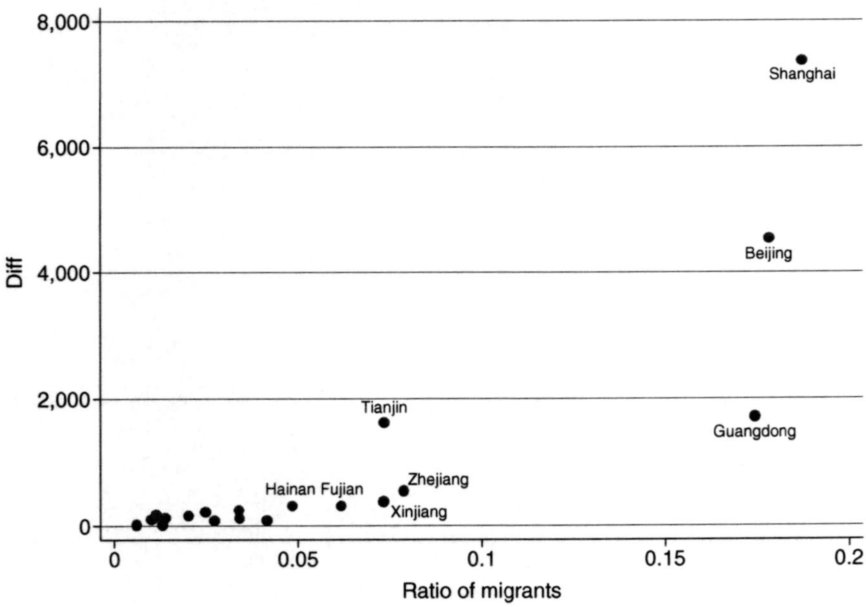

Figure 3.2 The difference in GDP per capita including and excluding migrants.

of the selected 23 cities in China (http://society.people.com.cn/BIG5/1063/4114454.html). Some commentators have cautioned that, to solve the problems of peasant workers shortages, the government and employers should face up and address the problem of peasant workers' lack of rights.

Social-political conflicts and the adjustments of the *hukou* system in the late 1990s

Social and political conflicts

In the pre-reform era, rural and urban residents were spatially segregated by the *hukou* system under which the majority of rural peasants lived in the countryside and urban residents lived in cities. Social and spatial boundaries are largely consistent with each other. The surging migration in the reform era has brought a visible social boundary into the cities. Migrants are socially and spatial segregated in urban China. They typically hold the menial jobs that local urbanites do not want to do, live in factory dorms, on construction sites, rent cheap rooms in remote suburban areas, and interact only with their fellow workmates from the same county.

The surging wave of migrants, despite the fact they offer cheap labour for the hosting cities, are often blamed for the untidiness, the crowdedness, for traffic congestion, and rising crime. Indeed, when the government decides to clean up the cities, these migrants are always affected. In particular, as the market reform proceeds further in urban China, many local workers have lost their jobs and privileges and become off-duty workers (*xiagang*), for whom the city government has the responsibility to provide employment opportunities. Local city governments have issued laws and regulations stipulating that certain jobs have to go to those with local *hukou*, openly discriminating against migrants. Migrants remain "strangers" in cities (Zhang 2001).

Such a discrimination policy against migrants has created special hurdles in socioeconomic integration not only for the adult migrants themselves, but also for their offspring, particularly in regard to their access to educational opportunities. First, in the 1990s, more city-born children of early migrants reached school age. Second, the new wave of migration has been bringing to the cities more children of school age, who migrate with their parents. In a survey conducted in 1997, school-age children constituted 12 per cent of the total migration population in Shanghai (op. cit. Liang and Chen 2005). Without local permanent registration status, migrant parents need to pay additional fees and surcharges to get their children access to local schools, a cost hardly affordable to many migrant families. A survey conducted in Beijing in 1995 reported that only 40 per cent of school-age children were actually enrolled in schools (op. cit Liang and Chen 2005). The provision of educational opportunities for migrants' children has been an increasingly important issue that concerns both the public and education policy-makers.

The institutional barriers and social exclusions associated with the *hukou* system create extra costs to some migrants who wish to bring their families with them. Many children are left by their migrant parents with their grandparents at home. Indeed, rural education finance reform in the 1990s has imposed extra economic burdens for families and have driven some parents to migrate for a cash income in order to support their children's education (Chao 2007).

Moreover, despite the fact that the benefits associated with urban *hukou* have faded away in the further market reform, the authoritarian government still has to rely on the *hukou* distinction for administrative control and police monitors (Wang 2004). Those migrants without stable jobs and residences are often arrested as "vagrants", and sent to labour camps for several months to earn the fare the government would spend to send them home. This practice has been condemned not only by the migrant workers themselves but also by educated urbanites. Public outrage culminated in an episode in 2003, when Sun Zhigang, a college-educated migrant in Guangdong province (who supposedly held non-local urban registration status) was beaten to death in police custody after being detained on suspicion of vagrancy (he indeed held a white-collar job). Sun's death gave impetus to the abolition of the Custody and Repatriation system (New York Times 2005).

The state policies in the 1990s neglecting rural areas and agriculture, coupled with the rejection of citizenship to migrants, have created a huge gap in income, wealth, and life chances between rural and urban China, which may jeopardize the social stability and the country's long-term development. In this context, the *hukou* regulations, after 20 years of reforms, began to adjust to accommodate the changes in labour markets.

Recent reforms on **hukou** *regulations*

Reforms of the *hukou* system in China seem to have intensified in the past few years. The elimination of the Custody and Repatriation system in 2003 had a significant impact on the *hukou* system, although it did not constitute a reform of the latter. For example, many provincial and municipal governments throughout China sped up their *hukou* reforms. The State Council's regulation ordered that migrant workers no longer be arrested for not possessing the right papers, and ordered police to provide urban residency documents to any migrant who can find a job.

Despite the regional variations, the qualifications required to obtain urban registration tend to be similar and often consist of having fixed residence and stable employment (usually one year on the job) in an urban area. State regulations introduced in 2001 made the *hukou* reform more of a local government responsibility than a national government-based one. By the beginning of the twenty-first century, local governments had almost complete control over population administration within their jurisdictions. Municipal governments in several large cities did not immediately implement the reform policies introduced by the national government in 1998, and their refusal to do so was tolerated by the national authorities. The high fees associated with obtaining an urban *hukou* in large cities, such as Beijing, Shanghai, Guangzhou, and Shenzhen, which are the most attractive to migrants, made access to these cities out of reach for most peasants.

Nevertheless, several provinces and major cities began to speed up local *hukou* reforms in 2003 (*South China Morning Post*, 8 July 2003). Beijing, for example, introduced further reforms in the summer of 2003, by issuing a new type of *hukou* registration called the Beijing Employment and Residence Permit, which would give its holders "rights to housing, education, investment, social and medical insurance, and a driver's licence" (*South China Morning Post*, 8 July 2003). In order to be issued such a permit, however, a person must be residing in Beijing, be employed, have a bachelor's degree, and two years of employment experience. This, according to the *South China Morning Post*, means that only "a select few will qualify". In March 2004, it was reported that the province of Guangdong was taking measures to protect the legal rights of its 23 million migrant workers and their families, including the rights to education and medical insurance. These measures included setting up offices across the province, at the provincial and local levels, to offer better services to migrants. An article in the *Shenzhen Daily* on 22 September 2004 also discussed the reforms taking place in the city of Guangzhou, where rural *hukou* holders with regular jobs and fixed residences would become eligible for Guangzhou *hukou.* Another article in the *China Daily*, 28 December 2004, discussed additional reforms planned by Guangdong province, which, according to an official at the Public Security Bureau, would lead to the total elimination of the agricultural *hukou* in the province in the years ahead.

Given these changes, has the effect of *hukou* on the drawing of social boundary in China's urban labour market been waning? In the rest of the chapter I analyse socioeconomic attainment in China, based on the data from the two national representative surveys, with particular attention paid to the role played by the household registration status.

Empirical analyses from two national representative surveys

Data and variable measurements

I analyse the data from two national representative surveys in 1996 and 2005 in China. The first data set is from the survey of *Life Histories and Social Change in Contemporary China* (1996), a multi-stage stratified national probability sample of 6,090 adults (including 3,003 rural cases and 3,087 urban cases) aged 20–69 from all regions of China (except Tibet). Rural and urban samples are drawn separately, and, with appropriate weight, form a national sample (see Treiman 1998: Appendix D) for details. The data were collected by UCLA in collaboration with Renmin University of China. The second data set is from the Chinese General Social Survey (CGSS), 2005, a collaborative project between the Hong Kong University of Science and Technology and Renmin University of China since 2003. The China GSS is an annual questionnaire survey of China's urban and rural households aiming to monitor systematically the changing relationship between social structure and quality of life in urban and rural China. About 5,900 urban samples and 4,100 rural samples are selected to form a national representative sample with weights. Because of funding limitations, the 2003 survey only covered the urban areas. The 2005 data contain both urban and rural components (*N*=6,098 and 4,274, respectively), with age ranging from 18 to 94.

Whereas both surveys were designed not specifically for *hukou* and migration studies, they contained relevant information on respondents' residence, registration status, and occupation and earnings. As far as we know, even to date, the data are unique in two respects. First, compared with China's population census data, the information on *hukou* status, occupation, work units, and earnings would allow us to conduct an in-depth analysis of the roles of spatial migration and *hukou* status in socioeconomic attainment. Second, compared with most survey data specifically targeting migrants on either rural or urban sides in limited areas, the national probability sample of the Chinese population could essentially overcome several weaknesses in previous migration studies in the sense that the whole process of rural–urban labour mobility, both spatially and socially, can be examined, and migrant workers can be compared to different groups in both rural and urban labour markets.

One main concern about the general population survey data is that migrants may be undercounted. Although the survey analysed here took special pains to try to identify migrants by sampling from the register of temporary residents as well as from the register of permanent residents, many migrants fail to register as temporary residents. However, the problem seems not be so serious. The 1996 survey data indicate that about 12.3 per cent of the urban populations are informal migrants without permanent urban *hukou* (see Table 3.1, column 1). Computations from the 2000 census yield a comparable estimate – 12 per cent of the urban population lacks a local *hukou*. In the 2005 survey, the non-permanent urban residents account for about 14 per cent of the population currently residing in Chinese cities, including 4.8 per cent who have already gained blue-stamp *hukou* or "self-supplied food grain" *hukou* in small towns, as a result of the *hukou* reform in the 1990s (see explanations in Chan and Zhang 1999).

While the 1996 data include relatively detailed historical information (*hukou* origins), the 2005 data include more information about the type of current *hukou* status, and working hours and fringe benefits provisions by the employers, as well as questions on the daily interaction with rural migrants (only urban residents answered the questions). Moreover, as significant reforms on the *hukou* system took place mainly in the later 1990s, the comparative analysis between 1996 and 2005 will enable us to conduct a basic evaluation of the consequences of *hukou* reforms. I restrict our analysis to the sample aged 20–60 years old in both surveys and focus on the effect of earnings determination and occupational attainment in urban labour markets and the role of *hukou* status in drawing the boundaries in urban labour markets.

I employ the same coding to the variables available in both surveys. Income refers to monthly earnings, which is taken logarithm. Education is measured years of schooling completed, which is a continuous variable. Age is the difference between the survey year and the reported birth year of the respondent. Party membership and gender are coded as dummy variables. So is current *hukou* status (urban=1).

I code current occupation into four categories (1=peasants; 2=ordinary workers; 3=ordinary professional/staff; and 4=middle rank professional/cadre). Work unit is also coded into four categories (1=state sector; 2=collective; 3=private; 4=missing or not applicable (mostly peasants or self-employed). In the analysis, they are treated as a set of dummy variables. Table 3.1 presents descriptive statistics for selected variables to be included in the following analysis.

As Table 3.1 shows, people in cities earn more than people in the countryside, in both 1996 and 2005. They are also more educated, and more likely to be Communist Party members working in state-owned work units with higher-status occupation. In particular, in the 1996 sample, 83.9 per cent of current urban residents hold urban *hukou* status, namely 16.1 per cent are migrants. In 2001, about 10 per cent of urban residents are rural migrants (probably undercounted).

Based on the current residence and *hukou* status, I conceptually characterize three types of labour market in China. The first is the rural labour market (only few urban *hukou* holders live and work in rural areas), specifically for non-agricultural employment. The second is the migrants' labour market in cities. Migrants hold rural *hukou* status but work in the urban sector. The last is the market for urban workers with permanent registration status. Table 3.2 describes the characteristics of wage workers within the three labour markets (full-time peasants are excluded).

Earnings include regular wages and bonus for employed workers. Income of the self-employed private entrepreneurs depends much more directly on the characteristics of their product markets, as well as on their entrepreneurial skill, access to capital, contact with suppliers, and other factors. Looking across columns, we found that in both years, the average monthly earnings of migrant workers is the highest, even higher than urban workers with permanent residents. Whereas this finding may be a bit surprising, it is indeed consistent with results reported by Yang and Chan (2000) and Maurer-Fazio and Dinh (2002) based on the data collected in some selected cities. A better indicator would be the hourly rate wage by taking account of working hours (Yang and Chan 2000). Unfortunately, the 1996 survey did not collect the information, but the 2005 survey did, which we shall examine separately, hereafter.

With respect to years of schooling, the migrants were less educated than rural non-farm workers in 1996; but up to 2005, out-migration seems to prevail and attracts the more educated. Communist Party members account for a tiny proportion among the migrants.

The empirical analysis is to test whether the social boundary is drawn along the spatial dimension or by the institutional (*hukou*) distinctions. Specifically, I test the patterns of earnings determination among the three presumed labour markets in 1996 and 2005. In transitional China, economic rewards are channelled through two main channels which represent two distinctive logics of distribution (Walder, Li, and Treiman 2000). As a result, scholars focus on returns to schooling and to the Communist Party membership to characterize the nature of a stratification system.

Table 3.1 Un-weighted descriptive statistics for variables included in analysis: urban and rural samples, 1996 and 2005

Variables	*1996*		*2005*	
	Urban sample	*Rural sample*	*Urban sample*	*Rural sample*
Current income per month (logged)	6.055 (0.568)	5.820 (0.628)	6.674 (0.847)	5.646 (0.654)
Years of schooling	9.207 (3.484)	5.785 (3.769)	10.57 (3.78)	6.000 (3.814)
Male	0.493	0.511	0.455	0.487
Age	38.40 (10.72)	38.57 (10.48)	39.98 (10.78)	41.43 (10.38)
Party member (yes=1)	0.151	0.058	0.114	0.058
Current urban *hukou* (urban=1)	0.839	0.037	0.908	0.053
Current occupation				
Peasant	0.026	0.794	0.025	0.788
Ordinary worker	0.619	0.160	0.662	0.143
Ordinary professional/cadre	0.216	0.031	0.254	0.060
Middle-rank professional/official	0.139	0.015	0.060	0.009
Current work unit				
State	0.434	0.004	0.464	0.029
Collective	0.102	0.029	0.103	0.016
Private	0.090	0.050	0.320	0.148
Missing/not applicable	0.373	0.883	0.114	0.807
N	2,665	2,738	4,868	3,619

Note
Figures in parentheses are standard errors for continuous variables. Data are un-weighted.

Table 3.2 Characteristics for wage workers in three labour markets

	1996			*2005*		
	Rural	*Urban*		*Rural*	*Urban*	
	Non-farm	*Migrants*	*Urban workers*	*Non-farm*	*Migrants*	*Urban workers*
Monthly income (yuan)	401 (223)	622 (379)	492 (398)	821 (950)	1,209 (2,966)	1,161 (1,557)
Years of schooling	8.452 (2.937)	7.400 (3.239)	10.19 (3.06)	8.225 (3.573)	8.542 (3.614)	11.06 (3.53)
Age	36.30 (10.61)	32.97 (10.77)	39.19 (10.12)	38.84 (10.39)	34.57 (9.37)	40.53 (10.75)
Party member (yes = 1)	0.154	0.086	0.220	0.109	0.024	0.132
Gender (male = 1)	0.713	0.617	0.532	0.660	0.482	0.479
Work units						
State	0.371	0.240	0.686	0.149	0.075	0.532
Collective	0.279	0.137	0.152	0.080	0.057	0.112
Private	0.268	0.400	0.038	0.727	0.786	0.293
Missing	0.081	0.223	0.124	0.044	0.081	0.064
Occupation						
Worker	0.671	0.868	0.518	0.648	0.714	0.659
Ordinary staff	0.245	0.090	0.295	0.305	0.286	0.270
Middle-rank manager/professional	0.084	0.042	0.187	0.047	–	0.072
N	261	175	1,608	685	332	3,918

Note
Figures in parentheses are standard errors for continuous variables.

Earnings determination in the segmented labour markets

The persisting role of the *hukou* in labour market attainment is treated as a hypothetical question. To verify it, I examine earnings determinations within three different types of labour market. If rural non-farm workers and migrant workers share a similar pattern in contrast to the urban workers, and, the most prominent difference exists between those who have urban *hukou* and those who do not, rather than between those who work in cities and those who work in the countryside, then the evidence supports the claims that the *hukou* system plays an important role in drawing the boundary in China's labour markets.

Table 3.3 presents estimates for earnings equations. Model 1 and Model 3 are additive models for 1996 and 2005, respectively. I include years of schooling, age, squared age, Party membership, gender, work unit, occupation, and workers in three labour markets. Education is a significant predictor of logged income. In 1996, the rate of return to an extra year of schooling is about 2 per cent, whereas it increased to 7.8 per cent in 2005. Age denotes experience, which affects income in 1996 but not in 2005. Communist Party membership had no effect in 1996 but brought about 7.6 per cent of income returns in 2005. The gender gap in income remains largely the same from 1996 to 2005.

The occupational and organizational hierarchies in income determination are not surprising, either. Professionals and cadres at middle rank or above earn significantly more than ordinary professional/staff, who earn significantly more than workers (peasants are excluded). Workers in collective work units earn less than their counterparts in the state sector, but workers in the private sector earn more than those in the state sector.

After controlling other factors, migrant workers still earn most among the three types of workers. Compared with rural non-agricultural workers, their earnings are 51 per cent higher ($e^{0.415-1}$) and those of urban workers are 29 per cent higher ($e^{0.256-1}$) in 1996, net of other factors. In 2006, the advantages of workers in urban labour markets over rural workers persisted. Migrant workers earn 26.2 per cent more and urban workers 25.9 per cent higher. The difference between migrant workers and urban workers becomes almost negligible.

To test returns as to education and Party membership in the three labour markets, I include interaction terms between worker type and the two variables of our key interests in Model 2 for 1996 and Model 4 for 2005. The results show that urban workers seem to differ from rural workers in returns, as to education, but migrant workers do not. In 1996, an extra year of schooling brought about little income returns for rural workers, 1.6 per cent for migrant workers, but 2.4 per cent for urban workers. Only the urban workers' advantage is statistically significant ($p<0.05$). In 2005, returns to education increased. For rural workers, the rate of return is about 4.7 per cent ($e^{0.046-1}$), for migrant workers, it is 6.9 per cent ($e^{0.046+0.021-1}$), which is not significantly different. For urban workers, the rate is 8.4 per cent ($e^{0.046+0.035-1}$), significantly higher than that for rural workers

Table 3.3 Wage determinations of workers in three labour markets in China

	1996		*2005*	
	Model 1	*Model 2*	*Model 3*	*Model 4*
Years of schooling	0.020*** (0.005)	0.001 (0.011)	0.075*** (0.004)	0.046*** (0.008)
Age	0.008*** (0.001)	0.008*** (0.001)	–0.009 (0.007)	–0.010 (0.007)
Age square*10	–0.031*** (0.008)	–0.031*** (0.008)	0.001 (0.001)	0.001 (0.001)
Party member (yes = 1)	0.020 (0.033)	–0.290 (0.089)	0.073* (0.034)	–0.027 (0.092)
Gender (male = 1)	0.220*** (0.025)	0.221*** (0.025)	0.220*** (0.021)	0.222*** (0.021)
Work Units (state omitted)				
Collective	–0.111*** (0.032)	–0.109*** (0.032)	–0.104** (0.036)	–0.097** (0.036)
Private	0.239*** (0.045)	0.225*** (0.045)	0.171*** (0.027)	0.169 (0.027)
Missing	–0.023 (0.073)	–0.034 (0.073)	–0.599*** (0.048)	
Occupation (worker omitted)				
Ordinary staff	0.073* (0.030)	0.081** (0.031)	0.104*** (0.024)	0.103*** (0.024)
Middle-rank manager/ Professional or above	0.192*** (0.040)	0.179*** (0.040)	0.322*** (0.046)	0.306*** (0.046)
Worker Type (rural worker omitted)				
Migrant worker	0.415*** (0.054)	0.243 (0.140)	0.233*** (0.048)	0.050 (0.123)
Urban workers	0.256*** (0.037)	–0.010 (0.110)	0.230*** (0.048)	–0.090 (0.081)
Interactions				
Migrant worker*schooling	–	0.016 (0.016)	–	0.021 (0.014)
Urban worker*schooling	–	0.023* (0.011)	–	0.035*** (0.009)
Migrant worker*party member	–	0.271 (0.170)	–	0.113 (0.273)
Urban workers*party member	–	0.351*** (0.093)	–	0.110 (0.098)
Constant	5.261*** (0.086)	5.459*** (0.119)	5.691*** (0.158)	5.933*** (0.167)
R^2	0.173	0.182	0.260	0.264
N	1,838	1,838	4,933	4,933

Note
*** $p < 0.001$, ** $p < 0.01$, * $p < 0.05$ (two-tailed tests).

(p<0.005). Similarly, with respect to returns to Party membership, only urban workers had significant advantages in 1996 (p<0.001) but in 2005 no difference is found among the three types of workers, though the additive model shows a positive and significant effect on income in general.

Overall, comparisons of earnings determinations among rural non-farm workers, migrant workers, and urban workers show that non-farm workers and migrant workers share more similarities, especially in terms of returns to education and Party membership. Despite the fact that both are in the "urban" labour market, the experience of migrant workers differs from that of urban workers. To a large extent, a boundary in the labour market can be drawn between those with urban *hukou* status and those without, rather than between those working in rural areas and those working in urban areas.

Hukou status and non-monetary benefits in urban labour markets

In descriptive statistics, we found that migrants tend to earn even more than urban workers. The gap should not be considered absolute since, first, migrant workers usually do not have benefits, which account for a significant portion of rewards urban workers receive; and second, migrants usually work longer hours than local urban workers. There is no relevant information in the 1996 survey data, but in the 2005 survey, such information is collected. Given adjustment of *hukou* policy in the late 1990s, the survey has also made a distinction between permanent urban *hukou*, and blue-stamped urban *hukou*. Hence, in urban China's labour markets in 2005, there were three types of workers, of different *hukou* status. Table 3.4 summarizes the monthly income, work hours, and a variety of benefits received by different types of workers.

As Table 3.4 shows, the average monthly income of rural migrants without urban *hukou* is the highest among the three groups, which can be explained by their long workings hours. While urban employees with permanent *hukou* status

Table 3.4 Summary of employment benefits provisions in urban labour markets, by *hukou* status, 2005

	Urban permanent	*Blue-stamped urban*	*Rural migrant*
Monthly income	1,164 (1,579)	1,110 (1,065)	1,209 (2,966)
Weekly working hours	48.5 (12.4)	51.7 (13.8)	55.8 (15.3)
Publicly-funded medicare	35.3	30.8	6.1
Basic medical insurance	50.4	36.0	8.9
Supplementary medical insurance	17.5	12.3	3.1
Basic pension	52.2	36.4	7.1
Supplementary pension plan	16.7	12.3	3.3
Unemployment insurance	29.7	19.0	2.5
Housing/housing allowance	27.3	20.1	5.6

work for 48.5 hours per week on average, employees with blue-stamped *hukou* work for 51.7 hours and rural migrants work for 55.8 hours per week. Note, the legal number of working hours per week in China is 40.

In regard to other benefits, while some urban workers no longer enjoy the full benefits they are entitled to, the percentages of those having the benefits are still highest among urban workers with permanent *hukou*, with a slightly lower percentage among those with blue-stamped urban *hukou*. However, few migrants receive such kinds of benefits, which include medical insurance, pension plans, unemployment insurance, and housing benefits.

Table 3.5 presents the results from logistic models of the likelihood of receiving various benefits on selected variables. Examining the coefficients across columns, we can see that work units and the respondents' schooling are consistently strong predictors of the likelihood of receiving all kinds of benefits mentioned: collective and private enterprises are much less likely to provide the benefits than state-owned, and people with more education are more likely to receive non-monetary benefits in addition to cash income. However, even net of all the individual characteristics, occupation, and work unit affiliations, migrant workers (with rural *hukou* status) are still significantly disadvantaged from access to the benefits (despite the difference between permanent and blue-stamped urban *hukou* access to certain benefits). Thus, the boundary largely exists between those who have urban *hukou* and those who do not.

Social segregation and social inclusion of rural migrants

The above analyses have demonstrated that rural migrants are mainly excluded from the urban formal labour markets and largely resemble their counterparts who stay in rural areas and work in non-farm jobs. Moreover, because of the stigma of their status, rural migrants are socially segregated from the urban world. In the survey, items are constructed to measure the interaction between urban permanent residents and migrants.

The left column of Table 3.6 presents the percentage of respondents who answer "Yes" to the five questions. As the results show, 61.7 per cent of urban permanent residents had experience of working with migrants, and 70.9 per cent of them had migrants living in their communities. The evidence suggests the presence of rural migrants in most urban working and daily life. However, only 36.6 per cent live closely with migrants, who are spatially segregated in the suburban villages, construction sites, and factory dorms; only 33.4 per cent had ever invited migrants to a home visit and 15 per cent had relatives/children dating with migrants.

To measure the attitude, the survey also asked a set of progressive questions whether the respondent is willing to accept rural migrants. The percentages of those who answered "yes" are presented in the right column of the table. Compared with the left column, except for the second question, all other percentages are clearly higher. For example, 57 per cent of urban residents are willing to have migrants living next door and 51.8 per cent are willing to invite migrants to

Table 3.5 Logistic regression on the benefits provisions in urban China, 2005 (N=4,728)

	Publicly-funded medicare	*Basic medical insurance*	*Supplement. medical insurance*	*Basic pension plan*	*Supplement pension plan*	*Unemployment insurance*	*Housing/housing allowance*
Hukou type (urban permanent omitted)							
Blue-stamped urban *hukou*	0.034 (0.154)	–0.425** (0.156)	–0.251 (0.205)	–0.482*** (0.152)	0.185 (0.205)	–0.408* (0.178)	–0.172 (0.179)
Rural *hukou*	–1.375*** (0.222)	–1.567*** (0.193)	–1.211*** (0.304)	–1.926*** (0.209)	–1.016*** (0.293)	–2.185*** (0.329)	–1.158*** (0.234)
Schooling	0.154*** (0.013)	0.202*** (0.013)	0.159*** (0.017)	0.188*** (0.012)	0.169*** (0.017)	0.160*** (0.014)	0.169*** (0.015)
Party member	0.310** (0.105)	0.388*** (0.119)	–0.059 (0.121)	0.254* (0.115)	–0.065 (0.123)	0.033 (0.109)	0.326** (0.109)
Age	0.031 (0.025)	0.013 (0.025)	–0.022 (0.031)	0.058* (0.024)	0.008 (0.032)	0.089** (0.027)	0.015 (0.028)
Age square*	0.003 (0.003)	0.008* (0.003)	–0.008* (0.004)	0.002 (0.003)	0.004 (0.004)	0.007* (0.003)	0.003 (0.003)
Gender	0.087 (0.072)	0.091 (0.072)	0.024 (0.088)	0.092 (0.071)	0.058 (0.089)	0.257*** (0.076)	0.081 (0.078)
Work units (state omitted)							
Collective	–1.628*** (0.157)	–1.846*** (0.137)	–1.670*** (0.131)	–1.670*** (0.131)	–1.237*** (0.209)	–1.939*** (0.185)	–2.268*** (0.217)
Private	–0.837*** (0.089)	–1.074*** (0.087)	–0.962*** (0.114)	–0.890*** (0.086)	–0.680*** (0.112)	–1.131*** (0.095)	–1.362*** (0.101)
Occupation (worker omitted)							
Ordinary staff	–0.083 (0.082)	–0.082 (0.082)	–0.057 (0.099)	–0.226* (0.081)	–0.133 (0.101)	–0.180* (0.086)	–0.164 (0.088)
Middle-rank manager/ Professional or above	0.263 (0.142)	0.651*** (0.178)	0.275 (0.150)	0.291 (0.165)	0.176 (0.153)	0.088 (0.142)	–0.249 (0.144)
Constant	–3.826*** (0.541)	–3.562*** (0.520)	–3.540*** (0.673)	–4.156*** (0.514)	–4.345*** (0.686)	–4.685*** (0.587)	–3.476*** (0.595)
Likelihood ratio χ^2	875.1	1,437.2	447.6	1,313.8	386.5	883.9	928.8
Pseudo R^2	0.147	0.220	0.108	0.201	0.095	0.161	0.175

Note
*** $p<0.001$, ** $p<0.01$, * $p<0.05$ (two-tailed tests).

Table 3.6 Urban permanent residents' interaction with and attitude to migrants, 2005

	Have you ever had experience? (yes = 1) %	*Are you willing? (yes = 1) %*
Working with migrants	61.7	73.6
Migrants living in the community	70.9	66.3
Migrants living next door	36.6	57.0
Inviting migrants home	33.4	51.8
Relative/children dating with migrants	14.9	40.9
N	4,083	4,083

their homes. Over 40 per cent are willing to accept the fact that their relatives or children date with a migrant.

This discrepancy suggests there is considerable room for social inclusion of rural migrants in cities. The exclusion faced by migrants is mainly from government-endorsed institutional restrictions, rather than discrimination against peasant migrants by ordinary urban residents.

Summary and conclusions

To sum up, this chapter has described the origin of the Chinese household registration (*hukou*) and its evolution in the economic reform era, particularly since the 1990s. I argue that the *hukou* system is a part of a socialist redistributive institution, which was employed as a means of social exclusion of the rural majority people from access to the socialist benefits that the state conferred on its citizens. In the process of market reforms and economic globalization, the *hukou* system continues to be used to maintain a pool of cheap labour for capitalist exploitation. Despite the increasing wave of migration from rural areas into cities, the boundary in Chinese labour markets is drawn between those with urban *hukou* status and those without, even within the urban labour markets.

Analyses of the two national representative surveys in China reveal that the patterns of earnings determination among local non-farm workers, migrant workers, and urban workers offer strong support to the segmented labour market based on their *hukou* status. In the urban sector, earnings determination is quite similar between migration workers and rural non-farm workers, in sharp contrast to urban workers. Migrant workers earn more than urban workers, mainly because they are segregated in the private sector, work for long hours and receive few fringe benefits. China's transitional labour markets are clearly separated by labourers' *hukou* status.

Despite the widely occurring presence of migrants in cities, they are socially segregated. However, it seems that there is room for social integration of this disadvantaged group. Their marginal position in the urban sector is to a larger extent due to the institutional barriers set by government policies, rather than due to urban residents' reluctance to accept rural migrants.

A quarter century of Chinese reform ironically was able to take advantage of various institutions as socialist legacies. In China's economic miracle, rural peasants have lagged far behind and migrants tend to fill the bottom of the urban social stratification system. This has led to the increasing inequality and to potential sources of conflict and social instability.

On 19 September 2004, the Chinese Communist Party officially put forward a historical goal to "build a harmonious society" at the Fourth Plenary Session of the 16th Central Committee. It was stated that such a society would be one in which "all the people can work to their fullest abilities, be paid according to their hard work, and get on well with each other". Speaking to a gathering of provincial leaders in February, the CCP General Secretary Hu Jintao urged the building of a social justice guarantee system based on "equal rights, equal opportunities, fair rules, and fair distribution". The social inclusion programmes of migrants in cities should be an important part of the government policy agenda.

Notes

* An earlier version of this chapter was presented in a conference Socialist China, Capitalist China: Social–Political Conflicts under Globalization", held at the Centre for Asia-Pacific Initiatives, University of Victoria, Canada, 16–17 October 2006. The research was supported by a Competitive Earmarked Research Grant from the Hong Kong Research Grants Council (HKUST6424/05H).

1 The 2000 census defines the floating population as individuals who have resided at the place of destination for at least six months without local household registration status. We now use a broader definition of the floating population. Under this definition which includes inter-provincial, intra-provincial (cross-county/city), and intra-county migrants, the floating population in 2000 totalled about 144 million. Among intra-county/city floating migrants, by far the largest group is intra-city migrants, who account for 21 per cent of the total floating population. They include all residential moves within a city, which is less relevant to the issue of rural migrants studied here (Liang and Ma 2004).

2 Residential (*hukou*) status need not be identical to residential location. People with agricultural status could and do live in cities, as have increasingly large numbers of migrant workers, beginning in the early 1980s. Similarly, people with non-agricultural status could live in rural areas, as do agricultural technicians, civil engineers, and school teachers.

3 By selling over-priced industrial products and buying under-priced agricultural produce, the Chinese government was able to reap a huge profit of about 20 to 30 billions RMB yuan in 1978 (Chan 1994:69), or 714 billion RMB yuan from 1952 to 1989 totally (Zhou and Yang 1999:107).

4 They include an identification certificate (*shenfen zheng*) and a temporary resident certificate (*zanzhu zheng*) issued by local police departments in originating counties and destination cities, an employment certificate (*jiuye zheng*) and an employment card (*jiu ye ka*) issued by labour bureaus of originating counties and destination cities, respectively.

Bibliography

Bernstein, Thomas P., *Up to the Mountains and Down to the Villages: The Transfer of Youth from Urban to Rural China*, New Haven: Yale University Press, 1977.

Bian, Yanjie, *Work and Inequality in Urban China*, Albany: State University of New York Press, 1994.

Cai, Fang, *Employment in Rural and Urban China: Issues and Options*, Beijing: Social Science Archive Press, 2002.

Chan, Anita, *China's Workers under Assault: The Exploitation of Labour in a Globalizing Economy, Asia and the Pacific*, Armonk: M. E. Sharpe, 2001.

Chan, Kam Wing, *Cities with Invisible Walls*, Hong Kong: Oxford University Press, 1994.

—— and Li Zhang, "The *Hukou* System and Rural–Urban Migration in China: Processes and Changes", *The China Quarterly* 160: 1999, pp. 818–55.

Chandler, Alfred D., *The Visible Hand*, Cambridge: MIT Press, 1977.

Chao, Loretta, "As China Booms, Millions of Children are Left Behind", *The Wall Street Journal*, 24 January 2007.

Cheng, Tiejun and Mark Selden, "The Origins and Social Consequences of China's *Hukou* System", *The China Quarterly* 139, 1994, pp. 644–68.

De Brauw, Alan, Jikun Huang, Scott Rozelle, Linxiu Zhang, and Yigang Zhang, "The Evolution of China's Rural Labour Markets during the Reforms", *Journal of Comparative Economics* 30, 2002, pp. 329–53.

Domanski, Henryk, "Labour Market Segmentation and Income Determination in Poland", *Sociological Quarterly* 29, 1988, pp. 47–62.

Fan, C. Cindy, "Migration in a Socialist Transitional Economy: Heterogeneity, Socioeconomic and Spatial Characteristics of Migrants in China and Guangdong Province", *International Migration Review* 33, 1999, pp. 954–87.

—— and Youqin Huang, "Waves of Rural Brides: Female Marriage Migration in China", *Annals of the Association of American Geographers* 88:2, 1998, pp. 227–51.

Hale, David and Lyric Hughes Hale, "China Takes Off", *Foreign Affairs*, November–December 2003.

Kalleberg, Arne L. and Aage B. Sorensen, "The Sociology of Labour Markets", *Annual Review of Sociology* 5, 1979, pp. 351–79.

Knight, John, Lina Song, and Jia Huaibin, "Chinese Rural Migrants in Urban Enterprises: Three Perspectives", in Sarah Cook and Margaret Mauer-Fazio (eds) *The Workers' State Meets the Market: Labour in China's Transition*, London: Frank Cass, 1999, pp. 73–104.

Lee, Ching-Kwan, "From Organized Dependency to Disorganized Despotism: Changing Labour Regimes in Chinese Factories", *The China Quarterly* 157, 1999, pp. 44–71.

Li, Lulu and Fenyu Wang, *Dangdai Zhongguo Xiandaihua Jingcheng Zhong de Shehui Jiegou jiqi Bianqian* (*Social Structure and Its Transformation in the Course of Contemporary Chinese Modernization*), Hangzhou: Zhejiang Remin Publishing House, 1992.

Li, Qiang, *Dangdai Zhongguo de Shehui Fenceng Yu Liudong* (*Social Stratification and Mobility in Contemporary China*), Beijing: Zhongguo Jingji Press [in Chinese], 1993.

Liang, Zai, "The Age of Migration in China", *Population and Development Review* 27:3, 2001, pp. 499–524.

—— and Michael J. White, "Market Transition, Government Policies, and Interprovincial Migration in China: 1983–1988", *Economic Development and Cultural Change* 45, 1997, pp. 321–84.

—— and Yiu-por Chen, "The Educational Consequences of Migration for Children in China." *Social Science Research* 36:1, 2007, pp. 28–47.

—— and Zhongdong Ma, "China's Floating Population: New Evidence from the 2000 Census", *Population and Development Review* 30:3, 2004, pp. 467–88.

Lin, Justin Y. F., Fang Cai and Zhou Li, *Zhongguo de Qiji: Fanzhan Zhanlue yu Jingjin Gaige* (*China's Miracle: Development Strategy and Economic Reform*), Shanghai: Sanlian Press, 1994.

Liu, Qiming and Kam Wing Chan, "Rural–Urban Labour Migration Process in China: Job Search, Wage Determinants and Occupational Attainment", University of Washington Center for Studies in Demography and Ecology, 1999, pp. 99–16.

Liu, Zhiqiang, "Institution and Inequality: The *Hukou* System in China", *Journal of Comparative Economics* 33, 2005, pp. 133–57.

Lu, Xueyi (eds) *Dangdai Zhongguo Shehui Jieceng Yanjiu Baogao* (*Research Report on Social Stratification in Contemporary China*), Beijing: Shehui Kexue Wenxian Chubanshe, 2002.

Maurer-Fazio, Margaret and Ngan Dinh, "Differential Rewards to, and Contributions of, Education in Urban China's Segmented Labour Markets", The William Davidson Institute Working Paper 508, Michigan Business School, 2002.

Meisner, Maurice, *Mao's China and After: A History of the People's Republic*, New York: The Free Press, 1999.

Meng, Xin, "Regional Wage Gap, Information Flow, and Rural–Urban Migration", paper presented at the Conference on Rural–Urban Migration, Beijing, 25–27 June 1996.

Murphy, Rachel, *How Migrant Labour is Changing Rural China,* Cambridge: Cambridge University Press, 2002.

National Bureau of Statistics (NBS), *Comprehensive Statistical Data and Materials on 50 Years of New China*, Beijing: China Statistics Press [in Chinese], 1999.

——, *China 2000 Census Data Tabulation*, Beijing: Zhongguo Tongji Press [in Chinese], 2001.

——, *China Statistical Yearbook, 2004*, Beijing: China Statistics Press [in Chinese], 2005.

Naughton, Barry, "The Economic Foundation of a Unique Institution", in Xiaobo Lu and Elizabeth J. Perry (eds) *Danwei: The Changing Chinese Workplace in Historical and Comparative Perspective*, Armonk: M. E. Sharp, 1997, pp. 169–94.

New York Times, "China to Drop Urbanite–Peasant Legal Difference", *New York Times*, 2 November 2005.

Parish, William L. and Martin King Whyte, "Collective Agricultural Organization", *Village and Family in Contemporary China*, Chicago: University of Chicago Press, 1978, Ch. 4.

——, Xiaoye Zhe, and Fang Li, "Non-farm Work and Marketization of Chinese Countryside", *The China Quarterly* 143: 1995, pp. 697–730.

Oi, Jean, "The Fate of the Collective after the Commune", in Deborah Davis and Ezra F. Vogel (eds) *Chinese Society on the Eve of Tiananmen: The Impact of Reform*, Cambridge, MA: The Council of East Asian Studies, Harvard University Press, 1990, pp. 15–36.

Parish, William L., Xiaoye Zhe, and Fang Li, "Non-Farm Work and Marketization of Chinese Countryside", *The China Quarterly* 143, 1995, pp. 697–730.

Peng, Yusheng, "Wage Determination in Rural and Urban China: A Comparison of Public and Private Industrial Sectors", *American Sociological Review* 57, 1992, pp. 198–213.

——, "Chinese Villages and Townships as Industrial Corporation: Ownership, Governance, and Market Discipline", *American Journal of Sociology* 106, 2001, pp. 1338–70.

Pun, Ngai, *Becoming Dagong Mei* Durham: Duke University Press, 2005.

Rawski, Thomas G., "Recent Developments in China's Labor Economy", manuscript obtained from Rawski, 2002.

Roberts, Kenneth D., "China's 'Tidal Wave' of Migrant Labour: What Can We Learn from Mexican Undocumented Migration to the United States?", *International Migration Review* 31, 1997, pp. 249–93.

——, "Female Labour Migrants to Shanghai: Temporary 'Floaters' or Potential Settlers?", *International Migration Review* 36, 2002, pp. 492–519.

Rozelle, Scott, L. Guo, M. Shen, A. Hughart, and J. Giles, "Leaving China's Farms: Survey Results of New Paths and Remaining Hurdles to Rural Migration", *The China Quarterly* 158, 1999, pp. 367–93.

Solinger, Dorothy J., *Contesting Citizenship in Urban China: Peasant Migrants, the State, and the Logic of Market*, Berkeley: University of California Press, 1999.

——, "Why We Cannot Count the 'Unemployed'", *The China Quarterly* 160, 2001, pp. 671–88.

South China Morning Post, "Permit Reform in Capital Offers Migrants First-class Benefits", *South China Morning Post,* 8 July 2003.

Stark, David, "Rethinking Internal Labour Markets: New Insights from a Comparative Perspective", *American Sociological Review* 51, 1986, pp. 492–504.

Stata Corporation, *Stata Reference Manuals*, Stata Corporation, College Station, Texas, 2003.

Treiman, D. J., *Life Histories and Social Change in Contemporary China: Provisional Codebook*, Los Angeles: UCLA Institute for Social Science Research, 1998.

Walder, Andrew G., *Communist Neo-Traditionalism: Work and Authority in Chinese Industry*, Berkeley and Los Angeles: University of California Press, 1986.

——, "Property Rights and Stratification in Socialist Redistributive Economies", *American Sociological Review* 57: 1992, pp. 524–39.

——, Bobai Li, and Donald J. Treiman, "Politics and Life Chances in a State Socialist Regime: Dual Career Paths into the Urban Chinese Elite: 1949 to 1996", *American Sociological Review* 65: 2000, pp. 191–209.

Wang, Fei-ling, "Reformed Migration Control and New Targeted People: China's Hukou Reform in the 2000s", *The China Quarterly* 2004, pp. 115–32.

Wang, Feng, Xuejin Zuo, and Danqing Ruan, "Rural Migrants in Shanghai: Living under the Shadow of Socialism", *International Migration Review* 36, 2001, pp. 520–45.

Wu, Xiaogang, *Institutional Structures and Social Mobility in China: 1949–1996*, unpublished Ph.D. dissertation, Dept. of Sociology, University of California, Los Angeles, 2001.

——, and Donald Treiman, "The Household Registration System and Social Stratification in China 1955–1996", *Demography* 41:2, May 2004, pp. 363–84.

——, and Yu Xie, "Does the Market Pay Off? Earnings Inequality and Returns to Education in Urban China", *American Sociological Review* 68, 2003, pp. 425–42.

Yang, Dennis, "Education and Non-farm Work", *Economic Development and Cultural Change* 45: 1997, pp. 613–32.

Yang, Quanhe, and Fei Guo, "Occupational Attainments of Rural to Urban Temporary Economic Migrants in China, 1985–1990", *International Migration Review* 30: 1996, pp. 771–87.

Yang, Xiaomin and Yihu Zhou, *Zhongguo Danwei Zhidu* (*The Chinese Work-unit System*), Beijing: Zhongguo Jingji Chubanshe (in Chinese), 1999.

Yang, Xiushi and Fei Guo, "Gender Difference in Determinants of Temporary Labour Migration in China: A Multi-level Analysis", *International Migration Review* 33, 1999, pp. 929–53.

Yang, Yunyan and Kam-Wing Chan, "Zhuanxi Laodongli Shichang de Fenceng yu Jingzheng" (Stratification and Competition in Transitional Labour Markets), *Zhongguo Shehui Kexue* no. 5 [in Chinese], 2000.

Yao, Yang, "Social Exclusion and Economic Discrimination: The Status of Migrants in China's Coastal Rural Area", Working Paper E2001005. China Center for Economic Research, Beijing University.

Zhang, Li, *Strangers in the City*, Stanford: Stanford University Press, 2001.

Zhao, Yaohui, "Labour Migration and Earning Differences: The Case of Rural China", *Economic Development and Cultural Change* 47, 1999, pp. 767–82.

——, "Rural to Urban Labour Migration in China: The Past and the Present", in West and Zhao (eds) *Chinese Rural Labour Flows*, Berkeley: Institute for East Asian Studies, University of California, 2000, pp. 15–32.

Zhou, Xueguang and Liren Hou, "Children of the Cultural Revolution: The State and the Life Course in the People's Republic of China", *American Sociological Review* 64: 1999, pp. 12–36.

4 Training the unemployed to become active job-seekers in post-Mao China

Feng Xu

Introduction

It is almost a truism to say that China's economic reform has led to spectacular economic growth, but also has created serious social and political problems. Unemployment (*shiye*) is one such social problem that demands immediate government attention. In various government announcements, employment is taken to be about "people's livelihood" (*minsheng*) and, consequently, the "nation's stability" (*guo'an*). Thus, unemployment is now deemed one of the most politically explosive issues to challenge the Chinese government's overriding priority of social stability. Despite only being officially acknowledged since 1994, unemployment, in the sense of a serious imbalance between the number of job-seekers and the number of jobs, is not an unprecedented policy problem.[1] According to recent government announcements, China has in fact entered the third of three employment peaks (*jiuye gaofeng*) since the death of Mao: the first peak hit China when sent-down youth of the Cultural Revolution returned to urban areas; the second peak was caused by *xiagang gongren* (off-post workers, or the so-called "40/50" – male workers over 50 and female workers over 40) who were hardest hit by state-owned enterprise (SOE) restructuring in the 1990s. That said, the current economic, social, and policy context means that the social, economic, and political implications of unemployment are unique.

How to solve unemployment in a country whose economy is increasingly dominated by market logic, but whose political system continues to be one-Party rule? As editors of this book point out, the Chinese regime exploits both the capitalist economy and the communist ideology to support its legitimacy, while leaving the benefits of socialism nowhere to be seen.[2] A conceptual framework that dichotomizes China either as capitalist or communist/socialist no longer captures the complexities of Chinese political, economic, and social landscape. In this chapter, I argue that unemployment is a policy area where the Chinese government mixes governance techniques of both neo-liberal and Chinese communist orientation. Specifically, I argue that although China is not a liberal democracy, it increasingly uses neo-liberal ways to govern, and that this has been true in the way China has addressed the unemployment issue. "Liberalism" in this context means a specific way of providing positive conditions for optimum economic performance at "minimum economic and *socio-political* cost"[3] One prominent feature of neo-liberal governance is the attempt to govern *through* the freedom of individuals. Indeed, the rationale behind this policy direction is the seemingly paradoxical one that freedom is necessary to governance. In neo-liberal governance, individuals are encouraged and steered in the parameters within which they govern themselves.[4] However, this argument does not imply that Chinese governance is shifting towards Western neo-liberal governance. It does argue that the Chinese government mixes and matches both neo-liberal and communist government rationalities to deal with challenges deriving from its "socialist market economy" programme.[5]

The post-Mao Chinese government continues to rely on campaign/*yundong* style of policy implementation, although campaign/*yudong* is now replaced with activity/*huodong*.[6] In the policy area of employment, for example, the Ministry of Labour and Social Security (MoLSS) has launched various nation-wide activities such as "Re-employment Assistance Month [Zaijiyye Yuanzhu Yue]" and "Spring Breeze Action [Chunfeng Xingdong]". Further, these government-sponsored activities make state power visible: the visibility of the state power is what distinguishes the Chinese state and neo-liberal state that must be seen to "govern at a distance". The Chinese state needs to make its power visible in order to claim itself as the sole legitimate player that represents the interests of the Chinese people. This chapter, however, focuses on the neo-liberal techniques the Chinese government is adopting in regulating the unemployed in order to address the unemployment problem. The research presented here suggests that unemployment has been a fertile ground for Chinese government experiments with administrative initiatives resembling neo-liberal ones in the West. The experiments include the emergence of community/*shequ* as a new space of local governance,[7] and services such as training and counselling that are designed to improve the employability of the unemployed and more generally to encourage the employed to seek self-employment and flexible employment.[8] These initiatives are seen to institutionalize (*zhiduhua*), professionalize (*zhuanyehua*) and humanize (*renxinhua*) its approach to governance, an approach that also meets international norms and standards in employment regulation.[9] Further, these international norms and standards fit nicely with the Chinese government effort to turn current and former state employees away from "organizational dependence" on such government programmes as social welfare.[10] Unemployment policy, like the wider framework for social policies, and the even wider problematic of governance, has been widely discussed in academic circles in China.[11] Yet outside Chinese policy and academic circles, very little analytical research has been conducted on the new forms of organizations involved in regulating Chinese unemployment or the mundane practices of unemployment regulation. This chapter is an initial report on this burgeoning area of job training centres, employment centres, community service centres, and the application process these centres employ for unemployment insurance and job counselling in Shanghai.

Data for this chapter is drawn in part from fieldwork conducted in Shanghai in the summers of 2004 and 2006. It has also been informed by Chinese government documents, publications on unemployment and career counselling published in China, Chinese newspapers, and expert and technical advice from such international organizations as the ILO, OECD, and World Bank,[12] and works by Chinese social scientists and social workers who inform government policies. The present interpretive analysis seeks to understand the discursive practices operative within and outside government, and to trace their origins and transformations.

Before beginning this analysis, a few caveats are in order. Shanghai is one of a handful of China's leading cities, both in prosperity, in outward orientation, and in sheer scale. What works in wealthy coastal regions such as Shanghai may not be applicable elsewhere in China; as the following discussion will show, successful public employment service centres require enormous financial and human resources. But national government documents and announcements do point to a wider turn away from political/ideological solutions to unemployment to technocratic ones. This technocratic vision of solving unemployment is certainly a leading element in the experiment at public employment service centres (*jiuyefuwu zhongxin*). Work at these centres emphasizes turning the unemployed from "government dependence" to the independence of self-steering individuals. But paradoxically, the government has felt itself obliged to intervene as the guarantor of self-steering individualism among China's unemployed, rather than allow the self-steering individualism of the market itself to exercise its own disciplining force alone.

The "retreat" of the state and the emergence of the social

In analyzing Europe's transition to capitalism in the eighteenth century, Karl Polanyi famously theorized that the emergence of the socially dis-embedded "self-regulating market" represents one movement within a society's transition to capitalist modernity. But Polanyi added that social and political forces, acting primarily in defence of the irreducibly non-market goods that underlie the fictitious commodities of labour and land, commonly arise as a second, stabilizing, counter-movement. The results of this double movement are social and political institutions that serve to contain or re-embed the market. He argues that self-regulating market as a coherent system was a practical impossibility, and that such a system would blow apart before being fully realized, without the second of these two movements. For this reason, Polanyi argues that "social not technical invention was the intellectual mainspring of the Industrial Revolution".[13]

The Chinese state, since it launched economic reform in 1979, has actively intervened to create a market society. After a number of interim stages, it has ultimately opted for a largely self-regulating market, in many respects very much in keeping with nineteenth-century Europe.[14] Against this trend, resistance to the full commodification of land and labour has arisen in both rural and urban areas. Increasingly, state initiatives such as social security policy, "community building", and government-mediated non-governmental organizations have sought to address some of the key perceived sources of such unrest. In a political system which rejects many of the classic organizational forms associated with Europe's "double movement", these state initiatives do nonetheless intend to help re-embed the market so that market economy can flourish in a stable social environment.

One of the state's tasks in creating a "self-regulating" market has been to create a labour market virtually from scratch – that is, to commodify labour – and it has had to do so in a form that is compatible with a cost-competitive, flexible-accumulation development strategy.[15] One of the prominent features of China's emergent labour market is the rapid increase in internal migrant workers, especially in coastal areas. Rural to urban migration was made possible by de-collectivization and by the loosening of the household registration system, both of which once limited people's freedom of movement. The SOEs, which operated both as economic institutions and as social ones, are being dismantled. The introduction of the contract labour system to SOEs in 1986, one of the first steps to replace the Maoist "iron rice bowl", was followed ultimately by the widespread privatization of SOEs in 1997. Even though workers are not allowed to form independent trade unions, workers' resistance is widespread in China, both in everyday forms and in protests and strikes more familiar in Western contexts. Protests and strikes are especially prominent in northeastern China and China's interior, where state-owned and heavy industries previously predominated.[16]

As the state "retreats" from providing for social welfare to its employees through the SOEs, "society"/"the social" (*shehui*) emerges as hegemonic discourse in policy and academic circles. But, in the Chinese context, what is society and what counts as the social? It seems at this moment in history, *shehui* in China is an abstract and reified vessel, or a black hole. It appears to mean whatever market and government deem not to be economic or political, and therefore, whatever lies outside the responsibilities of either of these institutions. This is a delicate position for the government to adopt, as it faces mounting social problems that it is inclined to police as a source of "social turmoil".

To solve this conundrum, the Chinese government calls on social forces (*shehui liliang*) to involve themselves in addressing social causes (*shehui shiye*). In general, social conduct now properly becomes a sphere for regulation by a much more complex web of actors – social scientists, professional social workers, and so on. Crucially, however, this notion of the "social forces" that are to address (non-state, non-economic) "social" problems does not distinguish between profit and non-profit organizations. Thus, the central dividing line in official government rhetoric about the sources of solutions is clearly the divide between government and non-government organizations, and not between market and non-market ones. Privatization and user fees are therefore considered efficient and desirable ways of delivering social services. Indeed, the profit motive constitutes the first principle of this new "subsidiarity": if companies are not now to deliver social services, social services are to be provided *as if* a company were providing them, in many instances in the sense that the for-profit form is applied to social service provision.

From the perspective of economic development policy, the logic behind this move is clear enough. Government, especially at the county and township levels, is reluctant to invest in social spending because it is seen to hurt economic development strategies that stress cost-competitiveness. That China's economic development model is based on cheap labour does not augur well for the demand for and creation of government social policies beyond the realm of the market. From a Polanyian perspective, however, this problem has the distinct disadvantage of addressing the consequences of market rationality by the further extension of market rationality. The logic of the Polanyian double movement seems to imply that the Chinese government's distinctive appeal for "social" forces of this market-oriented sort to deal with "social problems" would tend ultimately to exacerbate, rather than reduce, social polarization.

To some extent, the Chinese state realizes the danger of not dealing with social redistribution: rapid, market-driven social polarization has been officially discussed as a key source of large-scale social unrest. China's policy is not silent on the social implications of its population's encounter with the market system. In view of the need to build a social security system, the Ministry of Labour was changed to the Ministry of Labour and Social Security (MoLSS) in 1998. On the other hand, the Chinese leadership continues to view economic growth as the overriding national priority. Consequently, any social assistance schemes such as minimum living guarantee (*dibao*) and unemployment insurance are meant to be temporary, and are aimed at helping the unemployed to find jobs as soon as possible. Here is a transition from what Andrew Walder calls the "organizational dependence" of the *danwei* system under the socialist planned economy to active labour market policies. The latter aim at getting people off government assistance and employed as soon as possible. The "retreat" of the state from certain areas of economy does not mean the weakening of the state, rather it means the "regrouping" of the state – the state has been re-organizing so as to intervene in areas it deems essential, but leave areas that belong to "society" to be taken care of by "society".[17] As Lee points out, with the state's retreat from regulating employment relations,

> the increasing importance of the law [National Labour Law] and the market frees workers from their past economic and political dependence on a particular work unit or official department. Yet the "freedom" to choose and to change jobs comes at a high price.[18]

In fact, workers are encouraged to use their new-found freedom to become active job-seekers in the market economy, rather than cling to their old identity of state employees.

Let us now turn to consider the significance of such policies on a comparative basis. Welfare policies during the twentieth-century in most Western liberal societies may be construed as the state's response to those disadvantaged in the market, above all in order to contain class struggle. For Keynesians and for students of

"Fordism" alike, however, minimum income guarantees also serve to stabilize consumption in economies oriented primarily to a domestic market. But the classic Western welfare state does not have a more direct purpose with respect to entrenching the social preconditions for the market itself. Its primary functions are social and non-economic.

Neo-liberal government, by contrast, aids the worker by reinforcing market behaviour, actively re-inserting the subject of assistance back into the market. The classical example of this is the emergence of the Western workfare programme, but the turn in orientation is evident both substantively and at the level of policy "rhetoric". For example, The Canadian Employment Insurance Act of 1996 signalled the Chrétien government's turn from passive to active employment policy and its drastic reduction in overall policy coverage by substituting "Employment Insurance" for the former "Unemployment Insurance". In the United States, President Clinton signed into law the Personal Responsibility and Work Opportunity Reconciliation Act in 1996, better known as the Welfare Reform Bill. Such shifts to active employment policy reflect what Bob Jessop calls the "Schumpeterian Workfare State": welfare provision is devised with the aim of making the overall social formation more competitive in the market economy.[19] In other words, welfare provision focuses on the supply side of the labour market, emphasizing improvement in the employability of the unemployed through training and counselling.

When we consider the recent emergence of public employment service centres in China, it is also crucial to note the neo-liberal turn in global institutions and the impact of this turn on the roles and functions of public employment services (PES). The global transition from welfare state to workfare state is reflected in the changing roles and functions of ILO-mandated PES.

> The PES became involved in special employment measures to alleviate unemployment often on a much larger scale to their traditional job-brokering activities. Remedies for unemployment were increasingly sought in the supply side of the economy … [T]here was a belief that over-generous and indefinite systems of unemployment compensation were creating a problem of "benefit dependency". Renewed emphasis was given to the role of the PES in applying work tests to those drawing unemployment benefits.[20]

The OECD Jobs Study (1994) also suggested that Active Labour Market Programmes (ALMPs) should replace passive income support.[21]

Evidence emerging from my preliminary research and the still-limited literature on unemployment in China shows that government is increasingly opting for a market-oriented employment policy (*shichang jiuye*) and devolves the financing of employment programmes to local government.[22] The establishment of public employment service centres, active labour market policies, and wholesale departures from "standard employment norms"[23] are entirely in line with global trends. The ILO provides expert knowledge and advice on labour market mechanisms, of which PES is one. Shanghai municipality, in 1996, introduced the concept of informal employment (*fei zhengguijiuye*) from the ILO in order to help the city address large-scale restructuring of the SOEs and the increasing demand for people working in the ever-expanding service industries.[24] The two-way flow of information between the global and national levels is important to emphasize. The China Employment Forum, set up between China's Ministry of Labour and Social Security and the ILO, seems to be the main channel through which ILO expert knowledge and advice flow to China. On the other hand, statistics and experiences from China become part and parcel of the global knowledge base of employment policies and practices.[25]

From "iron rice bowl" (*tiefanwan*) to flexible/informal employment (*feizhenggui jiuye*)

"The shift to a service economy in many of the highly developed countries has resulted in a greater share of low-wage jobs than was the case when manufacturing was the leading sector".[26] This observation can be applied – with appropriate adjustments – to China, as well. In the Chinese government's push to restructure SOEs, every effort has been made to shrink state sectors and expand private sectors; as well as to shrink primary and secondary sectors and expand service sectors such as restaurants and tourism. The goal of expanding the latter service sectors tends to result from growth in high-tech and financial sectors (to list just two examples), above all, in big cities such as Shanghai.[27] The paradoxical coexistence of well-paid jobs in high-tech and financial sectors, and lower-paid jobs in service sectors is characteristic of global cities throughout the world.[28] But I would argue such a characteristic is not limited to global cities. What we are witnessing in any Chinese city is that the growth of the financial, and high-tech sectors, and of tourism, has created the need for many more people to clean office buildings, act as security guards (*bao'an*), clean hotel rooms (*baojie*), and so on. The growing middle class also creates spectacular market growth for fine dining, and hence, for appropriate waiters. The same can be said for a series of other services to the new middle class, as well as to the aging population, such as ground maintenance staff, and security guards at prosperous residential areas (*xiaoqu*), domestic work service, and so on.

To ensure the successful restructuring of China's economy, more and more people are channelled to such rapidly growing non-state, small- and medium-sized service sectors. In Polanyian terms, these new sectors are precisely oriented to guaranteeing the reproduction of (middle-class) labour by specifically market mechanisms. But, paradoxically, these sectors, as Sassen points out, tend to have "a greater share of low-wage jobs than was the case when manufacturing was the leading sector".[29] They, therefore, contribute to problems of labour reproduction in the new working classes.

One might also add that workplace ownership also affects wages in China, and disproportionately more women find themselves employed in informal sectors. Generally speaking, state sectors still have better-paid jobs, and hire disproportionately more full-time and permanent workers. But this sector is shrinking. Those employed in SOEs decreased from 50 per cent of all urban employees throughout the 1980s to 30 per cent by 1999. Women who were laid off took up 62.8 per cent of all the laid-off workers by 1997.[30] Those who were laid off from SOEs typically found less desirable "flexible" employment.[31] According to a survey of selected cities conducted by All China Federation of Trade Union, 80–90 per cent of laid-off workers who found re-employment by the end of 1999 were employed in the informal sectors.[32] Shareholding companies, joint ventures, individual households, (*getihu*) and private enterprises (*siren qiye*), in particular, prefer flexible employment, but these are the sectors that are growing.[33]

In order to encourage people to work in service sectors, which have disproportionately low-wage jobs, the government is no longer able to re-assign or otherwise compel them directly. It has to change people's attitude that part-time and informal/flexible jobs are "not real jobs". According to statistics from the fifth national census and the 66-city survey of employment and social security conducted by the Ministry of Labour and Social Security in 2002, fully two-thirds of those who found employment in the two years before the survey was conducted, had found temporary jobs (*lingshigong*).[34] Those who refused to work in these low-paid jobs are commonly characterized in both public and expert discourse as too picky and lazy, workers, in short, who are still "stuck in the past" with respect to what employment should be. One thing I heard the most while in China from staff working in employment service centres is that many jobs are available, and that, therefore, "it all depends on whether you want to work". Here, "many jobs" refer to many low-pay temporary jobs.

This line of analysis is popular among employment officials and experts, but does raise questions about the nature of the work available. Several independent front-line workers did say to me during my research trips that even workers on the minimum basic living guarantees (MBLG) would commonly refuse work. While this could be interpreted as laziness (or as a symptom of more general psychological depression over a life without hope or meaning) it could also be read as a perfectly rational individual calculation of the kind neo-liberal rationality encourages: what is the rational choice between the alternatives of receiving the MBLG, or receiving a similar amount in wages in return for many hours of service labour?

One problem I encountered with this line of analysis may be seen in a parallel analysis of youth unemployment, now being discussed openly as a particularly severe social problem.[35] A new term, "gnawing the old generation", (*kenlaozu*), refers to young employable men and women, usually in their 20s and 30s, who are unemployed, but are said to prefer to rely on their parents than to look actively for jobs. As staff in local community (*shequ*) offices told me in Shanghai, it is easier to get *xiagang* workers to actively look for jobs than it is to influence these younger workers. The older workers have a stronger sense of responsibility to their own families, and presumably a stronger lifetime commitment to paid labour. They are consequently characterized as being more willing to take up flexible employment in the service sectors than many who have never experienced non-market labour policy.

In sum, employment in China is undergoing a shift from "iron rice bowl" to "flexible" employment policy. The problem becomes one of making the workers flexible, as well. More and more people are subject to free market dynamics, and are thus more vulnerable. On the other hand, the existing social security system remains decentralized and the levels of assistance remain highly variable, a legacy of workplace-based welfare provision during the Maoist period. The new national priority of maintaining high economic growth is given as a rationale for the state's social security system emphasizing the re-insertion of the unemployed in the market, rather than shielding them from it.

From off-post/*xiagang* workers to the unemployed/ *shiyerenyuan*

The Chinese government only collects data on registered unemployed with urban *hukou*. Rural jobless migrants are not even counted as the unemployed because, first of all, it will significantly raise the already high unemployment rate, and secondly, to be recognized as unemployed is to have access to still-limited government services to help find jobs.[36] The unemployment rate also does not include off-post/*xiagang* workers because they are still considered part of the enterprises. As Solinger argues, there is simply no way to find out China's actual unemployment rate.[37] While it is the only officially stated figure, the unemployment rate of 4.5 per cent is widely considered far below the actual number, reflecting more the government target than the actual number.[38] Even though government increasingly turns to technical solutions to unemployment, unemployment rate is still considered a sensitive political matter.[39]

"Off-post" (*xiagang*) workers from SOEs and collectively-owned enterprises have lost their *danwei* as both economic and social institution, but their official relationship with their employers is not officially severed. These workers are considered a historical category unique to the Chinese situation, when these sectors of the economy were restructuring, but China's current social security system was not in place. In order to help off-post workers to make the transition, enterprises were required to set up re-employment service centres (*zaijiuye fuwu zhongxin*) for their workers. These centres were considered societal intermediary organizations (*shehui zhongjie*), namely, organizations that act between the government and the market.[40] But to be qualified as off-post workers, most workers have to have joined SOEs as full-time regular workers with tenure (*zhengshi gongren*) before 1986, when the contractual employment system was instituted. Furthermore, they must have been laid off because their enterprises had to restructure; they must not have terminated their labour relationship with enterprises, and must not yet have found employment. Those hired as contract labour, but whose contract had not yet come to term, were also qualified as off-post workers. It is clear that government is attentive to the needs of former "labour aristocrats", who have been considered in official Party discourse to have made great contributions to the society, and who are now making another sacrifice, this time for reform. Furthermore, of China's urban population, off-post workers are most likely to have experienced dramatic social dislocation. They, therefore, were most likely to complain about the present, and to feel nostalgic about the past.

In order to receive social insurance and medical care, these off-post (*xiagang*) workers had to enter a re-employment service centre established by the employer under government obligation, and sign a contract with the centre. By signing the contract, the off-post workers agreed either to look actively for work or to accept jobs referred by the centre. In return, these workers received a "basic living guarantee" of no more than 120 per cent of local unemployment insurance, and the centre continued to pay both for the workers' training and the employer's portion of the workers' previous social benefits. According to the contract, if the off-post workers twice refused work referred to them or did not find employment within three years, then all benefits would be withdrawn. In any case, under these contracts, off-post workers that were still unemployed would also end their relationship with their employers within three years. They would then have to look for jobs as regular unemployed workers, which entailed a much less generous level of support that itself lasted only two years.[41] In this sense, then, reemployment service centres were created to help off-post workers to make the transition from reliance on the state to independent, active job seeking in the labour market. This, however, was a privilege temporarily enjoyed by off-post workers who had worked as permanent SOE workers. By 2002, reemployment service centres for off-post workers were expected to have been replaced by public employment service centres modelled on ILO practices. Thus, in the new century, the unemployed seeking employment through the labour market becomes the standard category, but this practice is praised as China finally "connecting to the global track" [of employment policy practice]. And off-post workers' disappearance as a historical phenomenon coincides with China's shift to active employment policies. The transformation of off-post workers from "person of the plan" (*jihuaren*) to "person of the market" (*shichangren*), is, in Yang Yiyong's words, "a process of being reborn.... It is a silent revolution".[42] As the World Bank Employment Policy Primer writes,

> the objectives of active labour market programs (ALMPs) "is primarily economic – to increase the probability that the unemployed will find jobs or that the underemployed will increase their productivity and earning.... With economic reform, increasing liberalization of markets and growing concerns about the problems of unemployment, ALMPs have increasingly become an attractive option for policymakers.[43]

Besides encouraging a more flexible attitude to acceptable paid labour, active employment policies also aim to encourage people to seek self-employment (*ziwo jiuye*); government subsidies are available to encourage people to start and run their own small- and medium-sized businesses. These initiatives are uniformly called "Start and Improve Your Own Business" (SIYB) or "Start Your

Own Business" (SYB) found in Chinese newspapers and government documents and publications: as direct borrowings from ILO best-practices documents in the area of job creation, these acronyms signal China's convergence with "international best practices".[44]

This link to the ILO's programme is more than borrowing catchphrases. On the ILO official website, SIYB is described as "a globally recognized trademark and the program has been introduced in more than 80 countries" (www.ilo.org). The same website reports on a Chinese TV drama series called, "My Future is Not a Dream" (*Wode Weilai Bushi Meng*). This programme was a joint production between Sichuan TV Station, the Chinese Ministry of Labour and Social Security, and the ILO's SIYB Programme. The series is about how rural migrants start their own businesses and become successful entrepreneurs. As the chief technical advisor for SIYB-China Project points out, "the aim is to catch [migrants'] interest, encourage them to start their own businesses, and tell them about the training services available to help them make the first important steps" (www.iol.org). The key message is that rural migrants are as capable as urban people in starting their own businesses and becoming "modern" entrepreneurs in China's competitive market economy (www.ILO.org).

In turn, the ILO's SYB/SIYB programmes seem to have caught the attention of the government because they are seen to "kill two birds with one stone": the unemployed who become business owners solve not only their own employment problems but others as well. More significantly for government, the unemployed who turn to successful small- and medium-sized business owners act as "model citizens", and can be held up for the others to emulate: take your own initiatives to become entrepreneurs, but do not wait for the government to help you!

Briefly, then, active employment policies stress the supply side of the labour market. With them, government subsidizes training that is hoped to lead to employment. The training programmes are to improve the quality (*suzhi*) of the labour forces to meet the demands of an emerging "knowledge economy". The change from off-post/*xiagang* workers to unemployed/*shiye* is not just a change in terminology: instead, it signals a government shift in dealing with unemployment, from working through the state owned enterprise system to working through market mechanisms. The term "unemployed" (*shiye)* means that employers have terminated their relationship with employees, and that the expectation is now that they have to turn to the market to look for jobs. The Chinese government's employment policies put the individual's ability to find employment first, in combination with market-mediated employment. The government's role in employment is not to create employment, but to promote it. This promotional work favours multiple channels of employment (*duoyuanhua jiuye*), including self-employment, employment in private and foreign-owned companies, and diverse forms of part-time, temporary, and flexible employment.[45] Ultimately, individuals have to rely on themselves to navigate the labour market. Such employment policies are not unique to China, but are compatible with global trends. And the ILO, World Bank, and OECD countries are ready to provide expertise knowledge and policy advice.

Shanghai public employment service centres

The physical layout and its message

I visited public employment service centres in two districts in Shanghai in the summer of 2006. These centres shared a similar physical layout. When one enters the centre, one finds oneself in the middle of a large hall. The hall is clean, spacious, and open (*changkaishi*). There are stand-alone computers in the hall ready for those who know how to use computers to search jobs, construct resumés, and apply for jobs on the job net (http://jobs.12333.gov.cn). On the walls are large screen TV monitors that air Q & A sessions between clients and staff. On one side of the hall, there is a counter, and behind it, many small rooms with glass doors where many different services are delivered to individual clients. These services include help with constructing resumés on-line, techniques on how to conduct a successful job interview, and counselling those who have psychological barriers to successfully finding jobs. These small rooms provide one-on-one services, and despite their glass doors, their very existence in the Chinese context signals a desire to differentiate these services, and to protect clients' privacy. The physical layout of the centre signals a shift in governance approach: the impersonal bureaucratic architecture of earlier periods in modern Chinese history signalled an official orientation to handling standardized problems of undifferentiated hordes. The layout of these centres emphasizes human-centred services (*renxinhua fuwu*), designed specifically for clients with different needs. The openness of the main hall may be interpreted as an atmosphere of welcome, as if to say to clients that the officials are ready to serve them. In a word, the employment services centre's new rationality is to serve "clients".

Human-centred services (renxinhua fuwu)

As we have seen, PESs in China are modelled on ILO best practices,[46] and come under the jurisdiction of Bureau of Labour and Social Security. According to a public education brochure distributed in Shanghai's Public Employment Service Centre (*gonggong jiuyefuwu zhongxin*), the centre plays four roles: job brokering; labour resources management; unemployment insurance management; and assistance to those who desire to start their own businesses (*ziwo chuangye*). In other words, the centre's mission is not to create jobs, but to create favourable conditions for its clients to find employment on the labour market.

The centre's customers are Shanghai residents with Shanghai *hukou* status, or university graduates, whether they enjoy Shanghai *hukou* status or not. In the past two years, the Shanghai municipal government has started to stress assisting those who want to start their own businesses. My informants told me that this was done because those who start their own businesses create jobs not only for themselves, but also for others. The centre's mission is to provide services to clients, facilitating their job hunt in the labour market, or their start-efforts in business.

This implies that age-old coercive administrative measures (*xinzheng shouduan*) are assumed not to work any longer (if, indeed, they ever worked). In order to govern better and more effectively, the Chinese government, like its neo-liberal counterparts in the West, also assumes that it cannot govern everything. The concept and practice of human-centred service delivery is just one example of a more general shift in Chinese governance, one explicitly borrowed from recent trends in public administration in the West.[47] Humanization (*renxin hua*) in general is now officially described as being compatible with China's modernization, and the latter is expressed with a dual focus: first, on national strength; and second, on "individual comprehensive development" (*ren de quanmian fazhan*). "Individual comprehensive development" includes, among other things, individuals' ability to design their own lifelong project, or more narrowly, their career ambitions. Translated into employment, it means that individual clients must strive to become active job seekers. The PES centres provide services to help achieve that goal. Inherent in these services are the rationales (*linian*) that different clients have different needs, and that they must be divided up for different treatments.

Dividing practices (fenlei) and disciplinary power

To serve them better, clients have to be divided in order to be provided with different services – this is described as "human-centred service" delivery. Clients at these centres are divided into those who can navigate the site by themselves (self-steering), those who need help to navigate the site to fill out resumé forms, those who need face-to-face job counselling, and those who need psychological counselling.

This practice of dividing has an economic logic as well as a purely administrative one. I was told the dividing practice on the part of the government is to maximize its resources so that no resources are wasted on clients who can help themselves or need only some help. Such a rationale is provided as well by the World Bank Employment Policy Primer:

> PES can be organized into "tiers" with some general services available to everyone (e.g. job brokerage services) and more intensive programs only available to clients identified as needing those services. … Tiered service delivery can help allocate public resources as efficiently as possible.[48]

But the dividing practice is closely linked to disciplinary power, as Foucault warns us.[49] So, for example, those who can help themselves in navigating computerized labour market information do not need hands-on help from staff. Even for those who need help, there are different degrees of need. One staff member used the revealing analogy of medical patients to explain the rationality behind the PES centre's dividing practices. Patients, depending on their illness, can seek medical help ranging from over-the-counter medicines, to clinical help, to specialists. Similarly, the unemployed can be "diagnosed" as to how "sick" they are by the staff, and then are subject to different kinds of treatment, so that they might recover from "dependency syndrome" and conform to the new self-steering norms of subjectivity in an increasingly marketized economy.

When clients register with the centre, government has detailed knowledge about them. On the continuum of conformity with the latter norm of independent subjectivity, the most dependent (and thus most difficult to employ) are older people (anyone over 49 years old) with low education. Those people often do not even come to the centres, a lack of action which in itself demonstrates a degree of agency. Government needs different techniques to get to know those who do not come to the centre. Employment assistants (*jiuye yuanzhuyuan*) in communities (*shequ*) organizations were created to target this group of difficult, "inflexible", and passive cases. Usually in Shanghai, the most difficult to employ are provided with "public interest jobs" (*gongye xing*) as employment categories of last resort. These jobs include public hygiene, public security, and grounds maintenance (*baojie, bao'an, baolü*). District-level government usually pays the wage difference between the pay for these jobs and the municipal minimum living standard, and also pays for a premium on pension, medical and social insurance.

The job of employment assistants involves knocking on residents' doors, and getting to know every household that has an unemployed member. Once every month, these assistants have to update information on the unemployed. They then turn to finding job vacancies and matching them with the unemployed in their neighbourhoods. Employment assistants thus continue the tradition of resident committee work, but with different goals. This time, employment assistants collect detailed knowledge of each household's employment status, and try to match those unemployed with job vacancies available. Further, the employment assistants work on contract with local bureaus of labour and social security.[50]

Technologies of the self

Job counselling (*zhiye zhidao*) is a new service offered in Shanghai public employment service centres. The service targets the most difficult clients: those who face psychological difficulties are understood to have problems of personality type and/or (in strikingly Foucauldian terms) an improper understanding of the self. The job counsellor, armed with expertise in psychology, works with a client for a 1–2-hour session, sometimes with follow-up visits. Based on my observation of one such session and books on job counselling, it appears that job counselling is aimed at moulding clients' attitude and behaviour so that they have a "proper understanding of the self" (*ziwon de renshi*), so as to compete more successfully in the labour market.

More specifically, the job counsellor steers clients to properly understand their own capabilities and Shanghai's labour market conditions; figures out a client's pragmatic goals; and then outlines strategies to seek employment in the competitive labour market. To quote the main job counsellor I interviewed, a job counsellor's job is to readjust the client's understanding of self, and then to "reconstruct" that self. One book on job counselling told its readers (typically, university graduates) that a correct knowledge of oneself is a first step in helping university graduates to rationally design their career goals. The author of the book then quoted an American job counsellor expert in saying that career choice includes three steps: knowing self, knowing conditions for a successful career, and decision-making. The author then concludes that a correct assessment of one's own characteristics and of factors relating to one's career choices is an important precondition to choosing one's career correctly.[51]

All this should sound strikingly familiar to experts in contemporary reforms of Western welfare states. In analysing "advanced liberalism", Rose argues that,

> [I]ndividuals are to become "experts of themselves", to adopt an educated and knowledgeable relation of self-care in respect of their bodies, their minds, their forms of conduct and that of the members of their own families.... Those "excluded" ... are to be assisted not through the ministrations of solicitous experts proffering support and benefit cheques, but through their engagement in a whole array of programmes for their ethical reconstruction as active citizens – training to equip them with the skills of self-promotion, counselling to restore their sense of self-worth and self-esteem, programmes of empowerment to enable them to assume their rightful place as the self-actualizing and demanding subjects of an "advanced" liberal democracy.[52]

In turning the unemployed from dependence on government and family to independence, we see an array of techniques at work in Shanghai employment centres. Some of these techniques are borrowed from the advanced liberal societies, as exemplified by the ILO and World Bank; some are drawn from Chinese practices, such as the canvassing of mobilizing neighbourhoods to get to know the unemployed.

The successful individual in the modern market economy is someone who is constantly on the move to assess and maximize his or her capability and life chances in the ever-changing labour market. As Baum points out,

> it is individual men and women on their own who are expected to use, individually, their own wits, resources, and industry to lift themselves to a more satisfactory condition and leave behind whatever aspect of their present condition they may resent.[53]

The very media in use at these job centres speak to this model of flexible self-improvement. Computerized job-net systems in Shanghai's employment service centres facilitate this principle of flexibility: clients can constantly update their history of employment and change of skills through access to a personal computer file. Paper forms are in a sense part of an older order passing away: they cannot be changed, and can be difficult to locate. Flexible job markets – and hence flexible workforces – require a degree of agency on the part of individuals, but do not independently produce such agency.

Conclusion

China's policies towards unemployment cut across the distinction between authoritarianism and liberalism. In the area of active employment policies, the governance approach is of a new kind: freedom itself is being framed and mobilized to steer people to government's desired policy goals. The Chinese government does so for several apparent reasons. First, a growing consensus, mirroring an international consensus, claims that these policies seem to work elsewhere, and therefore provide valuable experience to the Chinese government in handling this potentially explosive political problem. Second, these policies are compatible with the government's effort to channel the unemployed away from "dependence" on government to becoming active individual job seekers in the labour market. Third, the Chinese government wants to show to the international community that it is "modernizing" and institutionalizing its employment policies, even though China is a late-comer in this area. Finally, mobilizing individual freedom in employment policies can be presented as simultaneously respecting the individual's agency, a value increasingly viewed as key to "individual comprehensive development", and as an integral part of enhancing overall national strength.

China is an authoritarian regime, but, as I argued in this chapter, it is increasingly adopting international norms and standards of employment policies common in the West, through the mediation of ILO, World Bank, and OECD standards and practices. Adopting neo-liberal ways of governing in this area, however, does not necessarily mean China is turning towards liberal democracy, any more than "people's courts" in an earlier stage of Chinese development were less repressive, simply by virtue of their insertion in a larger revolution with emancipatory intent.[54]

Aihwa Ong has recently made the provocative claim that neo-liberal practice is positioned as the "exception" in China and several southeast Asian countries, whereas it is positioned as the "norm" of the entire system of governance in Western liberal countries.[55] This certainly points to an important caveat in analysing such borrowings from a Western-influenced international rule system. But the distinction risks being dichotomized into a new post-Cold War Orientalism, one that exaggerates both the flexibilities of Chinese governance and the increasingly repressive rigidities of governments in the West. Restrictions on the participatory liberal-democratic character of the overarching system of Western governance, for example, has been a keystone of international neo-liberal practice that dates at least to the Huntington "ungovernability" thesis on Western democracy, presented to the Trilateral Commission in the early 1970s.[56]

Notes

1 Unemployment defined as the imbalance between the number of job seekers and the number of jobs has always existed in China, but it was never recognized officially. Unemployed rural migrants continue to be excluded from being considered as unemployed. During the Maoist period, unemployment was made "invisible" by

"over-staffing" SOEs, creating the category of "people who are waiting for jobs (*daiye renkou*), and sending urban youth to the countryside (the sent-down youth) after the peak of the Cultural Revolution. See, for example, Shaohui Chen, *From Employment under Planning to Employment under Market* [*Cong Jihua Jiuye dao Shichnag Jiuye*], Beijing: Chinese Finance and Economic Press, 2003; Edward X. Gu, "From Permanent Employment to Massive Layoffs: The Political Economy of Transitional Unemployment (1993–1998)", *Economy and Society* 28:2, 1999, pp. 281–99.

2 Guoguang Wu and Helen Lansdowne (eds), *Socialist China, Capitalist China: Social Tension and Political Adaptation Under Economic Globalization*, London: Routledge, 2009.

3 Graham Burchell, "Liberal Government and Techniques of the Self", in Andrew Barry, Thomas Osborne and Nikolas Rose (eds) *Foucault and Political Reason: Liberalism, Neo-liberalism and Rationalities of Government*, Chicago: University of Chicago Press, 1996, pp. 19–36.

4 Barbara Cruikshank, *The Will to Empower: Democratic Citizens and Other Subjects*, Ithaca: Cornell University Press, 1999; Michel Foucault, "'Omnes et Singulatim': Toward a Critique of Political Reason", in James D. Faubion (ed.) *Michel Foucault: Power*, translated by Robert Hurley and Others, New York: New Press 2000, pp. 298–325; Michel Foucault, "The Political Technology of Individuals", in James D. Faubion (ed.) *Michel Foucault: Power*, translated by Robert Hurley and Others, New York: New Press, 2000, pp. 403–17.

5 For a similar argument in understanding changing government rationalities in China, see *Economy and Society* special issue on governance and China, especially the introductory article: Gary Sigley, "Chinese Governmentalities: Government, Governance in the Socialist Market Economy", *Economy and Society* 35:4, 2006, pp. 487–508.

6 The rationale of campaign/yudong during the Maoist period, as Bennett points out, "is a government-sponsored effort to storm and eventually overwhelm strong but vulnerable barriers to the progress of socialism through intensive mass mobilization of active personal commitment", see Gordon Bennett, *Yundong: Mass Campaign in Chinese Communist Leadership*, Berkeley: Centre for Chinese Studies, University of Berkeley. Unlike *yundong* which involves large-scale mass movement and more coercion, *huodong* is a smaller-scale mass movement, targeting particular areas, and relying more on volunteering. On comparing *yundong* and *huodong*, also see Ellen Judd, *Chinese Women's Movement Between State and Market*, Stanford: Stanford University Press, 2002, p. 11.

7 David Bray, "Building 'Community': New Strategies of Governance in Urban China", *Economy and Society* 35:4, November, pp. 530–49; Feng Xu, "New Modes of Urban Governance: Building Community/*Shequ* in Post-*Danwei* China", in André Laliberté and Marc Lanteigne (eds) *The Chinese Party-State at the Turn of the Millennium: Legitimacy and Adaptation*, London: Routledge. Forthcoming.

8 Ministry of Labour and Social Security (MoLSS), *China's Active Employment Policies: Documents from National Re-employment Work Conference (2002)* [*Zhongguo Jiji de Jiuye Zhengce: Quanguo Zaijiuye Gongzuo Huiyi Wenjian Huibian*]. Beijing: China Labour and Social Security Publishing House, 2003; Ministry of Labour and Social Security (MoLSS), *Questions and Answers on Employment and Training Policies* [*Xinbian Jiuye yu Peixun Zhence Wenda*], Beijing: China Personnel Publishing, 2004.

9 Cf. C. Kasserly, *Employment Counselling, Career Guidance, Occupational Information Provided through a Public Employment Service*, Geneva: ILO, Labour Administration Branch. 1994. http://oit.org/public/english/employment/skills/empserv/public/publ/index.htm (25 September 2006); Phan Thuy, Ellen Hansen, and David Price, *The Public Employment Service in a Changing Labour Market*, Geneva: ILO, 2001; OECD, *Labour Market Policies and the Public Employment Service*, Paris: OECD, 2001; Ellen Hansen, *Career Guidance: A Resource Handbook for Low- and Middle-Income Countries*, Geneva: ILO, 2006.

10 Andrew Walder, *Communist Neo-Traditionalism: Work and Authority in Chinese Industry*, Berkeley: University of California Press, 1986.
11 See, for example, Keping Yu, *Incremental Democracy and Good Governance* [*Zenliang Minzhu yu Shanzhi*], Beijing: Social Sciences and Academic Press, 2005; Shangli Lin, *Institutional Innovation and the Development of Nation-State: China's Exploration* [*Zhidu Chuangxin yu Guojia Chengzhang*], Tianjin: Tianjin People's Press, 2005.
12 See, for example, OECD 2001; ILO, *An Employment Agenda for China: Background Paper for the China Employment Forum*. Geneva: ILO, 2004; World Bank 2002.
13 Karl Polanyi, *The Great Transformation: The Political and Economic Origins of Our Time*, Boston: Beacon, 1957, p. 84.
14 It does not mean that China has established a free labour market, as a rural–urban divide continues to exist, but rather, its desire to build a labour market has led to increasing commodification of labour. See, for example, Luigi Tomba, *Paradoxes of Labour Reform: Chinese Labour Theory and Practice from Socialism to Market*, London: Routledge, 2002; John Knight and Lina Song, *Towards a Labour Market in China*, Oxford: Oxford University Press, 2005.
15 Chen, *From Employment under Planning to Employment under Market*, 2003; Gu, "From Permanent Employment to Massive Layoffs", 1999.
16 Ching-Kwan Lee, "Pathways of Labour Insurgency", in E. Perry and M. Selden (eds) *Chinese Society: Change, Conflict and Resistance*, New York: Routledge, 2000, pp. 41–61; Yongshun Cai, "The Resistance of Chinese Laid-off Workers in the Reform Period", *China Quarterly* 170, June 2002, pp. 327–44; Dorothy Solinger, "Labour Market Reform and the Plight of the Laid-off Proletariat", *China Quarterly* 170, June 2002, pp. 304–26; William Hurst and Kevin J. O'Brien, "China's Contentious Pensioners", *China Quarterly* 170, June 2002, pp. 345–60.
17 Maria Edin, "Remaking the Communist Party-State: The Cadre Responsibility System at the Local Level in China", *China: An International Journal* no. 4, 2003, pp. 1–15; Dali Yang, *Remaking the Chinese Leviathan: Market Transition and the Politics of Governance in China*, Stanford: Stanford University Press, 2005.
18 Ching-kwan Lee (ed.) *Working in China: Ethnographies of Labour and Workplace Transformation*, London: Routledge, 2007, p. 4.
19 Bob Jessop, "Towards a Schumpeterian Workfare State? Preliminary Remarks on Post-Fordist Political Economy", *Studies in Political Economy* 40, 1993, pp. 7–39.
20 Thuy *et al.*, *The Public Employment Service*, 2001.
21 Ibid., p. 6.
22 Yiyong Yang, *The Employment Problem in the Transition Period of China* [*Zhongguo Zhuanxinshiqi de Jiuyewenti*], Beijing: China Labour and Social Security Publishing House, 2002; Chen, 2003; Yansui Yang and Zhao Jianguo, *Various Job and Flexible Employment Mechanism: A New Rule, Dream of Freedom*, Beijing: China Labour and Social Security Publishing House, 2006.
23 Vosko, Leah, *Temporary Work: The Gendered Rise of a Precarious Employment Relationship*, Toronto: University of Toronto Press, 2000.
24 Yang and Zhao, *Various Job and Flexible Employment Mechanism*, 2006, pp. 125–8.
25 See, for example, Jude Howell, *Good Practice Study in Shanghai on Employment Services for the Informal Economy*, Working Paper, Employment Sector, ILO, 2002; Ministry of Labour and Social Security, *Skills Training in the Informal Sector in China*, Geneva: ILO, 2002.
26 Saskia Sassen, *The Global City: New York, London, Tokyo*, Princeton: Princeton University Press, 1991, p. 27.
27 See, for example, Pamela Yatsko, *New Shanghai: the Rocky Rebirth of China's Legendary City*, New York: John Wiley & Sons, Inc. 2001; Andrew Ross, *Fast Boat to China: Corporate Flight and the Consequences of Free Trade, Lessons from Shanghai*, New York: Pantheon Books, 2006.

28 Sassen, *The Global City*, 1991.
29 Ibid., p. 127.
30 Qiufang Li, "Flexible Employment and Women's Rights" [Linghuo Duoyang de Jiuye Xingshi yu Funüliyi Yanjiu], in Lin Tan and Liu Bohong (eds) *Review on the Chinese Women's Studies in Recent 10 Years, 1995–2005* [*Zhongguofunuyanjiu Shinian*], Beijing: Social Sciences Academic Press, 2005, p. 237.
31 Jun You (ed.) *Blue Book of China's Employment Report* [*Zhongguo Jiuye Baogao Lanpishu*], Beijing: China Labour and Social Security Publishing House, 2005, p. 26.
32 Yongping Jiang, "Pay Attention to Gender Equality in the Labour Market" [Guanzhu Laodongli Shichang zhong de Xinbiepingdeng], in Lin Tan and Liu Bohong (eds) *Review on the Chinese Women's Studies in Recent 10 Years, 1995–2005* [*Zhongguo-funuyanjiu Shinian*], Beijing: Social Sciences Academic Press, 2005, p. 266.
33 Yang and Zhao, *Various Job and Flexible Employment Mechanism*, 2006; You, *Blue Book of China's Employment Report*, 2005, Chapter 5.
34 Ibid., p. 180.
35 See, for example, Yihua Huang, "China's Third Employment Peak is Under Way", *Jiangsu Workers' Daily*, June 24, A1; You, 2005, pp. 200–3.
36 There seems a policy shift towards providing migrants services such as training and counselling to help them find employment in cities, in accordance with the "people-centred" development and building "harmonious society" under the Hu leadership.
37 Dorothy Solinger, "Why We Cannot Count the 'Unemployed'", Research Report, *China Quarterly*, 2001, pp. 671–88.
38 Solinger, "Why We Cannot Count the 'Unemployed'", 2001.
39 I was repeatedly told, during my field research, that the unemployment rate is a sensitive issue.
40 Donghui Gu, *Support and Response: Research on Laid-Off Employees through the Lens of Social Work* [*Zhichi Yu Huiying: Shehui Gonzuo Shiye Zhong de Xiagang Zhigong Yanjiu*], Beijing: Social Sciences Documentation Publishing House, 2004, footnotes 7–12.
41 MoLSS, *Questions and Answers on Employment and Training Policies*, 2004; Grace Lee and M. Warner, "The Shanghai Re-Employment Model: From Local Experiment to Nation-Wide Labour Market Policy", *China Quarterly* 77, March 2004, pp. 174–99.
42 Yiyong Yang, *The Employment Problem in the Transition Period of China* [*Zhongguo Zhuanxinshiqi de Jiuyewenti*], Beijing: China Labour and Social Secuirity Publishing House, 2002, p. 35.
43 World Bank, *World Bank Employment Policy Primer* no 3, 2002, pp. 1–7.
44 See, for example, Bing Ding, "Suyu: SYB Enables Off-Post Workers Find 'Way out'" [Suyu: SYB ran Xiagangrenyuan Zhaodao 'Chulu'], *Jiangsu Workers' Daily*, 26 June 2006.
45 MoLSS, *China's Active Employment Policies*, 2003.
46 See, for example, Thuy *et al.*, *The Public Employment Service*, 2001.
47 Dali Yang, *Remaking the Chinese Leviathan: Market Transition and the Politics of Governance in China*, Stanford: Stanford University Press, 2005; Susan Greenhalgh and Edwin A. Winckler, *Governing China's Population: From Leninist to Neoliberal Biopolitics*, Stanford: Stanford University Press, 2005, pp. 176–81.
48 World Bank, *World Bank Employment Policy Primer*, 2002, p. 4.
49 James Lawson and Feng Xu, "SARS in Canada and China: Two Approaches to Emergency Health Policy", *Governance*, April 2007.
50 Cf. Michael Dutton, *Policing Chinese Politics: A History*, Durham: Duke University Press, 2005. As Dutton points out, China's policing has shifted from mass-line policing to contractual policing in the post-Mao era, Chapter 5.
51 Wei Wu (ed.) *Job Guidance* [*Jiuye Zhidao*], Shanghai: Eastern Normal University Press, 2005, p. 156.

52 Nikolas Rose, "Governing 'Advanced' Liberal Democracy", in Andrew Barry, Thomas Osborne, and Nikolas Rose (eds) *Foucault and Political Reason: Liberalism, Neo-liberalism and Rationalities of Government*, Chicago: University of Chicago Press, 1996, p. 59.
53 Baum, Baum, Zygmunt, *Liquid Modernity*, Cambridge: Polity, 2000, p. 135.
54 Michel Foucault, "On Popular Justice: A Discussion with Maoists", in *Foucault, Power/Knowledge: Selected Interviews and Other Writings, 1972–1977*, edited by Colin Gordon, New York: Pantheon Books, 1980, Chapter 1.
55 Aihwa Ong, *Neoliberalism as Exception: Mutations in Citizenship and Sovereignty*, Durham: Duke University Press, 2006.
56 Michel Crozier, Samuel P. Huntington, and Joji Watanuki, *The Crisis of Democracy: Report on the Governability of Democracies to the Trilateral Commission*, New York: New York University Press, 1975.

5 An institutional analysis of China's failed healthcare reform

Yanzhong Huang

Introduction

Since the late 1970s, the Chinese leadership began moving the economy from a sluggish, inefficient, Soviet-style, and centrally-planned economy to a more dynamic, liberal, and market-oriented system. The reform ushered in forces that dramatically changed China's socio-economic landscape. With an annual growth rate of more than 8 per cent, China is the fastest growing major economy in the world. Impressed by the country's economic growth, some China watchers claim that China's development model, dubbed "Beijing Consensus", offers a viable alternative to the Washington Consensus.[1]

China's health system reform began in the early 1980s, almost the same time as the economic reform was kicked off,[2] yet two and a half decades later, it is clear that the healthcare reform has failed to achieve significant improvements in terms of cost, access, and equality. While any reform produces its winners and losers, healthcare reform in China appears to lead to a situation in which none of the affected actors (patients, healthcare providers, governments, the new rich, the middle class, low-income groups) are satisfied.[3] A 2005 report released by one of the government's top advisory bodies publicly admitted that healthcare reform in the last two decades has been "unsuccessful".[4]

What is the main culprit in the failure of China's healthcare reform? Thus far, most policy analysts and health experts attribute the failure to a market-oriented health policy. The report issued by the State Council Development Research Centre (DRC), for example, asserts that commercialization and marketization are against the "fundamental law of the development of medical and healthcare cause".[5] While there is no doubt that the switch to a "market fundamentalism" (Joseph Stiglitz's words) is to blame, simply attributing the failure of the healthcare reform to a policy shift is problematic for at least two reasons. First, assuming the existence of an explicit and consistent "market-oriented" health policy, the policy failure thesis fails to capture the complexities of China's health policy process. Indeed, debates and conflicts over the direction of the reform abounded in China's health sector even during the heyday of market fundamentalism. Second, to the extent that marketization and commercialization have proved unworkable by theory and other countries' experience, as the DRC report has observed, the policy failure thesis cannot explain why China chose to "repeat a path that has been proved wrong".[6] Some China scholars, such as Shaoguang Wang, went a step further by emphasizing the lack of government commitment to primary healthcare.[7] Still, this line of analysis falls short of touching upon the fundamental question: why is the government unwilling and incapable of shouldering its responsibilities in the healthcare sector?

In this chapter, I provide a political/institutional analysis of healthcare transition in China. In particular, the chapter examines how changes in several key dimensions of China's political system affected the policy process and outcome of its healthcare transition. I hypothesize that a polity change from "bandwagoning" to "buckpassing" accounts for the content, form, and final outcome of China's healthcare transition.

A theoretical model

Bandwagon polity

Fifteen years ago, in one of the most methodologically sophisticated books on Chinese elite politics, Avery Goldstein identified bandwagoning, or the rush of political actors to back emerging winners in policy process, as an important domestic political phenomenon.[8] He explained the rise of bandwagoning as being a result of the variation in three structural dimensions: ordering principle, distribution of capabilities, and functional differentiation. According to him, bandwagoning prevails in "hierarchic realms in which the distribution of power is sharply skewed and functional differentiation is minimal".[9] Hierarchic ordering is conducive to bandwagon politics not only because "getting along" is the assumed motive in the pursuit of political interest, but also because it leads to the expectation that issues will be resolved in some sense and that a winner will emerge to allocate values or resources within the community. The prevalence of bandwagoning, however, is conditioned by the distribution of capabilities across actors and the type of functional differentiation among them. Tighter concentration of influential resources by political leaders creates more incentives for bandwagoning because it makes the leaders' promise of future payoffs or threats of reprisal more credible. The promises and threats gain further credibility under a relatively undifferentiated political structure (i.e. lack of specialization in political decision-making), under which alternative avenues for political advancement are usually absent.

A bandwagon polity has important implications for the public policy process. It increases state autonomy by enhancing the ability of political leaders to formulate and implement rules and policies that "do not merely reproduce current social practices or confirm the present distribution of advantage among groups in society".[10] Such a state is unlikely to be captured by special interest groups. Meanwhile, because the polity generates strong incentives for subordinates to be identified as early and enthusiastic supporters of the superiors' agenda, stalemate or foot-dragging in policy formulation is relatively rare. A bandwagon polity also facilitates policy implementation. Since the distribution of capabilities is skewed towards a superordinate official, needed policy resources (political and financial) can be mobilized in a relatively efficient manner. A political leader is also able to pursue a preferred policy because of the absence of significant veto points (due to the lack of functional differentiation) and because of the great influence he wields over the political fate of subordinates, who actively seek cues from him in order to be rewarded as early and enthusiastic supporters.

Applying this model to the China case, Goldstein suggested that the theory of bandwagon politics best explained Chinese elite politics prior to the Cultural Revolution (CR; 1949–66). But the bandwagon politics continued to dominate China's policy process even during the CR, in which the Red Guards quickly responded to Mao's call on rebellion and political purge. The stakes of defeat during the CR were high because of the dominance of a winner-take-all game structure. As State President Liu Shaoqi's death demonstrated, those who lost the game usually lost everything, even their lives. This zero-sum ordering principle, coupled with the sustained hierarchy and concentration of influential power in Mao's hands, ensured the continuation of bandwagon politics during the entire Mao era (1949–76).

Buckpassing polity

Significant changes in the three dimensions did not occur until after Mao died. Deng Xiaoping, himself a victim of Mao's personal dictatorship, concluded that it was not appropriate to over-concentrate power in the Party committees.[11] Concerns about the Party's legitimacy led to a shift of contentious issues from the political arena to the administrative "neutral" zone. This shift in responsibility increased bureaucratic autonomy in policy process, and reduced political leaders' commitment to certain policy matters. What is more, despite the sustained influence of the "winner take all" game (as demonstrated in the 1989 Tiananmen showdown[12]), elite political struggle has been increasingly seen as a non-zero sum one in which losers are invited to replay the game. The reduced stakes of defeat allows policy actors to look beyond immediate security concerns and pursue policy entrepreneurship, a significant deviation from the traditional "getting along" behavioural pattern in a bandwagon polity.

In the meantime, the political resources were further decentralized with the introduction of various reform measures. While market-oriented economic reform produced alternative sources of power and authority, fiscal and administrative reforms decentralized control over financial resources and, in some cases, supervisory and management control. The new developments made it increasingly difficult to skew the distribution of capabilities in favour of *one* superordinate actor. In consequence, the credibility of potential winners' promises and threats in policy enforcement is called into question.

The post-Mao era also saw the reassertion of specialized actors in policy-making. This began with post-Mao state rebuilding, which led to a rapid growth of the number of departments and personnel within existing "line ministries", the establishment of "stand-alone" administrative capacities by previously latent bureaucratic sectors (such as the State Family Planning Commission), and the creation of new regulatory agencies (such as the National Bureau of Statistics). In addition, state cadres were disaggregated into separate sectors – elite business, government, and nonprofit institutions, with different management methods developed for each sector.[13] The growing functional differentiation has created two consequences. On the one hand, it opens up multiple channels for political advancement, thereby reducing the incentive to win the early recognition and approval of political superiors. On the other hand, it also means that successful policy implementation is more likely to require securing the cooperation from several interdependent sources.[14]

The coexistence of the growing functional differentiation and the prevalent diffusion of influential resources in a weakened hierarchy eroded the patterns of bandwagon politics in which functional differentiation is low and political power is tightly concentrated in the hands of superior officials. For analytical purposes, I hereby propose a "buckpassing" model to characterize the post-Mao social policy process. Under this buckpassing polity, central political leaders moved more policy matters onto the politically neutral zone of administration and focused instead on policy issues of utmost legitimacy concerns (i.e. economic development). Meanwhile, with the involvement of multiple actors in different functional domains, having at its disposal useful policy resources, it becomes more likely for one bureaucratic official to shift responsibility and blame to others. In consequence, deadlock (due to heated opposition) or inaction (anticipating the difficulty of securing the cooperation of different actors) becomes more likely. This "buckpassing" polity potentially increases the preference discrepancy between central and political leaders, on the one hand, and local and bureaucratic officials, on the other, allowing the latter to pursue, in a strategic manner, their departmental or personal interests at the expense of the public interest. As a result, the policy process becomes more likely to be captured by special interest groups.

Applying this analytical framework to China's healthcare sector, I hypothesize that a polity shift from bandwagoning to buckpassing fundamentally changed the health policy structure in the post-Mao era. This polity shift in turn accounted for the divergent patterns of health policy process in the post-Mao era and was responsible for the failed healthcare reform in China.

Buckpassing polity and the healthcare reform

To assess the usefulness of this model in understanding healthcare transition in China, we need to demonstrate the correspondence between the buckpassing polity and its empirical referents in the post-Mao Chinese society. China's healthcare reform unfolded in a hierarchical setting quite different from that in the Mao era. With the death of Mao, health ceased to be a sensitive political issue in elite politics. As a matter of fact, the adoption of an economy-centred approach marginalized health issues on top leaders' development agenda. Instead, the locus of health policy-making was shifted to the Ministry of Health (MoH) and other bureaucratic agencies. While the State Council has the official authority to make decisions on "major guidelines and policy issues concerning national health work", MoH is entrusted to "propose the development blueprints and work plans for the public health cause".[15] The institutional change nevertheless also created a fragmented structure in which MoH is in a weak position to define policies and to exercise the stewardship, and regulatory and supervisory roles in the health sector. In addition to the Ministry of Health, the State Family Planning Commission is in charge of reproductive health; the Ministry of Labour and Social Security is responsible for the urban health insurance sector; the Ministry of Science and Technology on health-related research; and the Ministry of Construction, on urban water supply and sanitation.

The Party Centre also shook off its responsibilities in public health financing. Previously, under the vertical or *tiao* apportionment system, the central government collected a majority of the revenues and allocated a portion to the local levels through MoH. Now the central government no longer guarantees upper-level budget allocations for local spending. Instead, it would set up special funds to inaugurate and guide healthcare projects, with the local governments responsible for contributing the lion's share of government input and mobilizing mass participation.[16] As a result, localities must rely primarily on horizontal flows (*kuai*) to generate incomes to finance local public healthcare.[17] Preoccupied with GDP growth, however, sub-national leaders had few incentives to invest in healthcare. The local government incentives to provide health services were further reduced by the 1994 tax reform, through which the central state recentralized fiscal power but further decentralized fiscal responsibilities.[18] To reflect this marginalized status of healthcare at both the national and subnational levels, government health spending as a percentage of total fiscal spending dropped from 2.4 in 1980 to 1.71 in 2000.[19]

As the health policy process was no longer characterized by the constant and concrete involvement of the top leaders, health bureaucrats were in a more secure position to pursue their own agendas. In fact, since the populist health model in the Mao era was premised on minimized bureaucratic involvement, it became an easy target of the health bureaucrats rehabilitated in the post-Mao era. This was evidenced in the early 1980s, when the introduction of household farming ruined the rural healthcare system. Decollectivization and decommunization uprooted the financial base of the Cooperative Medical System (CMS) and created disincentives for individuals (including health workers) to participate in the system. As a result, the number of production brigades implementing CMS plummeted from 82 per cent in 1978 to 11 per cent in 1983.[20] With the work-point system gone, cash-strapped Barefoot doctors (BFDs) left the service or practiced privately. At the national level, the number of BFDs dropped by about 23 per cent.[21] Against the backdrop of the debilitated rural health system, the attitudes of the state became decisive, yet no action was taken by the central government. Not only did a Mao-style political intervention not occur, but the MoH leaders were determined to dissolve the system. State subsidies for CMS dropped from 100 million yuan in 1979 to 25.28 million yuan (current prices) in 1987, and after that the central government simply stopped funding CMS.[22]

In September 1980, the State Council approved the Ministry's report to legalize private practice, which had been phased out during the CR period. Very soon, private practising clinics flourished in the countryside. By the end of 1985 they had replaced collectively-run health stations as the dominant health institutions at the village level. The increasing competition from private practitioners saddled township health centres or THCs – the referral level between county hospital and village health clinics – with severe financial problems. Yet the MoH leaders simply called for the collapse of those ailing THCs. According to the then-Minister of Health, many such THCs were no different from collective village health stations, squandering too much money.[23] Not surprisingly, about 42 per cent of the THCs collapsed in the late 1980s.[24]

By highlighting the problems of low-quality healthcare in the Mao era, the Minister underscored the need to modernize China's healthcare sector. The process of modernization began in 1979, when the Ministry asked its provincial branches to "seize the moment to shift the work focus to medical and healthcare modernization".[25] In reality, though, modernization was no more than an excuse for the Ministry to shirk its responsibility in rural healthcare. For advocates of urban healthcare, the call for modernization provided new impetus to upgrade and improve urban health facilities. Prior to the CR, urban politicians, hospital administrators, and the Ministry had resisted rapid diffusion of resources out of fear that this would precipitate deterioration in urban health services. With the death of Mao, advocates of urban healthcare acquired sufficient security in articulating their interests. What occurred in the early 1980s, therefore, was the re-emergence of a coalition that Mao sought to break off in 1965. Ironically, the urban bias in healthcare was reinforced by the rational behaviour of peasants who opted to seek care in city hospitals when the rural health institutions were in decay. Driven by the increasing demand for urban healthcare, the National Seventh Five-Year Plan (1986–90) added 400,000 hospital beds to hospitals at or above county level.[26] Efforts to alleviate the burden of accessing urban healthcare services (*jiu yi nan*) resulted in the reversed flow of health resources to urban areas. Representing only 36 per cent of China's population, urban residents now claim nearly 80 per cent of the country's healthcare resources.[27] It was reported that in the city of Beijing alone, there are over 200 CT scanners, more than the total number in the United Kingdom.[28] By comparison, until the 1990s, 23.3 per cent of the township health centres nationwide still did not have X-ray machines, and 50 per cent of the health centres did not have any college-trained health personnel.[29] The urban–rural healthcare gap has been sustained because Party cadres themselves have a strong interest in high-end healthcare, which is concentrated in urban cities. According to an official survey, 80 per cent of the government health spending is used to serve the 8.5 million government officials (which consists of only 0.65 per cent of the population).[30]

In addition to the expanding rural–urban gap, fiscal and bureaucratic decentralization also created an upside-down pyramid structure in the distribution of health resources. As the healthcare budget at each level of government is intended for healthcare units at that level, an administrative unit at the grassroots level has only a small revenue base and, therefore, few healthcare resources at its disposal. Yet it is precisely at this level that the central policies are ultimately enforced and the costs of enforcement must be borne. Grassroots cadres are expected to fulfil a whole range of complex and often conflicting tasks assigned from above: promoting local economic development, collecting taxes and fees, financing public services, and organizing peasants to participate in other government-sponsored programmes. Overwhelmed by policy demands from above, local cadres have few incentives to comply with all of them.[31] Since economic development is used as a yardstick in measuring local government performance, local government officials often pursue economic development at the expense of social development such as healthcare. Buckpassing at the local level has not only contributed to the decay of grassroots public health institutions but also has forced the potential users to rely on healthcare services at higher levels. In 2000, hospitals at or above the county level accommodated 58.4 per cent of outpatient visits and 66.9 per cent of the inpatients. Both figures are higher than those for 1985 (51.4 per cent and 58.6 per cent, respectively).[32] This has generated additional incentives to invest health resources in a few large urban hospitals. It was estimated that 80 per cent of urban health resources are concentrated in large hospitals.[33]

Equally important, in a decentralized health financing structure, a health administrative department does not have formal power over its budget, nor does it have the power to determine the amount of public health resources its lower-level equivalents will receive. The difficulty in mobilizing health resources to pursue the modernization agenda thus generated strong incentives for the health bureaucrats themselves to "buckpass" – shifting the financial burden of modernization to other departments, healthcare units, and users of healthcare. In March 1985, the Ministry submitted to the State Council its "Report on Several Policy Issues Concerning Reform of Health Work". While reaffirming the state support for private practising, the document encouraged industrial and transport enterprises to run public health institutions.[34] The need to finance healthcare through multiple channels and in diverse forms was reaffirmed by a document issued by the State Council in 1992. Not surprisingly, new healthcare units (private hospitals, special healthcare services in public hospitals) boomed in China. Between 1980 and 2000, the number of health units increased from 180,000 to 320,000.[35] In encouraging the setting up of healthcare units by various departments, enterprises, sectors, and individuals at different levels, however, the government's regulatory power was further eroded. As Health Minister Gao Qiang admitted, health administrative departments at each level lack organizations and personnel to regulate hospitals and healthcare services.[36] Because of this poor regulatory environment, corruption has been rampant in the healthcare sector. While medical staff ask for "red envelopes" (monetary donations) from patients, pharmaceutical suppliers offer kickbacks to hospitals and health personnel in exchange for prescribing their products. According to the Ministry of Commerce, kickbacks and bribery involved in the purchase and selling of medicine amount to 772 million yuan per year, or 16 per cent of the annual tax revenue in the pharmaceutical industry.[37]

As part of the buckpassing process, the state also changed its approach to subsidizing public health institutions. Instead of subsidizing a health institution based on its personnel and facilities, the state would provide a fixed amount of subsidy. The hardened budget constraint nevertheless was not accompanied by changes in other revenue sources.[38] Because the costs of basic hospital services, consultation, inpatient stay, and simple operations were set below cost, the government for a long time allowed hospitals to charge drugs sold to patients at a markup of 15–20 per cent. Also, hospitals were allowed to make a profit from extra services, high technology investigations and treatment. Responding to the dwindling government financial support and the absence of reform in service charge and drug distribution, public health units turned to aggressive drug sales and extra, often high-tech services provision to recoup their loss and to fuel revenue growth. The information asymmetry between health providers and consumers, coupled with the business of peddling medicines to hospitals, only exacerbated induced demand and excessive services, leading to bulging prescriptions, abuse of antibiotics, excessive use of high-tech checkups and excessive application of operations on patients. In 1993, for example, drug sales accounted for 52 per cent of China's total health spending, compared with 15–40 per cent in most developing countries.[39] In the countryside, where many health units do not have the financial capability to update medical facilities and provide new services, the only legal and feasible profit-making method was to sell drugs. This may explain why the share of medicine revenue for township health centres was consistently higher than that for urban hospitals.[40] The end result is the rapidly growing healthcare cost. A national survey of health services suggested that between 1998 and 2003, the average annual medical expenses grew 13.5 per cent for urban residents and 11.8 per cent for rural residents. However, the average annual income increased only 8.9 per cent for urban residents and 2.4 per cent for rural residents.[41]

To be sure, the Party Centre never explicitly called for marketization of the health sector. Debates over the roles of state and market continued even within the Ministry of Health. In May 1993, Vice Health Minister Ying Daqui made it clear that he opposed marketizing healthcare services. In December 1996, the National Conference on Health Work issued the "CCP Centre and State Council Decision on Health Reform and Development" (hereafter "the Decision"). The Decision defined China's healthcare as "social public benefit undertakings in which the government implemented certain welfare policies".[42] It further stated that while "social forces" were to contribute to such a public good, the government assumed "important responsibilities" in this process. The problem is that the Party Centre failed to specify what responsibilities the state should assume in the healthcare sector, save to say that the government would increase public health spending annually, with the margin of increase no less than the increase in fiscal expenditures.

As policy debates and ambiguities went on, the urge of lower-level policy actors to take off the burden of public health financing continued unabated. With the publication of the "Guidelines on Urban Healthcare Reform" in February 2000, the binding power of the Decision was diluted and local strategic behaviour was encouraged. The 2000 document not only promoted "collaboration and merging" of all sorts of healthcare units, but also allowed the market to determine service prices for profit-seeking healthcare units. The same year, a city in northern Jiangsu province took the initiative of marketizing healthcare services by selling public hospitals. In the next five years, all but two public hospitals were bid out, leading to the "complete withdrawal of government capital from medical care undertakings".[43] With the reduced fiscal pressure, local government benefited the most from the process. The reform initiative actually received support from some senior officials in the Ministry of Health, who were arguing for the "significant" withdrawal of the state from healthcare.[44]

As the central government, the local governments, health bureaucracy, and public health institutions all shirk their responsibilities in healthcare, the end users have to bear the cost. Official data suggest that the share of out-of-pocket expense in healthcare increased from 20.8 per cent in 1978 to 55.5 per cent in 2003, while the government share dropped from 33.5 per cent to 17.2 per cent (Figure 5.1). By comparison, government spending accounts for about 44 per cent of health outlays in the United States and an average of more than 70 per cent in other advanced industrial states.[45] Unlike India, which has a similar government share in health spending, China distributes its health resources in a way that is strongly biased against people who most need them. Out-of-pocket share in total health expenses is much higher for rural than for urban areas. A 2003 national health survey shows

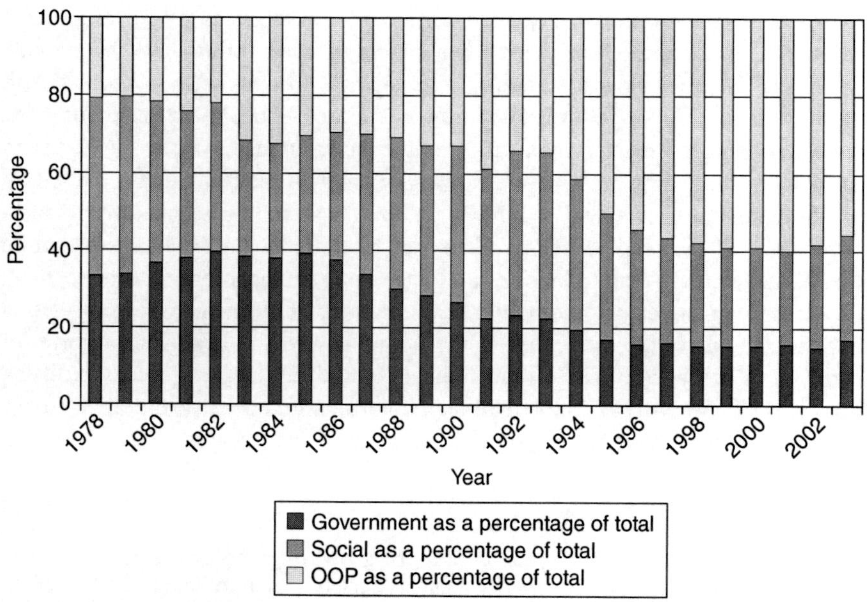

Figure 5.1 Composition of total health spending by source, 1978–2003.

that 79 per cent of the rural residents were not covered by any kind of health insurance, compared to 44.8 per cent for urban residents.[46] Admitted by a Vice Health Minister, 40–60 per cent of the rural patients dropped below the poverty line because of affordability problems in healthcare, while in the hinterland, 60–80 per cent of the patients end up dying at home because they could not pay.[47] Healthcare expenses have reportedly become the third largest consumption item for ordinary Chinese people, standing behind food and education.[48]

Conclusion

An examination of the political logic of China's healthcare transition suggests that the failure of the healthcare reform was caused not as much by marketization and commercialization as by a shift to the buckpassing polity. Unlike the bandwagon polity, buckpassing polity was a result of bureaucratic and fiscal decentralization, which restructured the rule of the game in the policy process, redistributed political capabilities and resources, and redefined bureaucratic functions in the political hierarchy. Under the buckpassing polity, central Party leaders, health bureaucrats, sub-national governments, and public healthcare units all have strong incentives to shirk their responsibilities in providing affordable, accessible, and equitable healthcare. What has emerged from the healthcare transition in China is a system that features poor regulation, widespread corruption, high inequality in health resources distribution, and lack of access to people who most need healthcare.

Thanks to the 2003 SARS crisis, the central political leaders have realized the importance of balancing social and economic developments and have placed increased emphasis on social justice, harmony, and the need to create a social safety net. In the area of delivering healthcare services, efforts have been made to reduce the price of medication and to separate the public, non-profit health units from private, for-profit health units. In the area of healthcare insurance, the state has tried to create a mandatory employee insurance system in the urban areas while launching an initiative seeking to have all the rural areas covered by a new cooperative medical system in 2008. These policy measures are commendable but they fall short of addressing the fundamental problems in public financing, central–local relations, and bureaucratic incentive structure. Such problems led state actors and public health units to shirk their responsibilities in healthcare and are the root cause of the failure of China's healthcare reform. In short, in the absence of some fundamental changes in the buckpassing polity, a policy shift away from marketization alone is unlikely to bring to Chinese people affordable, accessible, equitable, and quality healthcare.

Notes

1 Joshua Cooper Ramo, *Beijing Consensus*, London: Foreign Policy Centre, 2004.
2 Remarks of Cai Renhua, Chinese Economists Society annual conference, 3 July 2006.
3 Available online at http://politics.people.com.cn/GB/1026/3578733.html (access 17 August 2005).

4 Project Team of DRC, "State Council think tank's evaluation and advice on China's healthcare reform", 2005.
5 Project Team of DRC, 2005.
6 Ibid.
7 Shaoguang Wang, "State Extractive Capacity, Policy Orientation, and Inequity in the Financing and Delivery of Health Care in Urban China", paper presented at the International Seminar on "Reforming Health Social Security, Tokyo, 27–29 June 2005.
8 Avery Goldstein, *From Bandwagon to Balance-of-Power Politics: Structural Constraints and Politics in China, 1949–1978*, Stanford: Stanford University Press, 1991.
9 Goldstein, *From Bandwagon to Balance-of-Power Politics*, p. 45.
10 Roberto M. Unger, *Plasticity into Power: Comparative-Historical Studies on the International Conditions of Economics and Military Success*, Cambridge: Cambridge University Press, 1987, p. 80.
11 Deng Xiaoping, *Deng Xiaoping wenxuan, 1978–1982* (Selected works of Deng Xiaoping, 1978–1982), vol. 2, Beijing: Renmin chubanshe, 1983, p. 289.
12 See Tang Tsou, "The Tiananmen Tragedy: The State-Society Relationship, Choices, and Mechanisms in Historical Perspective", in Brantly Womack (ed.) *Contemporary Chinese Politics in Historical Perspective*, New York: Cambridge University Press, 1991, pp. 265–327.
13 John P. Burns, "The People's Republic of China at 50: National Political Reform", *China Quarterly*, no. 159, September 1999, p. 588.
14 Goldstein, *From Bandwagon to Balance-of-Power Politics*, p. 48.
15 *Zhongguo weisheng nianjian* 1983, p. 3.
16 *Zhongguo weisheng nianjian* 1994, pp. 4–5.
17 Christine P. W. Wong, *Financing Local Government in the People's Republic of China*, New York: Oxford University Press, 1997.
18 Qin Hui, "Big Government, Small Responsibilities", available online at http://column.bokee.com/85491.html (accessed 12 February 2006).
19 *Zhongguo xinwen zhoukan* (China News Weekly), 19 August 2005. Available online at http://guancha.gmw.cn/show.aspx?id=6238 (accessed 11 February 2006).
20 Author's database.
21 Ibid.
22 State Council Research Office, *Nongcun hezuo yiliao baojian zhidu yanjiu* (Studies on the Rural Cooperative Healthcare System), Beijing: Beijing yike daxue zhongguo xiehe yike daxue lianhe chubanshe, 1994, p. 18; *Zhongguo weisheng nianjian* 1989, p. 595.
23 *Weisheng jingji yanjiu* 1:5–6, 1987, p. 5.
24 *Jiankang bao*, 13 January 1991.
25 *Zhongguo weisheng nianjian* 1983, p. 12.
26 See *Zhongguo weisheng nianjian* 1986, p. 2.
27 *Renmin ribao*, overseas edition, 18 January 2006, p. 1.
28 See www.37c.com.cn/A1/200506/A143901305062809541 6.shtml (accessed 11 February 2006).
29 *Jiankang bao*, 11 December 1996.
30 *Zhongguo qingnian bao* (China Youth Daily), 9 October 2006, available online at http://zqb.cyol.com/content/2006–10/09/content_1531261.htm (accessed 13 October 2006).
31 Kevin J. O'Brien and Lianjiang Li, "Selective Policy Implementation in Rural China", *Comparative Politics* 31:2, January 1999, pp. 167–86.
32 *Zhongguo weisheng nianjian* 1986, 2001.
33 *Renmin ribao*, overseas edition, 18 January 2006, p. 1.
34 *Zhongguo weisheng nianjian* 1986: 390; Xinhua, 7 May 1985, in FBIS-China, 13 May 1985.
35 *Nanfang zhoumo* (Southern Weekend), 14 August 2005.

36 Gao Qiang's speech on healthcare reform, 1 July 2005, available online at http://news.sina.com.cn/c/2005–08–03/17427403708.shtml (accessed 11 February 2006).
37 *Renmin ribao*, 14 October 2005, p. 6.
38 The revenue of public health institutions in China mainly comes from three sources: government subsidies, medical service charges, and the profit margin from selling drugs.
39 Richard Tomlinson, "Health Care in China is Highly Inequitable", *BMJ* 315:4, October 1997, pp. 831–6.
40 Source: Chinese Ministry of Health, National Health Survey, 1993, 1998.
41 Source: Ministry of Health.
42 *Zhongguo weisheng nianjian* 1997, p. 5.
43 *Nanfang zhoumo*, 14 August 2005.
44 Ibid.
45 David Lague, "Healthcare falls short, Chinese tell leaders", *International Herald Tribune*, 20 August 2005.
46 *Zhongguo weisheng nianjian* 2004.
47 See www.farmer.com.cn/wlb/nmrb/nb6/200512290028.htm (accessed 12 February 2006).
48 *Hainan ribao*, 28 July 2005.

6 China, Christianity and the global market of belief systems

Carol Lee Hamrin

Over the past 25 years during China's reintegration with the world economy and society, and the gradual shrinking of the state sector, all religions have been spreading, with practitioners in most provinces and social strata, including the urban political and cultural elites. Today, there is a wide spectrum of collaboration, compliance, and contention between state and society, and growing competition among old and new belief systems, with much diversity of outcome in different spaces of this more complex society. This dynamic will continue under the impact of globalization.

In response to this social transformation, after decades of relatively lax supervision, the central state has revived its ambition to closely monitor and control the practice of religion in order to maintain its ideological and cultural hegemony, as intrinsic to its political monopoly. Yet it must operate under the constraints of domestic demand for greater social and cultural freedom and of international pressures in the same direction. So the state is adapting by experimenting with new regulatory methods. Religious rights defenders are becoming important to the negotiation of a new informal social contract and of new institutional relations between a society outgrowing socialism and a state experiencing a spillover effect from international economic and governance norms.

Religious belief and practice continue to grow almost exponentially in China, as part of the underlying dynamic intrinsic to globalization, whereby policy changes and institutional restructuring to support integration with the global market economy reshape the society and culture. In all spheres, the monopoly of state agencies and values is weakened by the growth of more autonomous organizations, including foreign actors, with diverse interests. To put it simply, economic markets for products and services go hand in hand with other markets – for education or health services, for lifestyles, for ideas and value systems for meaning and purpose. Once consumers get used to making choices about what to buy, where to go to school, and what work to do, they want to choose what to believe, as well.

Marketization produces social diversity

The most important social changes have been the growth of the educated urban middle class, the massive migration of rural people to the cities, and the huge disparities in wealth. All these are pieces of China's ongoing modernization that have counterparts in other countries at the same stage of development. These trends place great demands on the government to provide social services of new types and in greater quantity as well as quality. The state can no longer afford to provide them all for everyone, and is turning to non-state actors – domestic and foreign – to fill the growing gap. This explains the growing awareness of governments of the usefulness of what are vaguely termed "social forces", even faith-based social service providers and religious charities.

Social change promotes cultural pluralization

Prominent sociologist of religion, Peter Berger, in introducing a book based on a three-year study of globalization and culture in ten countries, including China, depicts globalization as a "cultural earthquake" affecting every part of the globe, prompting reactions ranging from full acceptance to militant rejection.[1] Isolation from global culture requires isolation from the global economy, a high price, indeed. Maintaining the middle ground of combining global economic participation with resistance against global culture, with China as the most important case, is a very difficult balancing act. The challenge to states with totalistic aspirations comes from a very important finding of Berger's study; global culture is carried by social movements and spurred by social activists using advanced communications technologies.

In China's peculiar hybrid "market Leninism", spiritual pursuits are thriving at the grass roots, while the government is adopting a reactive mode. Snapshots of the unexpected results include:

- Consumer culture is taking over, spread by the mass media. With the continuing Information Revolution, cable TV subscriptions are available with religious programming; ISBN numbers are being obtained for distributing materials with religious content outside the religious sector; there are satellite dishes even in some of the poorest tribal villages.
- Thousands of foreign and Chinese religious adherents travel each year into and out of China, often using tourist passports and visas for short-term training, education and cultural exchange, and cooperation in building churches or temples, or funding and running charitable services.
- From 1985 to 2005, 100,000 Chinese Muslims completed the pilgrimage to Mecca and the Protestant Amity Press published 40 million Bibles in cooperation with the United Bible Societies.
- Christmas has become a de facto national holiday, with a Western-style mix of veneration and consumption. In recent years, polls have found that 90 per cent of citizens in large cities had some sort of celebration on Christmas Eve.
- The cultural market place is awash with occult media, fortune telling, belief in UFOs, and spiritual cults. Recent showings of *The Da Vinci Code* were mobbed, despite the official Catholic Church call for a boycott. The government stepped in to withdraw the film from circulation only when it appeared

Hebei Catholics were planning action against local cinemas, and Catholic websites cited 2005 state regulations requiring religious publications to avoid contents that discriminate against or insult religious citizens.[2]

- The elected mayor of Zhenchuan gained his popularity not as a CCP member but the restorer of the local temple complex, with an amphitheatre seating 8,000. When its size attracted higher-level attention and officials insisted the temple register as one of the five authorized religions, Wang picked Taoism but resisted the dispatch of an authorized priest to ensure against "superstitious" practices.[3]

Hosting the Beijing Olympics 2008 has turned government attention to culture. The Organizing Committee is sponsoring a three-year campaign to teach good manners among youth, including the virtue of tolerance. The Olympics requires a re-thinking of how to define and promote Chinese culture. The former minister of the State Council Information Office has spoken of China's "cultural deficit", and a need to develop its cultural industries. Along with an attempt to reshape China's image as a harmonious and peace-loving country guided by Confucian values of peaceful coexistence, 100 Confucius Institutes are being set up world-wide to promote the study of Chinese language and culture, to beef up China's "soft power" in the global great power competition. China has hosted a meeting of the International Network on Cultural Policy, during which government cultural affairs officials signed a statement calling for protection and appropriate use of cultural heritage for social development, and announced that early in 2007, China will pass a new law for the preservation of intangible cultural heritage, with criteria for a list of protected masterpieces (such as folk craft, music, festivities, cuisines, oral histories, and endangered languages).[4]

The general growth of religiosity in Chinese society is fuelling both numerical growth in religious communities of China, and fragmentation within them as new forms of identity emerge – both for individuals and communities. There are new types of congregational or evangelical Buddhism; distinctions among Muslim sects; proliferating sects of "folk faiths", and more "streams" within Protestantism – factions within the official association, house church networks that are quasi-denominations, ethnic churches as Chinese–Korean, and the "emerging" or "third wave" urban fellowship groups growing out of campus Bible study groups in China or North America. Nearly all religious groups have transnational ties, including foreign travel for work, education and evangelism, and all are spilling over into society with cross-provincial activities and new levels of influence outside religious circles.

The widespread worry about corruption and social tension is creating a search for new moral sources of personal and social ethics by which to live. This can be seen in the utilitarian interest in Christianity, widely viewed as the basis for US power and influence, as a means of social cohesion and cultural power for China. It is also evident in a pilot moral education programme in public primary and secondary schools in 60 cities, partly based on ancient Confucian and Taoist classics, but in some cases (Shanghai) also including the *Bible*.[5]

Dozens of university religious study centres or institutes have been spawned by humanities departments (history, philosophy, and literature). Several leading universities offer intensive courses for business leaders that include Confucianism and Taoism along with Buddhist and Christian classics.

Peter Berger has best explained the explosion of cultural diversity and competition around the world, including in China.[6] He has retracted his support for an earlier paradigm of secularization as a central dynamic of modernization, a paradigm he helped form. More accurate, he contends, are the terms pluralization and individuation. As individuals and families become more mobile (geographically and socially), they are able to choose belief systems other than those ascribed to them by family origin or by a collectivity – whether the local village or the central state. Economic markets give birth to aspirations for greater freedom of personal choice in other markets, as well.

The China findings of sociologist Deborah Davis tend to confirm Berger's thesis. Her survey of middle-aged Shanghai residents (the Cultural Revolution generation), 90 per cent of whom were new homeowners, found that "one central theme of their consuming was the celebration of choice and individuation".[7] They took special pleasure in personalizing their new homes and socializing in that intimate sphere with their closest friends and relatives, completely separate now from their work units and work colleagues, so dominant in every sphere of life under China's former "work unit socialism". This pleasure, an outcome of economic and cultural globalization, was amplified by memories of political repression and meaningless sacrifice and served to claim a personal realm beyond the reach of the party-state.

Cultural diversity leads to competition

Growing cultural diversity and competition has spurred a renewed cultural nationalism in China, which is typical of the response to worldwide globalization. With exposure to new cultures, there is a universal redefinition and reorganization of traditional cultures, with a growth of local and regional variations. In China, this breakthrough of cultural hegemony is, by and large, a good thing but in terms of religion cultural nationalists do tend to use state power to favour Confucianism, Buddhism, and Taoism, and to portray Christianity as a foreign import that threatens (vaguely defined) traditional culture.

The worry among intellectuals and officials over the influx of pop culture and lack of interest by younger generations in traditional culture (which in the Mao era was attacked and severely weakened) is certainly legitimate, but their actions have some peculiar results.[8] In some tribal villages, Chinese officials and their foreign advisors are trying to reinstate pre-'49 (often pre-literate, animistic) cultures. An attempt to revive Confucianism led one prominent university political theorist to visit Qufu to worship at Confucius' temple, but apparently he inspired derision rather than a following.

Contrary to the fears of cultural nationalists, Berger's team concluded that there is not in fact a single American global cultural hegemony developing, but rather there is a diversity of global cultural strands clustered around four main global cultures, tensions among which help explain today's "culture wars". These are the two elite (business and intellectual) cultures and the two popular (commercial and Evangelical Protestant) cultures.

There is what he calls the Davos Culture of business and (some) political leaders, living a highly mobile and cosmopolitan international middle-class lifestyle that is a sort of "yuppie international". Here the values of the bottom line tend towards pragmatic outcomes-based strategy and project planning.

The values of the Faculty Club Culture of the Western(ized) intelligentsia are carried by academic networks, foundations, and NGOs, as well as by (some) governmental and intergovernmental agencies. They underpin the ideologies and social movements of human rights, feminism, environmentalism and multiculturalism.

A McDonalds Culture of consumerism is propagated by business enterprises and mass media cleverly tapping into the desire of locals to participate in global modernity, yet marrying it with familiar local traditions.

Finally, an Evangelical (Protestant) Culture, often charismatic in nature, is off the radar screen of most scholars but is considered by Berger and other sociologists as possibly "the most important movement serving indirectly as a vehicle of cultural globalization".[9] It exhibits great scope (a presence in nearly every country), scale (at least 250 million worldwide), and flexibility (indigenous to local cultures everywhere). Spurred and supported by an international missions enterprise centred in the US, of which the Lausanne Movement is one part,[10] its secret is the old Weberian Protestant work ethic that combines individualist self-expression, egalitarianism, and a capacity for creating voluntary associations, in all, "a morality singularly appropriate for people seeking to advance in the nascent stage of modern capitalism".[11]

A baseline for official numbers of religious adherents in China likely is an internal government census in the mid-1990s, prior to an official visit by the UN Special Rapporteur of the Commission on Human Rights on Freedom of Religion or Belief in November 1994. His team was provided the following official numbers: 100 million Buddhists (including seven million Tibetan Buddhists), 18 million Muslims (8.6 million Uighur; 7.2 million Hui), 11 million Christians (four million Catholics; seven million Protestants), and 50,000 Taoists.[12]

But continuing official PRC references to "over 100 million faithful" ever since then reflect a typical government tendency to mask the rapid religious growth so evident on the ground. Acknowledgement of reality would amount to admission of failure to win the ideological battle and thus suggest a need for policy change. When coupled with the opposite tendency of some religious groups to exaggerate their influence, this makes it difficult to parse reality.

Periodic glimpses of secret internal government figures indicate the government knows better. In 1998, for example, an official charged with monitoring religious activity acknowledged in an anonymous interview that Protestants likely numbered more than 50 million.[13] Even public figures from provincial Protestant associations add up to over 20 million, compared with the 17 million figure that central association leaders use.[14] Most recently, estimates in February 2007 based on a poll by professors at East China Normal University in Shanghai suggested there are 40 million Protestants and 300 million total religious adherents.[15]

And these numbers for authorized religions are dwarfed by the huge comeback of traditional folk religion in China. Focused on local deities and following a mix of Taoist and Buddhist practices, these actually may involve the majority of the population. Chinese officials and scholars now are studying "folk faiths" (a term that distinguishes these cultural practices from more organized, doctrinal religions) after decades of suppressing any discussion of this phenomenon. Certain local officials for some time have had to treat regional folk faiths as de facto legitimate religion, alongside the five authorized religions. Russian Orthodox worship is now authorized, but only in Heilongjiang; Fujian governments have sought to formally legitimize the widespread worship of the goddess Mazu.[16]

Charismatic practices of both rural house church quasi-denominations and folk religions echo those of traditional syncretistic sects. Over 20 have been banned in China since 2000 as "evil cults" (*xiejiao*) to be eradicated. The Falun Gong spiritual movement and the pseudo-Christian Eastern Lightning sect are examples. But this proliferation of sects seemingly is part and parcel of cultural globalization, since countries throughout the world are trying to understand and manage such new religious movements (NRMs). In times of rapid and radical social transformation, people seek new sources of meaning, purpose and community. And the internal and transnational mobility of people and ideas is the seedbed for novelty. Some Chinese while overseas have come to embrace the Mormon, Hindu, Greek Orthodox, Baha'i, and even Shinto faiths not authorized in China, and will want the freedom to practice them back home. Meanwhile, Olympics requirements for host countries to provide chaplains for visiting athletes was a challenge to the Chinese, given that Hinduism and Judaism are not recognized in China.[17]

China rejoins world Christianity

The series of government attempts since 1998 to impose tighter regulation on religion would appear to be a case of closing the barn door after the horse has escaped. The Protestant experience in China demonstrates this well. Influenced by the domestic impact of global trends, the Chinese Christian community, fuelled primarily by Protestant growth, continues to grow at a phenomenal rate, outpacing population growth. There were less than five million Christians in 1949, a little over 1 per cent of the total population of 450 million. By 1965, there no doubt were fewer than this under repression, and yet by 1980, the numbers were back up to four million and growth began escalating. As of 2005, Christians were approaching 5 per cent of the population, with guesstimates for 2020 of 10–30 per cent, all with virtually no public promotion, including no access to education or the mass media.[18] All religious scriptures are to be published and distributed only within registered communities, not public bookstores, although there is a growing demand, and therefore supply, of materials related to religion being sold there.[19]

Thus, it still is rare to observe public manifestations of Christianity other than crosses on church buildings symbolizing the presence of a registered community. There is also a growing number of faith-based nonprofits such as church-run clinics, elderly care homes, orphanages and social centres, which still are too few and too small to have significant impact on the larger society.

Yet, somehow, in this era of global transportation and information, Christianity has penetrated all sectors and levels of society to include prominent business leaders, artists and entertainers, intellectuals, and even government officials who technically cannot embrace religion in their status as Communist Party members and thus practice their faith in private.[20]

By far the majority of Christian communities (like the majority of all nonprofit organizations) are not registered with the relevant authorities and operate openly but independently from the Government's monitoring system and without any public Christian appearance. They conduct meetings in private homes or farmyards in rural areas ("house" church literally means "household" – *jiating*), and in urban apartments, factories, restaurants, or rented space in commercial, or even state, facilities. Summer camps and weekend retreats are popular. Both academic and business groups are beginning to reach out to help the downtrodden migrant communities. The church, thus, is a significant part of China's unofficial "second society", and its influence extends far beyond the visible religious activities and membership in the officially sanctioned churches.[21]

Transnational ties run both ways. Chinese Christian communities outside of Mainland China are also on the increase, paralleling the growth of a worldwide trend. The conversion rate among Mainland Chinese overseas is very high and increasing numbers of congregations that serve them are being established. (There are over 80 Chinese churches in Vancouver, for example). Chinese Christian communities, many with seminaries or Bible schools, are cropping up even in countries with no past record of a Chinese church, such as Mongolia and other former Soviet states, many Polynesian nations, all EU nations, many Middle Eastern countries, half of South America, and a dozen African countries. In Italy, Chinese Christian churches have formed their own national association.[22]

Many of these communities are in communication and partnership with churches in China; perhaps 80 per cent of Hong Kong churches have evangelistic training, or social service, programmes on the mainland. Overseas actors work with both registered and unregistered groups at the local level, bypassing the central and even provincial state-sponsored religious hierarchy. Thus the state's attempt to contain the mainland's national church interaction with the outside world within the confines of the monopoly association system continues to lose ground, as all wings of the church increasingly are becoming an active part of world Christianity.

There may in fact be a new and powerful cultural trend that marries the energies of global evangelism with the overseas Chinese business culture, combining the most modern business and technological expertise with traditional Chinese personalism. In the summer of 2006, prominent conservative commentator Marvin Olasky travelled through China and interviewed dozens of Christian

CEOs and other professionals.[23] Their small fellowship groups or training courses use materials downloaded from the Internet or circulating on DVDs. Many came to faith while travelling or studying overseas, or through the influence of family or friends who had been overseas. Government attempts to counter alleged infiltration by foreign Christians inside China thus would seem to be fighting only half the battle.

"Mutual adaptation" between state and society

The manifestation in state–religion relations of a broader tug-of-war between state and society reflects serious governance problems posed by globalization. The state challenge is to find new mechanisms with which to accommodate local realities and comply with international norms for religious freedom without opening the gate for intra- and inter-religious wars or inadvertently fuelling the fragmentation of society. Yet change in this sphere is slow, reflecting bureaucratic stagnation in the structure and policies of the United Front Department and its subordinate bureaus, including the State Religious Affairs Administration (SARA). Policies still require much more adaptation from society than from the state.

Post-Mao reforms of religious policy were introduced through Central Directive #18 of 1982. For ten years, from 1982 to 1991, the state authorized tolerance while re-establishing the Soviet-style religious affairs system of top-down control from Party United Front Departments through the State Religious Affairs Bureaus or sections at each level, delegating implementation to the official monopoly religious associations. This policy of the 1980s set up a zone of indifference as the state retreated from interference with marginal ethnic and religious minorities, as long as they did not challenge the state. There was a gradual and still incomplete shift away from class struggle against religion as a dangerous and counter-revolutionary ideology of the enemy, to viewing religious freedom as a temporary concession to minority social groups during an early stage of socialism. The assumption remained that economic development and scientific education gradually would do away with unscientific superstition and religion – according to the modernization paradigm that views secularization as a central element of modernization.

The Soviet approach remains quite evident in the PRC's current outdated and unpopular framework of social policy towards noncommunist groups, including religions.[24] The United Front system imposes indirect, hidden, Party control over social organizations through ostensibly independent associations. Intellectuals, democratic parties (vestiges of the 1940s), overseas Chinese compatriots, including in Hong Kong and Taiwan, and business entrepreneurs, each has its own bureau or section for overseeing. Matters involving religious and ethic minorities are dealt with in the same bureau or section, sustaining a mindset that religious rights are only for historical religious minority communities, not for all citizens.

The 1982 Constitution still in force defines freedom of religion very narrowly, as freedom of "religious belief" within a narrow private sphere of the home, family, and state-authorized local places of worship, greatly restricted in order to prevent either foreign dominance or involvement of religions in the rest of the public sphere. Intrusive monitoring and supervision is carried out by authorized monopoly agencies, the five so-called patriotic religious associations, which are viewed as social organizations serving members only. For example, there is only one Protestant national magazine and one national publishing house, to produce materials for distribution in special members-only channels. At every level, there are strict quotas for numbers of venues, personnel and publications.

From ideological struggle to cultural studies

The relatively lax attitude of the 1980s changed after 4 June 1989, and the collapse of European communism. Following a policy review, modifications emerged in Central Directive #6 of 1991 and two State Council regulations in 1994 governing domestic and expatriate religious communities. In an attempt to regularize the management of religious affairs, the ideological component of policy softened further as the state accepted the continued existence of religion as a persisting rather than temporary aspect of cultural life, and adopted a more pragmatic approach to governance. Bureaucratic regulations aimed to contain and re-shape religion to suit state purposes of economic development and international prestige. The top priority was to preclude the possibility of foreign use of religion against the state, separatism in the name of religion, or use of religion to spur mass demonstrations. Results included the state's enforcement of its preferred candidate for Panchen Lama over the Dalai Lama's choice in 1995, and public contention in 2000–01 between the state and the Vatican over appointments of Chinese Catholic bishops.

Very general central guidelines were to be fleshed out by provincial-level implementing regulations. Thus, the central state left local authorities to deal with what turned out to be a proliferation of religious groups and practices through the decade. This decentralization spurred a "buckpassing" phenomenon. The new approach authorized provincial-level religious associations to decide on foreign contacts and assistance up to one million yuan. To ensure political loyalty on the part of the associations, there was retraining of leading staff, faculty, and seminarians, and revision of doctrinal teaching to emphasize social ethics over supernatural elements of each faith. This fateful venture by the state into the mire of doctrine, after a decade of focusing mainly on control of organization and personnel, was to have major negative consequences over time by alienating believers even within compliant groups.[25] By July 1999, with the National Peoples Congress' ban on Falun Gong and other cults, the state had become the primary arbiter of orthodoxy versus heterodoxy, with arbitrary application by most local officials.[26]

As part of an effort to better understand the influence of religion overseas and in China, and to train religious affairs cadres, university courses on Western culture and religion were revived. Through the 1990s, dozens of religious study centres sprang up on major campuses, with growing budgets for field research and overseas exchanges. Religious affairs cadres retained a veto power over these academic initiatives, including editorial review of publications touching on religion, exercised by SARA's publishing arm. State funding through the annual and five-year planning process continued to shape the viability of such centres and their research agendas, as with all academic work in China.

Public discussion and distribution of studies on domestic religion remained taboo, however. In 1995, the State Council listed seven topics that should be classified as state secrets (pertaining to state security and national interests) and nine topics designated as *neibu* (internal only) matters.[27] The comprehensive list, interpreted broadly, pretty much covered any information about religion in China and much information about religion elsewhere. Yet despite these obstacles, the academic religious study centres, often with private funding, have brought the topic of religion from the margins into the mainstream public discourse in recent years.

A leading institution in religious studies is Renmin (People's) University in Beijing, the first to set up an Institute of Confucian Studies, as well as many others. It has been designated the "key centre" for the study of Buddhism; Zhejiang University in Hangzhou for Christianity; and Sichuan University in Chengdu for Taoism. It appears that universities have been encouraged to seek world-class scholars to head national research projects touching on religion, as well as other subjects. Even technical schools are getting into the act, such as Huazhong University of Science and Technology with its Centre for Research on the Taoist scripture, *Daodejing*.[28]

From cultural opening to rule by law

Since the turn of the century, there has been an overall effort by the party-state to regain central authority over society through more detailed regulations and closer supervision of local government implementation. Thus, civic organizations of all types face a bewildering and constantly changing set of regulations, at a time when their organizational capacity remains weak. Current religious policy was set forth at a decennial Party conference on religious affairs in December 2001. The first comprehensive regulations on religion followed, going into effect in March 2005. These should be viewed as one piece of a larger set that includes the new regulations on foundations, and regulations still in draft for membership-based social organizations and not-for-profit service providers, as well as new tax and audit provisions.[29] All of these regulations have gone through years of internal research and discussion, including consultation with at least the leaders of compliant constituencies.

The new religious regulations – not promulgated until March 2005 – were already in draft form in 2001. Like those on managing foundations (July 2004), they reflect the lowest common denominator, that is, those issues that people could agree on. The most important matters were also the most contentious and left unchanged or vague. Such regulations are a moving target for constant reinterpretation and renegotiation, as part of the more general hard bargaining underway between state and society. In fact, the lukewarm welcome at home and overseas for the religious regulations in March delayed the promulgation of implementing regulations at the provincial level. Such bureaucratic caution has produced a set of rules that are a poor match either for ensuring domestic nondiscrimination or meeting the full requirements of the UN's International Covenant on Political and Civil Rights (ICPCR), the new standard for China since its signing in 1998.[30]

The new regulations are an effort to shift from the local micro-management of religious issues on an ad hoc basis to a more comprehensive macro-regulation approach through standard public rules for registration and licensing, and post hoc supervision and inspection aimed at errant officials as well as errant religious groups. They are also part of an effort to address international demands for better governance in this arena. Beijing City in particular faced a challenge in regularizing religious affairs prior to the Olympics. For decades there has been an unwillingness to return former religious property or allow the building of new ones – no doubt seen as inappropriate in the capital of communist China. Before 1949, there were 72 Protestant and 65 Catholic churches in the city. Even with a recent building and renovation programme, there are still less than a dozen central city Protestant churches and 15 Catholic churches, with 3,000–4,000 unregistered fellowship groups that the government would like to bring above ground, but which are not inclined to register through the official associations.[31]

Meanwhile, a series of other policies and regulations in the security and propaganda sectors have had a decisively immoderate impact on religion: a campaign was conducted in 2005–06 to reinforce an ideology of atheistic scientific materialism (a modern secular worldview) among existing CCP members and potential elites (youth), in public education and media. The strong interest of university students in taking or auditing classes on religion also apparently prompted a moratorium on hiring, expansion, or construction of new religious study institutes.[32] A companion campaign to counter "foreign infiltration in the name of religion" – supported by alleged evidence of subversive political intent, such as a book by journalist David Aikman that posits a future Christian China that could change its red colour and support the US lead in international affairs, and a film by former 4 June activist Yuan Zhiming that revealed the extent of Christian faith within China's new elites. A continuing crackdown on cults also targets orthodox but unregistered religious groups, especially large movements that cross provincial lines.

The ongoing struggle against domestic and foreign religious forces by the state Religious Affairs apparatus was evident in July 2006 pronouncements by central Religious Affairs chief Ye Xiaowen that the role of the government was to "properly guide" the "more than 100 million faithful" to restrain their "negative elements", to help them adapt to the "socialist mainstream" of society, and "direct them to practice faith rightly". Ye made it clear that the government was behind the ongoing political campaigns to reconstruct Protestant theology, enforce the so-called democratic management of Catholic affairs, and promote a new human-centred Buddhism, in order to serve state goals of increasing social services, protecting the environment, and maintaining social stability, all under the latest policy mantra of building a harmonious society.[33]

Local politics and religion: compliance and resistance

A stereotyped Western view of the Chinese religious scene depicts zero sum warfare between collaborative state-run churches led by secret Party members and rebellious underground Christians. While this is a true picture for some groups in some localities, under the impact of globalization groups with different identities have a diversity of attitudes towards state authority and international actors. Most religious groups use a variety of tactics, depending on circumstances, many of which could be summed up as passive resistance. Most observers agree that alienation among religious groups is growing, as state policies require a degree of subservience that is inconsistent with religious convictions based on higher norms, contributing to the state's underlying legitimacy crisis.[34] Following are some examples of different types of state-religion relations.

Minority Christian cultures

The Lisu, Yi, and Miao, Christians in Yunnan, Korean Christians in the northeast, and Catholic villages in Hebei, represent small cultural communities on the margins of the conformist mainstream culture (defined as Confucian or socialist). Largely viewed by the Han majority as backward and superstitious, they suffer benign neglect or are afforded some state protection for their religious ethnic culture.

Compliant "patriotic" churches

The local churches and home meeting points that have registered through the monopoly associations vary in their relationship with the central and provincial association leadership from compliant to hostile. Many function rather independently through good local government ties and/or outside support.

Independent rural house church networks

In former mission bases in central China, especially Henan and Anhui, the post-Mao period has spawned an exponential increase of rural house church networks with a largely charismatic background that fits in well with traditional rural spiritual practices. By 1998, half a dozen of the larger networks had foreign ties to obtain training and scriptures, and sponsored a Unity Movement intended to articulate and defend the network interests in engagement with both foreign groups and with the Chinese government. The movement's manifesto of belief sparked a government crackdown in the name of fighting cults, which has continued ever since in a determined attempt to exterminate them. Former leaders are now either in labour camps or in exile abroad, while the networks have splintered into smaller groups under a new generation of leadership.[35] Smaller networks elsewhere, however, often are tolerated.

Transnational communities

Coastal religious communities have renewed their many historical overseas ties. Wenzhou, a prime example, is a municipality within Zhejiang province with a population of about seven million and the highest percentage of Protestant Christians among all municipalities in China, with official estimates ranging from 700,000 to one million (10 per cent to 15 per cent of population) and unofficial claims of at least one and a half million (20 per cent).[36] Visitors can observe churches, Catholic as well as Protestant, in every village, mingled with temples and mosques serving the highly religious population. Less well-known is the national and global nature of Wenzhou communities. At any given time, there are at least one million, possibly as many as two million, who are living as migrants in China or overseas doing business, setting up shops and churches from Tibet to Morocco to Bucharest, merging business with a missiological vision.

Urban fellowship groups

There are growing numbers of independent Protestant groups in China's cities, large and small. Most are apolitical, focusing their energies on prayer, study, and mutual support as they enter the professional world and raise young families. Their help for the urban poor, including migrant workers, or others disadvantaged in society is of a humanitarian and evangelistic nature. Many of the lay leaders have been mentored by elderly leaders of the pre-1949 independent churches who spent decades in prison, or by foreign professors in China, or while serving actively in churches while overseas. Members of the groups include students, high-level academics, media personalities, law professionals, business leaders, and philanthropists.

China's civil rights movement and religion

Controversial regulations, along with new administrative and civil law, have inspired renewed debate over constitutional reform and legislation, and opened the route to even bolder advocacy for religious rights.[37] There is growing pressure from China's human rights dialogue partners in Europe and the US to promulgate the ICPCR and fully implement other human rights covenants and mechanisms China has agreed to adopt, including the 1981 Universal Declaration of Nondiscrimination based on Religion or Belief. These norms mean freedom of belief of whatever kind for all citizens, not just for existing adherents of formal religious bodies.

Exposure to international opinion and practice has fuelled a new rights consciousness among religious believers. Younger, educated, and networked, urban believers are more willing and able to bargain with the government than flee repression. The boldness of believers is also inspired by a new awareness of their numbers and a sense of collective identity, both as a nation-wide movement and as members of a world religious community. Unregistered Christians are the largest autonomous social group in China, and the global Christian Church functions, in some ways, as a huge international NGO.

It is quite remarkable how Chinese Christians recently have surfaced in positions of influence within China's small circle of democrats. Consider, for instance, their influence in Hong Kong, which serves as China's de facto frontier for democratization. Although Christians in Hong Kong may be around 10 per cent of the populace they run most of the social service agencies and many educational institutions. Roman Catholic Martin Lee (from a prominent mainland family) heads the Democratic Party and Shanghai-born Cardinal Joseph Zen's diocese has the largest number of Chinese Catholics in the world.

Due to Zen's encouragement, many Christians participated in the December 2002 demonstration (60,000 persons) to protest a national security measure on which Beijing was insisting. As a result, Cardinal (then Bishop) Zen was voted Hong Kong's Person of the Year 2002 by 2,500 readers of the *Apple Daily*, who called him the moral conscience of Hong Kong and found in him a source of justice and hope, a symbol of "the struggle for truth, freedom, and universal love". News of his appointment as a Cardinal in early 2006 monopolized the Hong Kong mass media for days. Notably, almost all of the younger bishops on the mainland had been his students when he taught there part-time from 1989–96.[38]

In Beijing, a number of prominent national, civic, and environmental activists, critical writers and journalists, and legal advocates are relatively new Protestants, attracted by Christian principles of nonviolent resistance and of change fuelled by love rather than hate. They include Wang Yi and Yu Jie, founders of the China branch of the international writer's association PEN, which the government has refused to register. Along with lawyer Li Baiguang, the two met with President Bush privately in his White House living quarters in May 2006 to discuss matters of faith.[39]

The three above, along with poet Bei Cun, journalist Jiao Guobiao, and law experts Fan Yafeng and Gao Zhisheng are members of the independent Ark *(fangzhou)* Church in Beijing. These democrats tend to avoid street activism in favour of pragmatic efforts to build a legal culture through public awareness and peaceful pursuit of justice based on existing policy, law, and regulations. Several recent cases have given them hope for gradual progress.[40]

In this approach to advocacy, Christian activists are consciously adapting the nonviolent resistance principles of overseas Civil Rights Movements, and specifically the Christian principles of Dr. Martin Luther King.[41] Writer Yu Jie has expressed his admiration for peaceful democratic change in Taiwan and Hong Kong, and has called for the removal of Mao and his portrait from Tiananmen Square and for a process of national reconciliation and healing through religious faith prior to Beijing hosting the Olympics.[42]

The legal advocates' commitment to serve the cause of social justice, and their savvy use of international media, has positioned them as a potential link among multiple marginal groups suffering from abuses of official power. They have defended the right of free association, both with lawsuits on behalf of unregistered civic groups and by example – organizing the Ark Church and an

Association of Human Rights Attorneys for Chinese Christians in 2005. They are defending various local leaders of a national Chinese House Church Alliance established in 2004, reportedly with 300,000 members in 21 provinces.[43] Their chief celebrity lawyer, Gao Zhisheng, who had been rated by the Ministry of Justice as one of the country's "Top Ten" lawyers in 2001, has initiated lawsuits on wide-ranging matters. One result is that the Chinese social elite increasingly view the cause of religious rights not only as a legitimate element in the "basket" of human rights, but as a catalyst linking the rights of conscience, speech, and assembly, for all. Indirectly acknowledging the power of Gao's activism, however, the government disbarred him and shut down his law practice for alleged technical violations, not coincidentally, just prior to the visit to Beijing by President Bush in early 2006.[44]

One common grievance that has the greatest potential to bring together disaffected groups is defence of property rights. The 2003 amendments to the Constitution pledging to defend human rights and private property rights create a legal platform, and corruption in the redistribution of state assets and confiscation of property is a leading complaint at all levels of society. Religious groups are major complainants. In every locality there are properties nationalized in the 1950s and still not returned to their owners in contravention of 1982 policy directives. An example would be the Dongyue Miao, a vast Taoist complex dating to Kublai Khan, which was occupied by the Beijing Public Security Bureau until 2000 but even then not returned to the Taoist association. The Catholic Church, with its vast landholdings before 1949, had an estimated 130 billion yuan worth of property under dispute in 2005; foreign holders of deeds further complicate this issue.[45]

City officials favour developers by using the right of eminent domain to take over religious property. Egregious examples come from Xi'an, where in recent years the congregations of both the oldest Protestant church and the main Catholic cathedral in prime downtown locations were evicted and forced to accept less desirable locations for rebuilding, while their historic buildings were torn down. Hundreds of normally placid citizens in these registered venues demonstrated in protest, with little support from their respective association leaders. International attention followed the fierce beatings by hired thugs of 16 Catholic nuns, five of whom sustained permanent injury, prompting protests from international Catholic leaders and the European and Italian Parliaments.[46]

A recent episode in Xiaoshan near Hangzhou, Zhejiang demonstrates the latent power of property issues to galvanize a new level of civil rights activism. On 29 July 2006, over 3,000 Christians and supporters clashed with thousands of military police sent by the local government, along with trucks, excavators, and workers to demolish – for the second time in three years – a nearly completed sanctuary being built by the independent Dangsha Church congregation on land owned privately by a member. But this time, the congregation persisted in defending themselves. They retained prominent legal advocates from Beijing to defend their cause and called for an independent international investigation by human rights organizations and the UN Working Group on Arbitrary Detention.[47]

Conclusion

There is little doubt that the globalization process will continue to bring about further diversification in Chinese society and culture. Old and new alternative religions and belief systems, and cultural lifestyles will continue to contend for the loyalties of Chinese, with the state continuing to adapt in order to stay in the competition. For example, one scholar attached to the United Front Department has described the "diverse ideology of China's socialist society" as a combination of Marxism as the lead, Confucianism as a second major element, and Christianity as a core component.[48]

Under current trends, interest in religion will spread among new business and cultural elites with some influence also on political elites in the Party, government and even the military, often through children, spouses, and international peers bringing new ideas from overseas. A key link seems to be retirees who are freer to practice religion but still retain influence among former subordinates now in office. In 2000–01, there was internal debate about authorizing believers to be CCP members, which likely will resurface as a rights consciousness grows at all levels of society.

Domestic and foreign policy-makers will experience even stronger indirect pressures for change through the power of public and international opinion. China's educated and info-savvy urban populace have high expectations for China to become a responsible and peaceful world power that can match world class standards in all fields, including human rights and religious freedom; to promote political – legal – judicial reforms to address problems of social justice, corruption and abuse of power; and to create a "normal" robust civil society.

In response to these new expectations, the new leadership is turning to populist political themes, as was evident in slogans for the 2008 Olympics – a green Olympics, a hi-tech Olympics, and a people's Olympics, as well as in the new focus on human development and sustainable development. Societal regulations are using a new paradigm that no longer insists that the Party automatically knows and protects all social interests, but now admits that social groups have legitimate interests that are diverse and are not always respected by government regulators. The next ten years will witness the maturing of a civil rights movement focused on Constitutional reform and supportive legislation. It is likely that a Constitutional bill of rights lies just over the horizon in China, which will mark the abandonment of Communist cultural hegemony, just as the 1905 abolition of the Imperial exams marked the abandonment of state Confucian cultural hegemony and a period of openness to Western liberalism. Judging from global trends today, religiosity would then flourish, and the impact, direct and indirect, of religion on political life would increase dramatically, as it has elsewhere in the world.[49]

The question is whether this will be a positive or a negative development. Sociologist Richard Madsen is pessimistic, having studied isolated Catholic villages steeped in the martyr mentality of the underground church, noted Chinese attraction to millenarian, miracle-producing, faiths, and observed the hopes of Christian dissidents that their activism will weaken the socialist state in China, as in Eastern Europe. He believes "the signification of Christianity is the indigenization into many different fragments" of society, through the appropriation of the faith by many different groups for many different purposes. In his view, Chinese society, in general, and turbulent Christian communities, in particular, have returned to the early twentieth-century fragmentation Maoists tried to overcome.[50]

Historian Daniel Bays is more optimistic. His research on early twentieth-century Protestantism tells him that this is a force for good that is perhaps most compatible with the nature and needs of modern society. He sees churches meeting basic human needs with social services, urban middle-class Protestants in the modernizing areas of China taking a natural interest in local civic life, and business and other professionals building families based on Christian character. He also notes studies around the world of Pentecostals steeped in allegedly pre-modern faith-healing and other charismatic practices that have actually reinforced successful adaptation to economic modernization.[51]

As China enters into post-communist politics, many Chinese worry about the dangers of the continuing fragmentation of society, with tensions leading to greater violence given the existing power struggle culture of intolerance. Religious options will continue to enter into national debates on such weighty questions as what moral–cultural glue can hold society together until transformation reaches a new equilibrium; whether the European or American experiences can help China deal with culture wars; and what institutional framework could sustain a truly voluntary and, therefore, harmonious society.

Notes

1 The following discussion is based on Peter L. Berger, "Introduction: The Cultural Dynamics of Globalization", in Peter L. Berger and Samuel P. Huntington (eds) *Many Globalizations: Cultural Diversity in the Contemporary World*, New York: Oxford University Press, 2002, pp. 1–16.

2 "A Mystery: The Da Vinci Code in China", *Global Chinese Ministries*, OMF International, September 2006, citing *Xinhua*, 19 and 22 May 2006.

3 *The Washington Post*, 24 August 1998.

4 Antoneta Bezlova, "China's New Cultural Revolution", *Asia Times*, 29 July 2006. Available online at www.atimes.com/atimes/China/HG29Ad01.html.

5 Tang Yuankai, "Mindful of the Past", *Beijing Review* 21 October 2004, pp. 30–2. *Reuters*, 20 October 2004, cited a *Shanghai Daily* report on the Shanghai Education Commission's academic research office list of recommended summer reading for middle-school students, including the *Bible*.

6 Berger, "Introduction".

7 Deborah Davis, "Urban Consumer Culture", *The China Quarterly Special Issue on Culture in the Contemporary PRC* No. 183, September 2005, pp. 706–9.

8 For a discussion of cultural debates in the 1990s between neo-liberals and neo-leftists, spurred by cultural globalization, see Geremie R. Barme, "The Revolution of Resistance", in Elizabeth J. Perry and Mark Selden (eds) *Chinese Society, 2nd Edition: Change, Conflict and Resistance*, New York: RoutledgeCurzon, 2000, pp. 47–70.

9 Berger, p. 8. An example of the tendency of China scholars to consider religion separately from culture is evident in *The China Quarterly Special Issue on Culture*. Most

telling was the lack of reference to religion in the chapters; even one on "Uighur pop" focused on musical form and identity politics with little attention to religious values or practices. While the journal had produced a special issue on religion in China earlier, there was no cross-referencing. See Daniel L. Overmyer (ed.) *Religion in China Today*, London: Cambridge University Press, *The China Quarterly* Special Issues New Series No. 3, 2003.

10 See the history and documents of the Lausanne Committee for World Evangelism at www.lausanne.org/Brix?pageID=12722.

11 Berger, p. 8.

12 Annual Report to the UN Commission on Human Rights by the Special Rapporteur on Freedom of Religion or Belief, 22 December 1994. For all such documents, see www.unhchr.ch/html/menu2/7/b/religion/documents.htm.

13 *Compass Direct*, October 1998, pp. 26–9.

14 Tony Lambert, "How Many Christians in China?", *China Insight*, August–September 2005.

15 "Special Report China: Chinese Survey Finds Religion Booming", *Guardian Unlimited*, 7 February 2007. Available online at www.guardian.co.uk/china/story /0,2007690,00.html.

16 Kim-kwong Chan, "Accession to the WTO and State Adaptation", in Jason Kindopp and Carol Lee Hamrin (eds) *God and Caesar in China: Policy Implications of Church–State Relations*, Washington, DC: Brookings Institution Press, 2004, p. 64.

17 See Chan in Kindopp and Hamrin, pp. 61ff., for a discussion of these factors.

18 Daniel H. Bays, "State and Religion in Historical Context in China – Christianity", in unpublished remarks at a conference in Washington, DC, 19 January 2005, spoke of 40–50 million Protestants and 12–15 million Catholics. The upper range would be 5 per cent of 1.3 billion, with growth to 10 per cent of 1.4 billion in 2020 adding up to 140 million. David Aikman, *Jesus in Beijing: How Christianity is Transforming China and Changing the Global Balance of Power*, Washington, DC: Regnery Publishing, Inc., 2003, p. 285, posits 20–30 per cent of the population by 2030.

19 During the past 25 years, the China Christian Council in cooperation with the International Bible Society has printed 40 million copies of the Bible and overseas Christian groups have brought in large quantities. There are also an unknown number of Bibles privately printed in China, as revealed in the 2006 sentencing of a Beijing Christian publisher for "illegal commercial activities". At that time, the director of the State Administration for Religious Affairs (SARA) told Hong Kong's *Ta Kung Pao* on 8 July 2006, that Cai in recent years had illegally published 40 million copies of the Bible and other tracts (matching the official church production of Bibles since 1985), as cited in *Forum 18* 24 August 2005.

20 The right of freedom of religious belief does not extend to Party members in Government, Party, military or law enforcement agencies. This major departure from international norms obviously is intended to limit the public influence of non-communists.

21 For creative research on the political economy of religion in China, see Fenggang Yang, "The Red, Black and Gray Markets of Religion in China", *The Sociological Quarterly* 47, 2006, pp. 93–122.

22 Kim-kwong Chan, "Missiological Implications of Chinese Christianity in a Globalized Context", *Quest* 4:1, November 2005, pp. 55–74.

23 "Wildfire", *World*, 24 June 2006, pp. 18–21.

24 See Tong Zhan, "The United Front Work System and the Nonparty Elite", in Carol Lee Hamrin and Suisheng Zhao (eds) *Decision-making in Deng's China: Perspectives from Insiders*, Armonk: M. E. Sharpe, East Gate Studies on Contemporary China series, 1995, pp. 66–75.

25 For example, in 1998 the leading Protestant Jinling Theological Seminary in Nanjing suffered internal rebellion over the imposition of Bishop K. H. Ting's theological reconstruction campaign, resulting in the ousting (and banning from further religious

employment) of dozens of staff, faculty, and students, many of them relocated to North America by 2005. Similar but even harsher re-education campaigns took place in Tibetan Buddhist and Muslim circles.

26 See state documents on the ban on cults in *Chinese Law and Religion Monitor* 1:4, October–December 2005, and "Selection of Cases from the Criminal Law: Banned Protestant Groups", *Occasional Publications of the Dui Hua Foundation* no. 12, February 2003.

27 Public Notice from the State Council's Religious Affairs Bureau and the State Classified Secrets Bureau, 12 October 1995, excerpted in "Regulations on the State Secrets and Specific Classification Limits in Religious Work", *Dialogue* Spring 2003, p. 5.

28 Personal communication with Chinese and Western scholars of religion in Beijing and the US, October 2006 and March 2007. Sichuan University started a global search for directors of three projects including "Religion in Society", according to *Xinhuanet*, 9 May 2005.

29 State Council Decree No. 426, 30 November 2004, *Xinhua*, "Religious Affairs Regulations (Authorized Release)", 18 December 2004. See "Regulations on Religious Affairs", translated by Peter Barry, in *Tripod* XXV:136, Spring 2005, pp. 5–18, with commentary.

30 For more detailed analysis of the 2005 regulations and their implementation, see "China's New Regulations on Religious Affairs: A Paradigm Shift?" (03/14/05 Roundtable) and "China's National and Local Regulations on Religion: Recent Developments in Legislation and Implementation" (11/20/06 Roundtable) at www.cecc.gov/pages/roundtables/index.php.

31 A report from Voice of the Martyrs, in *Crosswalk.com*, 2 November 2004, cited a survey done by leaders of the registered church at the request of the Beijing Religious Affairs Office that found around 3,000 unregistered Protestant groups. According to personal communication with a member of one network of such groups, the police contacted the network after a thorough investigation of their activities and (minimal) foreign ties with a request that they register independent of the official association. The police broke off this dialogue in early 2006, with the untenable excuse that the district already had sufficient numbers of churches.

32 "Crossing the Communists", *The Economist*, 21 April 2005.

33 *Xinhua* report cited in *China Church Quarterly*, Summer 2006, p. 5.

34 See Pitman B. Potter, "Belief in Control: Regulation of Religion in China", in Overmyer, pp. 26–31 for his conclusion that bureaucratic stagnation in China is contributing to a continuing decline of legitimacy.

35 Aikman discusses the early history of these central China networks and in Appendix A, pp. 293–307 includes an English translation of several statements they issued in the Fall of 1998.

36 Much of the following information on Wenzhou comes from Chan, "Missiological Implications..". Chan travelled to Kotor, a medieval town in Montenegro in August 2004, and visited with a Wenzhounese who operated a shop in the local market. See Kim-kwong Chan and Tetsunao Yamamori, *Holistic Entrepreneurship in China*, Pasadena: William Carey International University Press, 2002, on Wenzhou Christians in Qinghai province.

37 An internal conference at Qingdao in late 2005 brought together well-known reformers from the 1980s under the umbrella of Hu Jintao's call for "constitutional politics", a slogan that disappeared from the public media shortly thereafter. Government harassment prompted the organizer, economist, and lobbyist Cao Siyuan, to leave the country. Among the papers presented was one on amending Article 36 on freedom of religion to fully protect the manifestation of belief.

38 Gianni Criveller, "Bishop Zen, Hong Kong's Person of the Year", *Tripod* XXVI:128, Spring 2003, pp. 29–31, and "A Cardinal in Hong Kong", *Tripod* XXVI:141, Summer 2006, pp. 55–8.

39 Sarah Schafer and Jonathan Ansfield, "Strength from their Faith", *Newsweek International*. Available online at http://msnbc.com/id/13879416/site/newsweek.html. There are precursors to this Christian leadership for dissent dating back to at least 1988–89. Seminary students in Beijing and Nanjing marched in the demonstrations carrying a cross, and a popular pastor in the Haidian church was later dismissed for harbouring congregation members who had been involved (including at least one lawyer active today). Through the 1990s, a surprising number of prominent dissidents who fled the country converted to Christianity in Europe or the US, including the founder of the China Alliance for Democracy in 1978, 1989 activists Yang Jianli and Peng Ming (all three now in prison in China), Zhang Boli, Yuan Zhiming, Wang Xizhe, and even the elderly Wang Ruowang before his death.

40 Through 2005, the First People's Intermediate Court of Beijing was forced to postpone trials and then to provide a second trial, with family present, for house church pastor Cai Zhuohua. Cai was accused of illegal business activities despite his claim that the Bible and other religious material he published were distributed free of charge rather than for commercial gain. On the eve of President Bush's November 2005 visit to China, Cai and two others received relatively light sentences and strong pressure not to appeal further. See the trial results in *Compass Direct*, 16 November 2005, and more details on the case in *Chinese Law and Religion Monitor* 2:1, January–June 2006.

Elsewhere in Henan, according to a press release from China Aid Association of Midland, Texas, 25 September 2006, a district court in August revoked a "Re-education through Labour" decision against a house church Christian, who had pursued his right to request an administrative review and, when that failed, lodged a lawsuit with the court. China Aid press releases referenced in this chapter can be found at www.chinaaid.org/english/press_release.php (through 2005) or www.monitorchina.org/english_site/rss/feed.php (after 2005). Find issues of the Monitor at www.monitorchina.org/english_site/index.php.

41 Tony Carnes, "China's New Legal Eagles", *Christianity Today*, September 2006, reports that King's activities are part of the public school curriculum, and his speech, "I have a dream", inspired the Olympics' slogan, "One World, One Dream". Recently a play about King's civil rights leadership opened in Beijing.

42 Verna Yu, biographical sketch of Yu Jie, *South China Morning Post*, 31 July 2003.

43 Press releases from China Aid Association, 25 November 2005 and 1 March 2006.

44 Gao defended cases involving a Shaanxi oil spill, Shaanxi coal miners, Guangdong farmers losing their land, evicted courtyard homeowners in Beijing, house church members brutalized by police in Xinjiang, members of Falun Gong, and a group of villagers who sought to recall their elected village chief for corruption. After Gao released an open letter to Hu Jintao in October 2005 reporting on atrocities of mental, physical and, sexual torture of FLG and other alleged cult members, the confrontation escalated. Gao's colleague, Guo Feixiong, was detained in Guangzhou for "illegal business activities" and a Chinese film maker and Internet activist from the US was detained just before a planned meeting with Gao. After several dangerous run-ins with police thugs, Gao released a statement of withdrawal from the CCP and joined an AIDS whistle-blower in a fast to protest persecution of rights activists. In August 2006, police in his hometown in Shandong detained Gao and his family incommunicado. Dissidents overseas joined Tiananmen activists in China led by writer Liu Xiaobo, to register their protest over his treatment, prompting the government to release him (no doubt still with restricted movement).

45 The *South China Morning Post*, 19 February 2002, reported that a number of historic religious sites are being restored in Beijing, but are not being returned to religious bodies as Central Directive #18 of 1982 directed. An example is the Bada Chui Buddhist complex (with eight temples) in the Western Hills. See *Tripod* XXVI:140, Spring 2006, on church property issues in China.

46 Report by Philip Pan, *The Washington Post*, 1 December 2005.

47 Information on this Zhejiang case is taken from news releases by China Aid Association, 2 and 9 August 2006. When hundreds were injured and over 50 church leaders were detained by police without any information provided to families, the congregation requested a list and details of arrests; medical treatment and release of detainees; a permit for a proper place to worship; and a public apology and reimbursement for losses. Five of those detained were issued formal notification of criminal detention for instigating violence and obstruction of the law (with 20 remaining in detention). On 2 August, the Chinese House Church Alliance released a statement through China Aid Association that called for international intervention and detailed the history of this confrontation. The Dangsha congregation was founded by missionary Hudson Taylor in 1867 and labelled "counter-revolutionary" in 1956, after the government occupied its property. Decades of harassment followed with endless haggling over compensation and permits for either rentals or acceptable sites for a new building.

48 Li Pingye, in *Dangdai Zongjiao Yanjiu* no. 1, 2004, cited in *Spotlight on China*, March 2005, p. 3.

49 Timothy Samuel Shah and Monica Duffy Toft, "Why God is Winning", *Foreign Policy*, July–August 2006, pp. 38–43. Shah's views are based on a major set of 13 case studies of evangelicals and politics around the world.

50 Richard Madsen, "Chinese Christianity: Indigenization and Conflict", in Elizabeth J. Perry and Mark Selden (eds) *Chinese Society, 2nd Edition: Change, Conflict and Resistance*, New York: RoutledgeCurzon, 2003, pp. 271–88.

51 Daniel Bays, "Chinese Protestant Christianity Today", in Overmyer, pp. 196–7.

7 *Super Voice Girls* and *Freezing Point*

Media, hegemony, and domination in the new China

Barrett McCormick

This chapter considers a success in China's commercial television and failures in Chinese newspapers as a means of assessing China's transformation from a hierarchical Leninist or socialist society towards a more open society with a market-based economy. Media is a particularly important sphere in this transition, as in modern society the media have an enormous impact on what people know and in particular on their perceptions of the state. In Leninist China, the communication media were a critical means by which the Party and state mobilized power, were integrated into state hierarchies, and disseminated information and perspectives, more or less as state leaders found appropriate. In contemporary China, these media are now expected to succeed in competitive markets. This has created new incentives for media entrepreneurs, which has led to importing global culture and disseminating critical news. This challenges China's still-authoritarian leaders. Is it possible to craft a decentralized system of media regulation that will result in a public sphere that sustains the political status quo? Is it possible to blend hierarchical control over media content with modern media technologies and global media markets? Is control over the public sphere fraying in ways that portend a general unravelling of the state's political power?

There is a great deal of social and political theory that links modernity with flattening hierarchies, the substitution of consent for coercion and violence, and an increase in individual autonomy. Traditional modernization theory had what may well be the most optimistic version of this argument. Talcott Parsons, for example, argued that modern society, which by his estimation is the most complex society ever, could only be held together by shared values.[1] Other scholars have been far more sensitive to inequalities in wealth and power, but still find that modernity entails an increasing measure of autonomy and consent. Michel Foucault, for example, contrasted "punishment" and "discipline", with the former being traditional and violent, and the latter a modern alternative that depends on the dissemination of certain forms of knowledge that lead individuals to restrain themselves.[2]

In this chapter I shall draw on Gramsci's "hegemony", a concept which is not unrelated to Parsons' "values" and Foucault's "discipline". Gramsci's use of "hegemony" was shifting and contradictory,[3] but in general refers to "the consensual basis of an existing political system within civil society" and importantly,

> is understood in contrast to the concept of "domination": the state's monopoly on the means of violence ... Gramsci contended, however, that only weak states need to rely very often on the threat or use of force implied in their domination. Strong states rule almost exclusively through hegemony.[4]

China's reforms are partly an attempt to realize the benefits of this kind of modernity. Prior to reform, Chinese society was built around Lenin's "vanguard party", an institution which, as Kenneth Jowitt, Andrew Walder, and others have explained, had at least one foot in the world of rational-legal organization, but which also entailed enough charisma to ensure that rule of law was always kept at arm's length. The resulting politics were modern in the sense that people were mobilized to participate in politics, but this style of participation depended on an unsustainable charisma and threats of violence. The result was a gradual but sure drift towards "communist neo-traditionalism", in which patronage replaced charisma, leaving a visibly corrupt and economically inefficient hierarchy.[5] The transformation began when new leadership replaced Mao, and reached the conclusion that all Chinese, including the leadership, would be much better off in a society with less hierarchy and more economic efficiency. The results of the last 20 years have borne abundant testimony to the wisdom of that choice.

This course raises the question of just how far flattening and autonomy will go and in particular whether or not the authorities can regulate the rate, degree and nature of change in ways that protect their power and prerogatives. Several strands of current research lead to the conclusion that China faces little need to replace domination with hegemony. First, those who see China as the latest version of the "East Asian Model" argue that certain types of authoritarian states are actually better at promoting economic growth and modernization than democratic governments.[6] Second, a growing body of literature on political organization in contemporary China argues that by promoting fear among the elite that a more open society would lead to chaos and/or redistribution, the current regime has successfully won their support for substituting authoritarian corporatism for a more open pluralism.[7] Another strand follows from the allegedly authoritarian consequences of neo-liberal globalization and finds that China's openness to the world economy creates inequalities that can only be sustained by authoritarian government.[8] Finally, several studies of new media technologies have found, contrary to the expectations of Internet utopians, that by and large, the Chinese government has been able to turn the introduction of such technologies to its own benefit.[9] These views are summarized by Bruce Bueno de Mesquita and George Downs. While they recognize that modernity requires the provision of public goods that allow autonomous individuals to be productive, they claim that some authoritarian states have become adept at withholding those that have political implications while providing those that are necessary for economic growth. The result, they say, is that while dictatorships like China's have given some ground, they have managed to postpone any crisis over the contradiction between economic growth and authoritarian stability.

Super Voice Girls

The success of the hit television series, *Super Voice Girls*, could be conclusive evidence that the Chinese government can carefully distinguish between the public goods that are necessary for economic growth and those that are politically sensitive. *Super Voice Girls* exemplifies the autonomy of Chinese entrepreneurs and consumers and suggests that ever larger portions of Chinese culture are driven by markets and consumer choice, rather than being directed by a domineering state. This television series offered the pleasing spectacle of young women competing to become a national "pop idol". The format – stretching from awful performances in early rounds to avid fan clubs in later rounds – is closely related to similar shows that have run in many countries around the world. The enthusiastic response in China mirrors that of television audiences in other countries where similar shows had similarly high ratings. The production was distinctly entrepreneurial and the format gave considerable weight to contestants' individual aspirations and involved fans in unofficial social activities. While some Chinese commentators argued that the audience voting to choose winners and losers is a harbinger of democracy, this actually seemed of much less concern to the state than the ostensible vulgarity of the entire spectacle.

The format that eventually became *Super Voice Girls* is one of the global TV market's greatest successes ever, having been broadcast in over 50 markets worldwide. The first such show, *Pop Idol*, reached its first climax in the UK in February of 2002. It was produced by Simon Cowell, formerly a leading figure in the British music industry. Cowell's new format was based on *Popstars*, a format originated in New Zealand in 1999 in which the audience chose among auditioning musicians to create a new band. The *Popstars* format was a great success with versions broadcast in many countries.[10] Cowell modified this format to choose a single singer rather than a band. His production was the show of the year in the UK,[11] but Cowell and his partners only succeeded in selling the show in the United States when they won support from Elizabeth Murdoch, who as manager of BskyB, an important satellite TV firm in the UK, was well aware of the show's success in Britain. She was able to persuade her father, Rupert Murdoch, that he ought to buy the show for his Fox Network.[12] The resulting show, *American Idol*, has consistently won enormous ratings in the American market. In a recent quarterly report *American Idol* was cited as the main reason that profits had doubled over the same quarter a year earlier, not just for the broadcaster, Fox Television, but for all of News Corp.[13]

Chinese television has come a long way to be capable of successfully producing such a show. At the time of Mao's death, Chinese television was more of a curiosity than a mass medium. Broadcasts were limited to a few hours a day in major cities and enjoyed reception in only a very few locations. But post-Mao China proved fertile ground for television. While in 1980, only 0.4 per cent of urban households had a television, by 1997 there were more than 100 televisions per 100 households.[14] Production of television shows grew at a similar rate. In 2001 alone, the Chinese produced nearly 3.5 million hours of television.[15]

The growth of the consumer economy created an advertising industry eager to organize and pay for the production of commercial television. In Mao's China, advertising had been condemned as capitalist. By most accounts, it was in January 1979 that Shanghai TV broadcast the first advertisement – a plug for some wine – to appear in any Chinese media since the Cultural Revolution. Television broadcasters were soon able to claim enormous revenues. For example, CCTV, the national network operated by the central government, generated nearly 4.25 million dollars of revenue from one broadcast, the Chinese national soccer team's opening match in the 2002 World Cup.[16]

This growth would not have been possible without decentralization of state-owned television interests, the participation of private firms, and the growth of competitive markets. In 1978 Beijing Television was renamed China Central Television (CCTV) and became the national network. By 1980, officials determined that provinces would take the lead in developing television. In 1983 they established a four level system with county, city, provincial, and national television broadcasters. Lower levels were allowed to invest and hire personnel with relatively limited supervision from above. In 1985 television stations were granted the right to keep a portion of any profits they generated, and by 1992 were made responsible for their own profit and loss. While a national Ministry of Radio and Television was organized in 1982, provinces already had a running start at autonomy. Most importantly, provincial rather than central authorities could approve shows for broadcast, and approval in one province was valid in others.[17]

This institutional framework resulted in more or less competitive markets. To be sure, there are serious limits to market competition. Despite the *relatively* convenient regulatory framework, there are still stiff regulations on what can be broadcast. This includes political restrictions, limits based on moral grounds, and on taste. Television stations' links to provincial authorities lead to restrictions on market entry and access. While privately-owned firms are allowed to participate in the television industry, since all broadcasters are owned by provincial authorities, the private firms are almost always in the weaker position. This said, the growth in the television industry and the broadcasters' need to attract audiences has created a robust market for television programming. Some of this market has been met by private production firms. Advertising agencies were among the most important early pioneers, often putting together television shows and distributing them to television stations as a means of generating product that could be sold to advertisers. This ensemble of participants has collaborated to create a lucrative and growing industry.

Hunan Satellite TV, which broadcast *Super Voice Girls*, is one of the most successful provincial stations. Founded in 1997 under the ownership of the television and broadcast offices of the Hunan Provincial Government, the company enjoyed steady growth through 2000, and managed to win landing rights on the cable systems found in cities in every province in China. The broadcaster's success lured others to copy its formats and profits fell from 2000–03, prompting a change in strategy to emphasize entertainment like *Super Voice Girls*.

From the early 1980s on, Chinese television has imported television content from international sources. Already in 1980, *The Man from Atlantis*, which was terminated in the US after a quick 13 shows in 1977, proved a sensation in China. Later imports, such as *Hunter* and various Latin American soap operas, would prove similarly popular. The American NBA has won enormous audiences from its broadcasts on Chinese TV. Foreign imports, though, face various political and economic restrictions.[18]

Chinese television has also imported formats. While Hollywood has succeeded in producing movies that appeal to global audiences, television audiences usually prefer shows that are produced in local languages and to suit local cultures. In response, there is a global trade in television formats. Using an off-the-shelf format saves development and production costs, but nonetheless allows a local flavour.[19] Michael Keane reports that Chinese television has copied formats from Hong Kong, Taiwan, Europe, and the United States. He finds the result – such as the 2001 television series *Shangri-la*, in which three teams of six people went on a 30-day trek across the fringes of the Himalayas, supplied with only ten-days of matches and food – to be lacking in creativity and quality.[20]

This brings us to the success of *Super Voice Girls*. Hunan Satellite TV ran a first season of the show in 2004, but did not win exceptional ratings. It did, however, attract the attention of Sun Jun, a marketer working for Mongolian Cow, a firm that sells, among other products, Mongolian Cow Yogurt. Sun had been hired to triple sales of the already popular yogurt from 700 million to 2.5 billion *yuan* within the year. After unsuccessful attempts to make deals with various celebrities, Sun chanced upon the existing show. Aware of *American Idol*'s success and seeing that young women were the main market for yogurt, Sun pitched the idea to his superiors. Once he overcame their initial resistance, he then worked to persuade Hunan Satellite TV that with an infusion of cash from Mongolian Cow, their show could be as successful as it had been in other countries. When Hunan Satellite TV agreed, Sun organized a marketing campaign that included advertisements on television, the Internet, print media, and posters in grocery stores. The *Super Voice Girls* logo was prominently displayed on Mongolian Cow Yogurt packaging. Sun exceeded his sales goals and Mongolian Cow Yogurt went from third to first place in China's yogurt market. Other firms benefited as well, including telecommunications firms that handled the text messaging required for voting, advertising agencies, and the media firms such as Internet portals that carried the ads.[21]

Super Voice Girls adjusted the *Pop Idol* format to suit Chinese tastes. As in versions broadcast elsewhere, the Chinese version included: awful performances in early rounds,[22] a panel of judges that comments on performances, sympathetic endorsement of contestants' dream of a career as a "pop idol", presentations of training sessions designed to improve the contestants' skills, interviews, and commentary that gave contestants "back story", and dramatic tension over who would be voted off the show. But *Super Voice Girls* was nonetheless constructed as a Chinese show. It started with regional competitions in provincial cities and towards the end included a vision of "global China" in the form of groups of

Chinese fans of *Super Voice Girls* shouting encouragement in recognizable international settings such as Sydney Harbour. The Chinese show adopted vocabulary from Chinese video games, "PK" for "player kill", and created a special "PK stage" where contestants at risk of "PK" were required to stand while at risk. While ejecting players from the show is a focus of dramatic tension in all versions, the PK moment was tearful in a manner that American audiences might find excessively feminized.

The Chinese public was overwhelmingly enthusiastic. The series had higher average ratings than CCTV's news show, *Xinwen Lianbo* (新闻联报) and Hunan Satellite TV was able to charge commensurate rates for advertising.[23] The final achieved the extraordinary distinction of coming close to, or even overtaking, CCTV's *Spring Festival Gala*, formerly the most watched show on Chinese television. As with *American Idol*, fans attached themselves to individual contestants. As Ben Marcom and Jeremy Goldkorn explained, Super Voice Girl terminology entered the Chinese lexicon:

> "Fan" is sometimes rendered in Chinese as fen si (粉丝 – Chinese vermicelli). The fan group of each semi-finalist Super Voice Girl competitor were given their own names, with each name related to the word *fen si*:
>
> *Yu Mi* (玉米 – corn): Li Yuchun's fans
> *Fen Bi* (粉笔 – chalk): Zhou Bichang's fans
> *Liang Fen* (凉粉 – bean jelly): Zhang Liangying's fans
> *He Fan* (盒饭 – take-out food): He Jie's fans
> *Jia Mi* (佳迷 – Ji Minjia addiction): Ji Minjia's fans
>
> The fans have been crazily supporting their idols, arguing with each other and slandering their competitors. There have been scandalous stories about the competition's judges, allegations that Li Yuchun is a lesbian, and enough gossip online to keep *Super Voice Girls* at the top of Baidu's most popular search terms for weeks on end.[24]

Exactly what this means for Chinese politics and culture was the subject among leading intellectuals of an avid debate that was largely found on-line, but which also spilled into some newspaper columns.[25] Some were sceptical that any good could come from commercial culture and noted that the choice of what entertainment to consume was hardly the same thing as democracy, and that democracy was discredited by the choice of a winner who did not sing all that well. Others charged that even then the Party had interfered with the course of the show, alleging that a round of patriotic songs sung by the contestants at the end was the result of such intervention. Others, such as Xu Jilin, pointed out that the procedures used for selecting winners and losers were less than democratic, as in early stages, judges appointed by the sponsors were able to change outcomes and while the rules were changed for later stages to give power exclusively to the voting audience, the changes were made arbitrarily.[26] Others, though, argued that *Super Voice Girls* had had a beneficial effect. Liu Qing argued that the show helped young people learn how to deal with success and failure in competition.[27] Liu Xiaobo argued that the show demonstrated that Chinese were capable of acting autonomously outside government authority, and could be very enthusiastic about democracy.[28]

The authorities evinced more concern over the show's alleged vulgarity than any putative trend towards democracy. In July of 2005, CCTV held a conference on "vulgar sensationalism" (低俗化) which may have been in response to a policy speech delivered by the deputy director of the State Administration of Radio Film and Television and which initiated a series of attempts to regulate this format. In response, *Super Voice Girls* adjusted aspects of their costume, stage design, choice of songs, and the style of judges. New regulations were issued on the eve of the 2006 series. These specified that in future such shows should establish a healthy world view and good values, avoid vulgarity, maintain appropriate aesthetic standards for dress and appearance, and should be judged fairly. Judges were prohibited from issuing criticisms that would humiliate contestants. They also specified that local satellite stations are not allowed to broadcast the preliminary rounds of national contest shows held in their locality.[29] While this caused a flurry of concern, Hunan Satellite TV once again achieved high ratings. In 2007 the authorities imposed further constraints, first limiting the duration of such contests to two and a half months as opposed to the previously customary four and a half months,[30] and later banning weirdness, vulgarity, and low taste, and limiting contestants to singing songs that are healthy and ethnically inspiring, and banning gossip.[31]

The irony is that it could very well be that the censors' intervention is more destabilizing than their ostensible target and may well not accomplish much. The weight of opinion in many countries is that flooding media with entertainment commodities facilitates political passivity. David Mindich, for example, points out that during *American Idol*'s premier season, Americans under 30 were likely to know far more about *Idol* contestants than candidates in the concurrent Presidential primaries.[32] Of course, post-Mao or post-totalitarian China is on a different trajectory than is the United States. Compared to Mao's China, the *Super Voice Girls* model, where entrepreneurs with no clear political intent import commodities from global cultural markets, represents a high degree of social and cultural autonomy. It could be that allowing ordinary Chinese the opportunity to consume and participate in this spectacle allows them to re-imagine their lives and China in ways that ultimately contradict the Party and its purposes. For example, the choice of cities for regional finals – Guangzhou, Changsha, Zhengzhou, Hangzhou, and Chengdu – and holding the finals in Changsha suggests a different map of China than is usually projected from Beijing. That the *Super Voice Girls* finals drew as large of an audience as CCTV's *Spring Festival Gala* suggests a certain displacement. But this is all speculative, indirect, and at most, a distant threat. What seems far more likely, is that heavy-handed intervention by nativist cultural conservatives angers people who might otherwise be perfectly content to remain passive consumers of entertainment commodities. Finally, these restrictions will certainly incite a great deal of passive and covert opposition. There have been over 500 reality TV productions since the inception of *Super Voice Girls*, and the lure of the profits they have generated will doubtless ensure that there will be many more entrepreneurs like Sun Jun to come.

Newspaper editors dismissed

The *Super Voice Girls* story suggests that, contrary to Bueno de Mesquita and Downs' argument, it is difficult for states to carefully manage the use of repression. When culturally conservative or xenophobic censors are not accountable and have ready access to a repressive apparatus, they are likely to use it at will. Consideration of more serious acts of repression in China's newspaper industry shows why censorship cannot be accountable or managed by legal standards.

Over the last 20 years, commercial newspapers have displaced the Party's organ papers. While the newspapers are still owned and operated by government and party agencies, their structure and content is quite different. At the outset of reforms, the most authoritative papers were the "organ papers" published by territorial Party committees. These papers' leading role started to fade with the reintroduction of evening papers (the organ papers are typically morning papers) in the early years of reform. In contrast to the stale political news that dominated organ papers, evening papers were allowed to abridge political reports and emphasize softer fare, including sports, fashion, home, personal advice, cultural news, useful information for urban residents, and so forth. This content made these papers the most widely read, and with the onset of advertising, generated large revenues for their publishers. This in turn meant that they could publish more pages of content which attracted more readers and more advertisers. Meanwhile, the organ papers lost readers and struggled to attract advertisers.

Those stuck with the burden of publishing organ papers found respite in publishing supplemental papers such as a weekend edition that were not subject to the content regulations imposed on the organ papers. One of the most successful supplemental papers, *Southern Weekend*, was published by the same body that published the Guangzhou Provincial organ paper, *Southern Daily. Southern Weekend* made a name for itself by exposing scandals and publishing reports closer to the edge of what the authorities were willing to tolerate than other papers were willing to risk. This, a mix of advertisements and content oriented to an increasingly affluent white collar readership, and national distribution made *Southern Weekend* an enormous economic success, but also led to repeated criticism from political authorities.

Beginning in the late 1990s, "the metropolitan paper" became the dominant format. The leading example was the *Southern Metropolitan Paper*, another entry from Guangdong province, which like *Southern Weekend*, risked censure to win market-share. In content and format, metropolitan papers resembled urban papers in other countries, such as the *Washington Post* or *New York Times*, and demonstrated that television was not the only medium that could learn from foreign formats.

The commercialization of China's newspapers has created a limited space and strong financial incentives for critical journalism. Commercialization is not without serious problems. Most commercial content is soft. Sensationalism is also relatively common, and has at times incited aggressive nationalist passions. Corruption is widespread, with some editors and reporters accepting payoffs for stories favourable to commercial interests or eliciting blackmail to prevent critical reports. However, while still owned by official organs, and still subject to rigorous scrutiny, newspapers like *Southern Weekend*, *Southern Metropolitan News*, and *Beijing News* have developed a lucrative market for commentary more critical than that found in other papers. *Beijing News*, for example, exceeded expectations by becoming profitable within a year of its founding.

The rapid growth of China's Internet has had an important impact on both the content and the economics of newspapers. Chinese newspapers had enjoyed a steady growth in circulation that newspapers in Europe and the United States could only envy. In the last couple of years, though, like their Western counterparts, they have suffered the loss of younger readers and advertising dollars to the Internet. Equally important, the Internet allows information to circulate in ways that change the boundaries of what can be published in newspapers. The Internet both makes more content available for newspapers to report and helps journalists to communicate with each other. As will be seen below, this has had an important impact on the authorities' ability to regulate newspapers.

The intrinsic characteristics of newspaper and Internet technologies make these media more difficult to regulate than television. Television technology as yet makes it the quintessential "few to many" media. Print media and especially the Internet allow more senders to send more messages at a lower cost than television. This, coupled with the structural incentives for critical journalism described below has created serious problems for Party media managers.

The authorities have established an enormous infrastructure for regulating media content. This system still bears the legacy of China's Leninist past when the authorities orchestrated virtually the whole of the public sphere. Media regulation is multi-tiered and thorough. The authorities still organize campaigns offering financial and career incentives to those who will report selected issues the way they want them reported. There are still extensive ownership and licensing regulations that mean that most media properties, especially in print and broadcast media, are formally owned by the Party or government organs. This means that political authorities generally have the ability to suspend publication or close a property. They also have the ability to transfer or fire editors and reporters. Open-ended laws restrict constitutional guarantees of freedom of speech. Many journalists report that local press and propaganda authorities put out a steady stream of directives with instructions on how some topics should be reported and ban reporting other topics altogether. Party authorities closely monitor the press and Internet to make sure that their injunctions are followed.[33]

Many special provisions apply to the Internet. "Firewalls" mounted between the Chinese Internet and the global Internet block the retrieval of foreign web pages from specified addresses. Filters mounted at various places in the Internet interdict the flow of certain combinations of words, regardless of their source. The authorities hire individuals to pose as ordinary Internet users and post messages to chatrooms and BBS that help to turn the flow of discourse in directions favoured by the authorities. Internet users, whether at home or in Internet cafes, are required to register. Internet content providers are required to keep logs of who posted what and, unless otherwise licensed, are restricted from doing their own reporting to create new content.

This far exceeds what American journalists would call a "chilling effect". International monitoring groups such as the Committee to Protect Journalists and Reporters Without Borders are aware of at least two or three dozen journalists and about 60 Internet users in detention or incarcerated.[34] This is more journalists detained than any other country, but still indicates that the vast majority of journalists have chosen to avoid doing anything that would cause trouble with the authorities. On the other hand, this set of controls is not a self-regulating system.

Jiao Guobiao's 2004 criticism of the Propaganda Department is polemical but points out a fundamental problem in the Party's system of media management. A system that imposes secrecy and obscures pertinent ideas and points of view cannot be held to any meaningful standard of accountability or reliably incorporate rule of law.[35] Such a system is inevitably open to arbitrary abuse and manipulation. One website manager, for example, complained that it is difficult to predict exactly which postings will draw a response from the authorities that watch his website. Very often, he said, the problem was a local problem, such as a report regarding a specific locality that drew a response from the authorities in that locality who in turn were able to reach the authorities responsible for monitoring the website in question. Moreover, the interests protected by censorship could well be the personal interests of the leaders who complain rather than the public interest of the Party or government.[36]

In his essay, "Propaganda Culture", Sha Yexin presents evidence that the lack of a legal framework for censorship is an intentional strategy for maintaining control. Sha cites Zhong Peizhang, a former head of the News Bureau of the Central Propaganda Department, who in turn attributed the following to a named high-level power holder:

> During the time that the Guomindang ruled, they drafted a press law and we Communists carefully studied its text, seized its shortcomings, and drilled into its gaps. Now that we have power, I think we do not want a press law in order to avoid having people drill into our gaps. If there is no law, we have the initiative, and whatever we want to control, that is what we will control.[37]

The contradiction between a state possessed of a blunt and arbitrary means of control and media with increasing space and incentives for critical reporting has been illuminated by a series of incidents in which prominent journalists have been forced to leave their posts or have had their publications suspended. In one such incident, on 28 December 2005, *Beijing News*' editor-in-chief, Yang Bin, was forced to step down. Different reports identified reasons ranging from the personal ire of Central Propaganda Department Chief Liu Yunshan to displeasure over reports on the violent repression of villagers in Dingzhou to speculation that the Guangming Daily Group wanted more control of the increasingly profitable new paper.[38]

What was unusual in this case was that, following Yang's suspension, 100 of the paper's journalists went on strike and only returned when two assistant editors who had originally been dismissed along with Yang were allowed to return. The incident was widely discussed on China's Internet, where Yang and his staff were widely supported and the authorities broadly condemned.

On 24 January 2006, the authorities suspended publication of *Freezing Point*, a weekly magazine supplement to *China Youth Daily*.[39] The supplement had been created in 1994 and after starting with mostly soft news, came to offer a steady stream of thoughtful commentary on politics, culture, and other topics. The editor, Li Datong, estimated that 40 per cent of *China Youth Daily*'s subscribers only subscribed because of *Freezing Point*.[40]

That Li and his deputy, Lu Yuegang, were able to edit such a prominent supplement is evidence of structural tensions. Both have histories such that their superiors must have known what sort of paper they would edit. Li had been suspended for leading protesting journalists in 1989. After that, he was the founding editor for the controversial magazine, *Orient*, from which he resigned in protest over his superior's conservatism after publishing the first issue. Even so, *Orient* was eventually forced to close. Li's tenure at *Freezing Point* was tempestuous. He had circulated a criticism of the management of *China Youth Daily* earlier in 2005. He not only seemed to escape sanction, but seemed to have induced the management to retract a bonus scheme that Li had charged would lead to flaccid journalism.[41] Lu was the author of a banned book and had been among the problems that led to dismissing an editor-in-chief at *Southern Weekend* some years before. No-one with experience in Chinese journalism could have been unaware of these circumstances, and it seems very likely that they were recruited precisely because of their ability to push the envelope.

The article that evidently triggered the crackdown was an historical piece by Yuan Weishi which charged the histories taught in Chinese textbooks with dangerous distortions that inflame nationalist passions. Li and Lu also reported that the authorities were critical of an article posted to the paper's intranet by Lu complaining that Liu Binyan – regarded by many as China's greatest investigative journalist, a reporter at *China Youth Daily* prior to falling victim to the Anti-Rightist Campaign in 1957 and recently deceased in exile – should not be erased from contemporary media history. Li was sceptical that the historical article was really the problem, telling a foreign journalist that "That's just an excuse, they needed an excuse to close me down, and they chose that particular topic, history, because that's an area they can easily manipulate public opinion on."[42]

Li and Lu were transferred to a think tank and the supplement resumed publication under another editor, but Li and Lu refused to go quietly. Instead, they wrote a letter of appeal to Party authorities, gave angry interviews to the international media, and circulated statements on the Internet.[43] While Li and Lu proved at least temporarily beyond rescue, a group of 13 prominent intellectuals signed an open letter to the Party Central Committee citing, among other things, the Chinese Constitution's guarantee of free speech. As in the case of Yang Bin, the *Freezing Point* incident was widely discussed on China's Internet.

At about the same time, Chen Jieren was demoted from his position as editor of a smaller paper, *Public Interest Times*. Although officials stated that the actual reason for his demotion was incompetence, Chen issued a public statement claiming that the reason was a series of critical articles such as one that criticized a locality for pocketing disaster relief money meant to be distributed to victims, and capped by an interview with an English professor claiming that an English language website maintained by the Ministry of Civil Affairs had numerous errors in translation and grammar.[44] Chen's statement, titled "Despicable Intrigue, Ridiculous Game" described Chen's superiors as scrambling to retreat from even the slightest hint of controversy for fear of arousing the ire of high-level leaders at the Ministry of Civil Affairs. He argued that his leaders were far more interested in personal prestige and avoiding trouble than in correcting mistakes or protecting the public welfare.

The contradictory results of the commercialization of Chinese media and the legacy of Leninist controls is that on one hand, the authorities have retained the ability to intervene almost anywhere in the media at will. They can and do suspend publications, dismiss journalists, and from time to time, arrest, slander, and beat those who challenge their authority. On the other hand, commercialization has created structures that, at least so far, have continued to generate incentives and opportunities for journalists who would challenge official interpretations. Some individuals, like Li Datong and Lu Yuegang, take great personal risks but have somehow survived calamities to do similar work in other settings. Moreover, the rise of the Internet means that they and others like them have the opportunity to tell their side of the story. Repression remains effective, but is more visible and open to public challenge than at any time since 1989.

Conclusion

Living in Mao's China was not just violence and coercion but required a great deal of discipline. The "mobilization regime" involved almost the whole of society in politics, and set a wide range of exacting standards for how they should conduct their politics. Citizens had to keep close watch on their behaviour. But as Michael Dutton argues, politics in Mao's China was founded on Mao's stark question, "Who are our enemies and who are our friends", and while the incentive to maintain the discipline was in part the utopia promised to friends, it was also the fear of being designated as an enemy.[45] The importance of this threat to maintaining that state means that Mao's China was far more of what Gramsci called "domination" than "hegemony".

The momentous changes that followed Mao's death were predicated on taking some of the danger out of ordinary people's lives. China's post-Mao leaders, who had themselves suffered the terror of Maoist politics, determined that there might be more to be gained by reducing the level of fear and allowing more people more autonomy. Much of the activity chronicled in this chapter, including the entrepreneurial and creative efforts of people like Sun Jun and Li Datong, follow closely from those decisions. Post-Mao China's most important success is surely lifting hundreds of millions of people out of degrading poverty but creating space for meaningful endeavours such as these is surely also an important historical achievement.

The conclusion of these stories has to be that these changes have as yet only gone so far. It is noteworthy that none of the journalists involved in the incidents at the *Beijing Times*, *Freezing Point*, and *Public Interest Times* was sent to prison. But it remains that the state's coercion is a major factor in keeping China as it is. In the case of *Super Voice Girls*, cultural conservatives quite possibly corrupted by economic interests are able to apply ineffective but consequential regulations almost at will. Analysis of cases of newspaper editors dismissed in early 2006 demonstrate that the power to censor is, and must be, highly arbitrary and beyond any accountability or rule of law. While politics are no longer as violent and coercive as they once were, the distinction between friends and enemies still casts a threatening shadow. This in turn strongly suggests that it is very difficult to create institutions that carefully distinguish between the public goods needed for economic growth and those with political implications.

In the meantime, the discipline of Mao's China is in decay, if not in ruins. The structural contradictions of contemporary Chinese media offer powerful incentives to violate political standards, and these cases demonstrate the existence of highly entrepreneurial serial violators. Readers and audiences, too, are eager to violate both the Party's standards of taste and its political norms. There is clearly an enormous demand for "vulgar" entertainment and critical news.

Moreover, changes in Chinese media mean that leaders' use of coercion is visible to a broader and broader public. The journalists involved in these incidents not only avoided prison, but were also able to post their stories to the Internet and to read public letters of support.

I conclude that if restraints were lifted, China's public sphere would undergo dramatic change. It could be that the existing state could adapt to those changes, but there is also a strong chance that it could not. In other words, for all that Chinese leaders have created spaces for economic and cultural entrepreneurs, the state is still not hegemonic.

None of this necessarily means that China will experience political change in the immediate or even foreseeable future. The more a state relies on domination – coercion and violence – to maintain stability, the more extemporaneous its politics and the more likely that a single error in judgement will lead to an unexpected outcome. But that does not doom dictators to making mistakes. Some dictatorships last for decades. On the other hand, if in Gramsci's words, hegemony can be likened to "a powerful system of fortresses and earthworks", the Chinese state as yet lacks those bulwarks.[46]

Notes

1 Talcott Parsons, *The System of Modern Societies*, Englewood Cliffs: Prentice Hall, 1971.

2 Michel Foucault, *Power/Knowledge: Selected Interviews and Other Writings 1972–77*, Brighton: Harvester Press, 1980.

3 Perry Anderson, "The Antinomies of Antonio Gramsci", *New Left Review* 100, November 1976–January 1978, pp. 5–78.

4 Walter L. Adamson, *Hegemony and Revolution: A Study of Antonio Gramsci's Political and Cultural Theory*, Berkeley: University of California Press, 1983, p. 170. See also Antonio Gramsci, *Selections from the Prison Notebooks*, New York: International Publishers, 1971.

5 Kenneth Jowitt, *The Leninist Response to National Dependency*, Berkeley: Institute of International Studies, 1978; Andrew G. Walder, *Communist Neo-Traditionalism: Work and Authority in Chinese Industry*, Berkeley: University of California Press, 1986; and Barrett L. McCormick, *Political Reform in Post-Mao China: Democracy and Bureaucracy in a Leninist State*, Berkeley: University of California Press, 1990.

6 Alice Amsden, *Asia's Next Giant: South Korea and Late Industrialization*, London: Oxford University Press, 1989 and Robert Wade, *Governing the Market: Economic Theory and the Role of Government in East Asian Industrialization*, Princeton: Princeton University Press, 1990.

7 Bruce J. Dickson, *Red Capitalists in China: The Party, Private Entrepreneurs, and Prospects for Political Change*, New York: Cambridge University Press, 2003 and Margaret Pearson, *China's New Business Elite: The Political Consequences of Economic Reform*, Berkeley: University of California Press, 1997.

8 Wang Hui, *China's New Order: Society, Politics and Economy in Transition*, Cambridge: Harvard University Press, 2003 and Mary Elizabeth Gallagher, *Contagious Capitalism: Globalization and the Politics of Labour in China*, Princeton: Princeton University Press, 2005. Note that Gallagher concludes with foreign investment has delayed democratization, change may yet come.

9 Nina Hachigian, "The Internet and One-Party East Asian States", *Washington Quarterly* 25:3, Summer 2002, pp. 41–58 and Taylor Boas and Shanthi Kalathil, *Open Networks, Closed Regimes: The Impact of the Internet on Authoritarian Rule*, Washington, DC: Carnegie Endowment for International Peace, 2003.

10 See Screentime: Formats at www.screentime.tv/. Retrieved 15 May 2006.

11 Bill Carter, *Desperate Networks*, Garden City: Doubleday, 2006, see especially pp. 181–95.

12 Ibid.

13 "American Idol boosts News Corp profit" *Sydney Morning Herald* 11 May 2006. Retrieved from www.smh.com.au 11 May 2006.

14 *China Statistical Yearbook, 1998*, Beijing: China Statistical Publishing House, 1999. At the same time, over 90 per cent of rural households had a television.

15 *China Statistical Yearbook*, 2002.

16 See "China–Costa Rica Match *Earns* CCTV US$6,000 Per Second in Ad Income", *China Online* at www.chinaonline.com. Accessed 6 June 2002.

17 This history is recounted in greater detail in Liu Qing and Barrett McCormick, "Cinema and Television: Leninist Institutions, Commerce, and the Private Sphere" unpublished manuscript.

18 For a history of the internationalization of Chinese television, see Junhao Hong, *The Internationalization of Television in China: The Evolution of Ideology, Society and Media Since the Reform*, New York: Greenwood Press, 1998.

19 Albert Moran, *Copycat TV: Globalisation, Program Formats and Cultural Identity*, Luton: University of Luton Press, 1998, vol. II, no. 30.

20 Michael Keane, "As a Hundred Television Formats Bloom, a Thousand Television Stations Contend", *Journal of Contemporary China* 11:30, February 2002, pp. 5–16. See also Christopher Bodeen, "China-Survivor" *Associated Press*, 22 June 2001.

21 孙隽, *超级策划*, 合肥: 安徽人民出版社, 2005.

22 At this writing, a video clip of one such performance could be found at http://news.wenxuecity.com/BBSView.php?SubID=news&MsgID=245231.

23 王冰子, "2005 湖南卫视超级女声节目的研究和启示". Retrieved from www.monternet.com/moneditor/cs/subject/zwtx/mwgc/ 3462/10064.html, 22 March 2006.

24 Ben Marcom and Jeremy Goldkorn, "The Final Week of TV Sensation Super Voice Girls", *Danwei*, 24 August 2005. Retreived from www.danwei.org, 15 April 2006.

25 A compendium of such commentary can be found in translation in the EastSouthWest-North blog's "Super Girl and Democracy" at http://zonaeuropa.com/20050829_1.htm.

26 许纪霖, "戳穿" 超女民主 "的神话", [http://211.157.100.62/viewthread.php?tid=20336].

27 刘擎, "超级女声与生活世界的成功神化" [[原载 2005 年 08 月 18 日新京报]. Retrieved from www.cc.org.cn/newcc/browwenzhang.php?articleid=4618, 15 February 2006.

28 刘晓波, "超女粉丝的民间自组织意义" [www.boxun.com/hero/liuxb/429_1.shtml].

29 Miao Di, "Struggling Between Propaganda and Commercials: Chinese Television Today" presented to Changing Media; Changing China conference at University of California, San Diego (5–6 May 2006) Thanks to Miao Di for allowing me to read this paper. For the text of these regulations, see 广电总局关于进一步加强广播电视播出机构参与、主办或播出全国性或跨省(区、市) 赛事等活动管理的 通知[www.law-lib.com].

30 David Bandurski, "SARFT orders TV networks to limit 'competition show' durations to two and a half months" (27 February 2007). Retrieved from *China Media Project* http://cmp.hku.hk, 1 March 2007.

31 "China gives thumbs-down to 'American Idol' imitators" (9 April 2007). Retrieved from *ChannelNewsAsia.com* www.channelnewsasia.com/stories/entertainment/view/269289/1/.html, 1 May.

32 David T. Z. Mindich, *Tuned Out: Why Americans Under 40 Don't Follow the News*, New York: Oxford University Press, 2005. See also Neil Postman, *Amusing Ourselves to Death: Public Discourse in the Age of Show Business*, New York: Viking Penguin, 1985.

33 The best account of controls over Chinese media can be found in 何清涟, "中国政府如何控制媒体" 中国人权研究报告 2005. Retrieved from ChinaAffairs.org at www.chinaaffairs.org, 1 July 2005.

34 "Reporters Without Borders", *China – 2004 Annual Report*, www.rsf.org, accessed 10 October 2004 and *Internet Under Surveillance 2004: China*, www.rsf.org, accessed 9 August 2004; Committee to Protect Journalists, "China, Cuba, Two African Nations are Top Jailers of Journalists" 13 December 2005. Retrieved from www.cpj.org, 28 March 2006.

35 Jiao Guobiao, "Taofa Zhongxuanbu" (Declaration of the Campaign against The Central Propaganda Department) available in translation at *EastSouthWestNorth* (5 May 2004), www.zonaeuropa.com/weblog.htm, accessed 23 June 2004 and in the original language at *Guancha* (China Information Center, 9 April 2004), www.guancha.org, accessed 23 June 2004.

36 Interview in Shanghai, January 2006.

37 Author's translation. Sha Yexin, "'Propaganda' Culture" (宣转文化) (16 June 2003), retrieved from TECN at www.tecn.cn/index.php on 18 May 2007. Sha cites Zhong Peizhang, "Going Forward in the Same Boat" (同舟共进) in Guangdong Political Consultative Publication (广东政协刊物) (February 2003).

38 Congressional-Executive Commission on China, "Chinese Authorities Crack Down on Progressive Newspaper Publisher", 3 January 2006. Retrieved from *Congressional-*

Executive Commission on China, www.cecc.gov, 3 February 2006 and Reporters Without Borders, “Restless Journalists at Beijing News Kept Under Close Surveillance”, 3 January 2006. Retrieved from *Reporters Without Borders*, www.rsf.org, 3 February 2006.

39 The author is grateful to Nico Volland for being allowed to read his excellent unpublished manuscript, “The Freezing Point Controversy and the Modernization of the Chinese Media Sector”, 2006, which was very useful in writing this section.

40 Mark Magnier, “In China, Free Speech Shows Its Teeth” *Los Angeles Times*, 17 February 2006. Retrieved from www.latimes.com, 18 February 2006.

41 Christine Kwok, “China: Freedom Row at China Youth Daily”, *South China Morning Post*, 16 August 2005. Retrieved from AsiaMedia, www.asiamedia.ucla.edu/article.asp?parentid=28286, 20 September 2005.

42 Philip J. Cunningham, “Li Datong Meets the Press” *Danwei*, 24 February 2006. Retrieved from www.danwei.org/media_and_advertising/li_datong_meets_the_press_by_p.php, 26 February 2006.

43 A translation of Li and Lu’s statement, a link to the original, and the text of the memo announcing their dismissal can be found at “The Li–Lu Statement On Freezing Point”, *EastWestSouthNorth*. Retrieved from www.zonaeuropa.com/20060218_2.htm, 10 May 2006.

44 Chen’s statement can be found at 陈杰人, “无聊的游戏 卑劣的伎俩 – 就本人被解除“公益时报》主编职务并遭总编辑刘佑平恶意中伤事件告天下书”, *Academic Criticism*, 10 February 2006. Retrieved from www.acriticism.com/article.asp?Newsid=7619&type=1001, 15 April 2006. The ostensibly offending article can be found at 黄卫峰：对外宣传工作任重而道远 – 评“中国政府网”英文网页中的表达问题 [学术批评网创办五周年纪念征文]” *Academic Criticism*, 2 February 2006. Retrieved from www.acriticism.com/article.asp? Newsid=7566&type=1000, 15 April 2006.

45 Michael Dutton, *Policing Chinese Politics: A History*, Durham: Duke University Press, 2005.

46 Gramci, *Prison Notebooks*, op. cit. p. 238.

8 Granting or refusing the right to petition

The dilemma of China's *xinfang* system

*Keyuan Zou**

Chinese society has been in a relatively unstable state in recent times, with more social protests and unrest resulting from its fast economic growth and rapid social changes. The *xinfang* system is a mechanism for Chinese citizens to air their grievances, but it faces a serious challenge as the number of *xinfang* is said to have reached "flood peak" in 2003 and is expected to continue climbing. The dilemma rests with the fact that the Chinese government and the Communist Party are using the *xinfang* system to maintain their close links with the masses, but they are afraid that the *xinfang* activities of the people could jeopardize the social stability of the country. The recent attempt to put it under legal rein has the purpose of balancing the two contradictory elements. However, it is doubtful whether this measure is effective in practice.

The right to petition: an essential element to build a harmonious society?

Recently, with the fast economic growth and rapid social changes, Chinese society has been in a relatively more unstable state with many social protests and disturbances spotted around the country. The uneven distribution of economic wealth among the Chinese has created a lot of social and personal grievances. It is said that "numerous social conflicts may surface when per capita gross domestic product (GDP) enters US$1,000–3,000 stage".[1] All these unstable factors obviously constitute another new challenge to the Chinese government, resulting from greater demands from Chinese citizens. It is thus imperative for China to have a mechanism for its citizens to air their grievances.

It is to be remembered that after the succession of the Chinese leadership, the new generation centred on the Hu–Wen leadership which put forward the new government policy of building a harmonious society in China. In this ideal society, according to the Chinese government, harmony in eight areas should be achieved: the development of democracy, the rule of law, justice, sincerity, amity, and vitality, as well as a better relationship between the people and the government and between man and nature.[2] The 6th Plenary Session of the 16th Central Committee of the Chinese Communist Party put the strategic goal of "building a harmonious socialist society" on its agenda, which as is defined, would be "a democratic society under the rule of law, and based on equality and justice. It will also be an honest, caring, stable, vigorous, and orderly society in which humans live in harmony with nature".[3] The application of the *xinfang* system becomes an indispensable component of China's efforts in building such a society since it can be used to alleviate the tensions in Chinese society.

On 4 November 2005, a special conference on *xinfang* was held in Beijing and jointly chaired by Zhou Yongkang, member of the CCP Political Bureau and Hua Jianmin, member of the State Council. According to Zhou, the *xinfang* work needs to be strengthened and improved under the guidance of the Deng Xiaoping Theory and the Three Represents Thought. It needs to be regularized and legalized. He called Party committees and governments at all levels to prioritize the *xinfang* work so as to fulfil the goal of "building a harmonious socialist society".[4]

There are at least three signals coming from the above news. First, the *xinfang* system remains imperfect despite the fact that the *Xinfang* Regulations have been in effect since 1 May 2005. Thus, it still needs improvement. Second, the new *Xinfang* Regulations just came into effect in May. People, including ordinary citizens and governmental officials, are not yet familiar with this new law, much less with how to implement the new regulations in an effective manner. The central government wanted the *xinfang* system to be incorporated into the Chinese legal system (纳入法制化轨道) as early as possible, though it takes time to realize this. Finally, there is a trend of increasing unrest and tension in Chinese society, which would correspondingly increase the volume of *xinfang* activities, thus putting the government under tremendous pressure. The emphasis of strengthening the role of the *xinfang* system carries a critical goal of maintaining the stability of Chinese society.

The term "*xinfang*" literally means "letters and visits or calls" in Chinese, a short term for "people's letters and visits". As defined by law, *xinfang* is an activity of a citizen, a legal person, or organization to provide information, submit proposals and opinions, or express grievances and petitions to the relevant departments of the government at all levels, subject to the handling of the relevant administrative organs and in accordance with law, by means of letters, email, fax, telephone, or visits.[5] The inclusion of email as a method of petition is praised as a "major progress" since it not only increases efficiency, "but also greatly reduces petitioners' economic costs by saving them the trouble of visiting offices in person".[6]

While the definition includes reports or proposals and opinions as part of *xinfang*, the current *xinfang* system mainly deals with petitions submitted by citizens who have grievances and have suffered unjust treatment, largely by local officials or government departments. Thus, in this context, the *xinfang* system is in fact a petition system with Chinese characteristics. Yet, *xinfang* should not be confused with the term "*shangfang*", which is only one component of "*xinfang*", as *xinfang* can be conducted through letters, emails, visits, and telephone calls.

The *xinfang* system can be traced back to the 1930s when the Chinese Communist Party (CCP) was in Yan'an. As recorded, Mao Zedong himself handled a collective petition case in 1938 concerning injured soldiers.[7] In

August 1949, the CCP Centre set up an office of political secretary in charge of people's letters and visits. The system is inherently connected to the CCP tradition of "following the mass line".

After the founding of the People's Republic of China (PRC), the Central Government as well as the CCP Central Committee established corresponding organs to deal with *xinfang* matters.[8] However, the milestone document – the Decision on the Work of Handling People's Letters and Receiving People's Visits, issued by the State Council on 7 June 1951, is generally regarded as the official establishment of the *xinfang* system in communist China.[9] The government and the Party encouraged *xinfang* as a way to overcome bureaucratism and to establish a close connection with the masses. During the Cultural Revolution (1966–76), the *xinfang* system was paralysed and dysfunctional.

After 1978, together with the economic reform and openness to the outside world, the *xinfang* system has been gradually restored and relevant working procedures, including the Detailed Rules of the People's Supreme Court on Receiving Visitors by the *Xinfang* Division in June 1980, and the Detailed Rules of the People's Supreme Procuratorate on Appeals in December 1980, were adopted.

In 1995, the *Xinfang* Regulations were for the first time promulgated to regularize the *xinfang* system. Following these regulations, ministries and governments of provinces and cities adopted corresponding regulations, measures, and procedures. Corresponding *xinfang* departments were established within the government, as well as within the Party organization.

Though it is new in modern China, the *xinfang* system has a strong connection to Chinese traditions. People in traditional China were afraid of power-sharing due to the suffering it brought them by corrupt officials. Their only hope rested with a wise Emperor who would deliver justice to them.[10] On the other hand, there was no court in the modern sense until the turn of the twentieth century in Chinese history. People would go to beat a drum outside the government offices (衙门) to appeal their grievances, petition a visiting Imperial envoy,[11] or go directly to the capital to appeal to the Emperor (告御状 *gao yu zhuang*). Thus, for the ordinary people in today's China, there is little difference between the means of *xinfang* and traditional means of petition.

The *xinfang* system has faced a serious challenge recently, since the number of *xinfang* has increased for the last 13 years. As reported, the number culminated in 2003 in a *xinfang* "flood peak", with more than 12.72 million (piece or person), 4.1 per cent increase over the previous year. Among them, the increase for central government departments was 46 per cent. More serious is the great increase of collective visits to the higher authorities (*jiti shangfang*), involving more than seven million people, an increase of 44.8 per cent over the previous year. A record for a single visit to Beijing involved more than 800 people.[12] According to Xiao Yang, President of the People's Supreme Court, his Court handled 147,665 cases of petitions in 2004, up 23.6 per cent year-on-year.[13] It indicates that even after the "flood peak", the *xinfang* cases have been increasing until very recently, in 2006.

For the above reason, the Chinese government has tightened this system by taking a series of measures including legal regulations so as to improve this system, as officially claimed. In August 2004, according to the instructions from Hu Jintao, the Central Government set up a mechanism of Joint Meetings specifically to deal with *xinfang* matters.[14] The most important move is the promulgation of the new *Xinfang* Regulations, which came into force on the 1 May 2005, and replaced the 1995 Regulations.

Institutional structures and government mandates

There is a comprehensive network of *xinfang* work in China, comprising *xinfang* bureaus and offices within governments and departments at all levels above and including the county. The highest is the State Bureau of Letters and Calls, officially subordinate to the State Council, but maintaining a close link to the CCP Central Secretariat.

The main responsibilities of the State Bureau include, *inter alia*, (1) the handling of letters and calls from people within and outside China; passing important suggestions, opinions, and problems to the Central Government; and putting forward proposals concerning related policies by analysing and studying *xinfang* information; (2) the handling of *xinfang* matters entrusted by Central leaders and supervising the implementation of the instructions of the Central leaders; entrusting local governments and ministerial departments to deal with *xinfang* matters; (3) coordinating the handling of inter-regional and inter-departmental *xinfang* matters and collective visits to Beijing or abnormal and sudden *xinfang* incidents; (4) guiding the national *xinfang* work; studying and drafting policies and regulations concerning *xinfang*; (5) organizing the training of *xinfang* cadres; and (6) responsibility for the propagation and publishing on *xinfang* and coordinating external activities and exchanges.[15]

Similar institutional organs have been established at the local level. For example, the Office of Letters and Calls of the CCP Beijing Municipal Committee and the People's Government of Beijing Municipality is responsible for handling letters, visits and calls to the Mayor from the masses. Under the Office, the establishments include: the Secretariat; the Division of Personnel and Education; Division of Letters Processing; Division of Visits Receiving (with the external name as Room of Receiving People's Visits of CCP Beijing Municipal Committee and the People's Government of Beijing Municipality); Division of Telephone Calls Handling; Division of Comprehensive Investigation and Study; Office of Assisting Disputes Settlement; and Office of Collecting People's Proposals.[16]

The relevant official responsibilities are prescribed in the 2005 *Xinfang* Regulations. What is remarkable is the change in the Regulations to strengthen the role of the *xinfang* offices by granting them a power of supervising, urging, and inspecting the handling of the *xinfang* matters.[17] Any administrative organ should respond to the suggestions from the *xinfang* office and should give reasons why they have not adopted the said suggestions.[18]

In addition, governments at all levels should establish and improve the *xinfang* work responsibility system and any misconduct, dereliction, or malfeasance is subject to corresponding punishment. *Xinfang* work should be considered in the performance evaluation system for civil servants.[19]

Xinfang matters should go through the process within 60 days; for those more complicated, extension of time is allowed, but not exceeding 30 days. This is to say, for any *xinfang* case, whether simple or complicated, the relevant *xinfang* office must complete it within 90 days. The more recently revised *Xinfang* Regulations of the Beijing Municipality, which came into force on 1 January 2007, have even stipulated that people's congresses and government organs of the city must reply to a *xinfang* matter within 15 days.[20] It may raise a doubt as to whether the *xinfang* office can properly handle all the *xinfang* cases within this short period of time, as some *xinfang* officials may rush the cases in order to meet the timing requirement without thorough investigations and fact-findings.

Administrative organs should not conceal any urgent *xinfang* matters or information, otherwise, they are subject to punishment. In addition, any of the following conduct by government officials will be subject to administrative punishment, or even to penal punishment: (a) abuse of power to encroach on the legitimate rights and interests of petitioners; (b) the circumstance that the administrative organ is obliged to act but does not act and, therefore, causes an infringement of petitioners' rights and interests; (c) the infringement of petitioners' rights and interests by misusing laws and regulations or breaking the prescribed procedures; and (d) the refusal to implement the opinion of the competent administrative organ to support a petitioner's request.[21]

Another big change in the new regulations is the insertion of a new principle which requires the government at all levels to manage the *xinfang* work within their respective territorial jurisdiction (属地管理).[22] Related to the principle that "who is in charge, is responsible", the new policy and law for the *xinfang* system tend to resolve *xinfang* problems at the grassroots level (it is so-called "把信访问题解决在基层") so as to reduce the existing *xinfang* pressures on the Central Government or higher level authorities.

In recent years a new method was experimented with in Henan and Shandong by the Supreme Procuratorate, i.e. the introduction of a public hearing system to the *xinfang* system. It is helpful for enhancing judicial fairness, increasing the quality of the judicial personnel, as well as case-handling, and settling the relevant cases permanently.[23] This type of experimentation has been endorsed by the newly-promulgated *Xinfang* Regulations which provide that the *xinfang* work department may utilize various methods such as consultation, education, negotiation, conciliation, and hearing in handling *xinfang* cases,[24] and that public hearing can be particularly used for "major, complex or knotty" problems raised by petitioners.[25]

Accordingly, the government encourages public hearings for *xinfang* cases. Based on the relevant provisions of the *Xinfang* Regulations, Zhejiang province, as it is reported, became the first province to invoke the provisions on the *xinfang* hearing system on 31 May 2005. The Bureau of Letters and Calls of Yiwu City held a public hearing on a case on the protection of employees' rights and interests.[26] It shows the public hearing can bring transparency and enhance the exchange of views of the petitioners and relevant enterprises or government departments. More and more localities now use this mechanism as a more effective means of settling *xinfang* problems.[27]

Besides the above government establishments and arrangements for *xinfang*, the CCP organizations have their own institutions in this regard. Some CCP internal regulations emphasize the importance of earnestly dealing with *xinfang* problems. For example, the 2003 Intra-Party Supervision Regulations (Trial) has one section on how to handle *xinfang* matters. It provides that Party committees and disciplinary committees at all levels exercise their supervision over lower level Party organizations and leading cadres through the handling of *xinfang* and study the important issues raised from letters and visits. For important *xinfang* matters, they should provide supervision and inspection until the matters have been properly dealt with.[28] According to one statistic, during the five-year period to 2004, the Party disciplinary committees at all levels had handled more than eight million *xinfang* reports, and disciplined 465,000 Party cadres.[29]

Legal measures and their implementation

With the country marching towards the rule of law, laws and regulations are indispensable in the management of the *xinfang* work, as officially pledged that legalization of the *xinfang* system is the only way to give the system vitality.[30] The earliest regulations governing *xinfang* is the 1951 Decision on the Work of Handling People's Letters and Receiving People's Visits. Then there came the 1995 *Xinfang* Regulations, which mainly governed the *xinfang* activities and handlings, but it was later replaced by the newly adopted Regulations in 2005.

The 2005 *Xinfang* Regulations is currently the most important legal document guiding the substance and procedures of *xinfang*, both for relevant government departments and for ordinary Chinese citizens. Compared with the 1995 version, the 2005 Regulations contain many significant changes, including, *inter alia*, innovative *public hearings* which may be held to handle "major, complex or knotty" problems, *accountability system* requiring the relevant department in charge to address any petition within 60 days from the time it is accepted, and that any negligence of officials be subject to punishment.

In line with the relevant constitutional norms of citizens' protection, the 2005 Regulations for the first time provides that any individual or organization must not retaliate against petitioners, on penalty of facing legal action. This is significant since many of the *xinfang* people had bitter experiences in being deprived of their jobs and properties, and in physical and psychological sufferings. Yet it is unknown whether relevant local officials will resort to other means for de facto retaliation since the *Xinfang* Regulations contain a series of measures constraining *xinfang* activities.

The Regulations specify the *xinfang* items which petitioners can refer to the relevant administrative organs and which concern: (a) administrative organs and their personnel; (b) organizations with statutory functions of public management and their personnel; (c) enterprises or public organizations (*shiye danwei*) which provide public services and personnel; (d) social organizations or personnel who are appointed or dispatched by the State administrative organ to enterprises or public organizations; and (e) villagers' committees and residents' committees and their members.[31] It is interesting to note that CCP organizations are not expressly included. Therefore, there is a doubt whether and how a petition concerning a Party organization is dealt with under the new regulations.

On the other hand, the new regulations set a number of limitations on petition visits. It encourages petitioners to use letters, email, or fax, but when petitioners want to pay a visit, they should go to the relevant organ or designated reception place. Furthermore, the number of collective visits should not exceed five persons.[32] Among all the *xinfang* cases, the greatest headache for the Chinese government is the collective petition, which, if it is not handled properly, could endanger the social stability and the CCP authorities. The limit of five persons embodies expressly the purpose of preventing any potential for large-scale demonstrations, or even riots from happening.

In order to further control petition activities, the Regulations provide that petitioners must abide by the law, should not damage the State interest and legitimate rights of other citizens, and should maintain the social public order and *xinfang* order. The following acts are prohibited: (a) to illegally gather together in a public place or in the surroundings of the State organs, or besiege, or assault State organs or government vehicles, or block the traffic; (b) to carry dangerous goods or controlled articles; (c) to insult, beat, or threaten State organ personnel, or illegally constrain the personal freedom of other people; (d) to overstay or create trouble at the *xinfang* reception places; (e) to incite, make by establishing ties, force, entice with incentives somebody else to *xinfang*, or manipulate behind the scene; and (f) to disturb public order or jeopardize the State or public security.[33]

For the violations of the above provision, the State organ personnel first resort to the means of persuasion and prevention, criticism and education; if this is not workable, the public security organ will give warnings or put the illegal *xinfang* activity to an end; those who violate the law of demonstration or the regulations of public security will be liable and subject to punishment.[34]

On the other hand, some of the provisions in the *Xinfang* Regulations are not pragmatic in practice. For example, Article 11 requests the State *xinfang* working organ to establish a national *xinfang* information system so as to provide conveniences for the petitioners to know the handling process. However, even if such an information system were established, it is doubtful whether petitioners or the majority of them could use it since they belong to the "disadvantaged group of people" (弱势群体). While they have difficulties in maintaining their basic needs for daily life, how can they have the luxury of using the Internet or owning a computer at home?

Following the Central regulations, local governments and departments have also enacted relevant laws and regulations to govern *xinfang* activities within their territorial jurisdictions. Based on the principle of administration in accordance with law (依法行政), some localities have taken a "sunshine" policy in terms of local legislation. Hubei province recently issued a circular and posted its draft *xinfang* regulations on its website, seeking for opinions and suggestions from the public in order to improve the quality of the regulations.[35]

Most of the local laws or department regulations are simply passed for the purpose of implementing the 2005 Regulations. Some such laws do contain tougher measures against petitioners. For example, the Xi'an Government recently issued the Opinion on Maintaining the Order of Collective Visits to the Higher Authorities in dealing with disorderly visits by petitioners.[36] It seems that local governments used the new Central regulations to control *xinfang* activities in their localities, rather than sincerely resolve the problems raised by the petitioners.

Military disciplinary rules are even stricter. For example, the Central Military Committee issued the Supplementary Provisions on the Implementation of the CCP Regulations on Disciplinary Punishment in August 2005, in which it is clearly provided that any military person who organizes, attends or supports demonstrations, silent sitting, petition, or visits to the higher authorities (*shangfang*) in society is subject to severe punishment.[37]

In order to make necessary preparations for the better implementation of the *Xinfang* Regulations, the Central Government (sponsored by the CCP Ministry of Organization, the Law Office of the State Council, the State Administrative College and the State Bureau of Letters and Calls) organized a special workshop during late February and early March 2005 before the entry into force of the Regulations, which relevant officials at the provincial level attended.[38]

Another point worth mentioning is the role of the people's congress in the *xinfang* work. As is stipulated in the *Xinfang* Regulations, the main responsibility rests with the government. The people's congress becomes a "transfer station".[39] However, the people's congress is the body which takes the function of supervision over the government, the court and the procuratorate. In fact it receives large quantities of *xinfang* cases each year (see Table 8.1). It is hoped that with the adoption of the Supervision Law in 2006[40] the *xinfang* work in the people's congress can be significantly strengthened.

Seeking a breakthrough in the conundrum

The Chinese government and the CCP have utilized the *xinfang* system to maintain its close link with the masses, but are afraid of any social instability caused

Table 8.1 Number of *xinfang* received by the National People's Congress in the first half year of 2004

Letters	*Complaints*	*Seeking for decisions*	*Accusations*	*Suggestions*	*Others*
Letters (42,298)	13,313 (31.47%)	17,201 (40.67%)	4,702 (11.12%)	5,770 (13.64%)	1,312 (3.10%)
Visits (12,220)	9,698 (79.36%)	1,720 (14.07%)	575 (4.71%)	74 (0.61%)	153 (1.25%)

Source: *People's Daily*, 4 August 2004, at 15.

by people's *xinfang* activities. The attempt to put it under legal rein has the purpose of balancing the two contradictory elements. The ideal model of the *xinfang* in its mind would be like "a bird in a cage".

However, it is doubtful whether this can work effectively in practice, despite the official claim that after the entry into force of the *Xinfang* Regulations there have been several positive changes including the *xinfang* channels which are further smoothed; the *xinfang* order which has turned out to be better; and the intensified efforts in solving *xinfang* problems.[41]

There are several dilemmas the Chinese government faces and for which it needs solutions. The first dilemma is related to the dual function of the *xinfang* system: on the one hand, it allows ordinary people to exercise the right to petition, but on the other, it gives priority to maintaining social stability. Despite the efforts made in the legal field, "resolution of grievances will continue to be compromised by the inherent lack of independence of the system and the risk that officials may side with powerful vested interests, including political and business concerns".[42] It is recalled that in recent years, petitioners, in the eyes of some governmental officials, are trouble-makers; and some corrupt local officials, for fear of their dirty dealings being discovered by petitions, tried their utmost to obstruct or repress the petitions.[43] For example, the Shanghai-based lawyer Zheng Enchong was sentenced to a three-year imprisonment under the charge of "leaking state secrets to foreigners" in October 2003.[44] It is now revealed that he was persecuted, at least partly due to the fact that he attempted to unearth a corrupt case in which Chen Liangyu was involved.[45]

The second dilemma is that the *xinfang* system is a product of "rule of man" which was established during the time of the planned economy. It is also linked to the Chinese cultural tradition that while the local officials are corrupt, the Emperor is always good. In that culture, the Chinese people depended upon a wise Emperor or, at present the Central leader, to offer them justice and relieve their grievances. This clearly contravenes the ongoing legal reform towards the rule of law and is detrimental to the building of the legal awareness of the Chinese citizens and of a rule-of-law society.

The third dilemma is the relationship between the *xinfang* system and the judicial system. The most ideal way to realize the remedies and justice for grievances is the resort to the court, as is practiced in many rule-of-law countries where most, if not all, of the social disputes are settled in courtrooms. While it has to be noted that the current legal system in China is not effective in resolving the social disputes within its mandate, it is necessary to build people's confidence in using legal means to defend their legitimate rights and interests.

There are two main issues in this regard. One is judicial corruption and the other concerns litigation costs. For the former, there were two cases reported in *Outlook News Weekly*: both of petitioners who first sought justice through the judicial mechanism, but because of the corrupt judicial officials, they were finally forced to resort to petition (*shangfang*).[46] For the latter, in comparison with *xinfang* (which is free except for personal expenses of the petitioners themselves), the resort to the court needs a large amount of money, including fees for judicial proceedings, lawyers' retainers, etc. As most of the *xinfang* people are poor and disadvantaged, they usually cannot afford the legal fees.[47] The current legal aid system in China is far from enough to provide legal assistance for the needy people.

The link of *xinfang*, especially visits to the higher authorities, and to the judiciary cannot be ignored since more and more cases are related to problems involving the judiciary. Among 187 unusual visits to Beijing in the second half of 2003, 125 were related to the judiciary, accounting for 70 per cent.[48] For the first half of 2005, 80 per cent of the petitions were related to law enforcement and litigation, mainly resulting from petitioners' dissatisfaction with the court decisions or from the non-enforcement of court judgments in cases which petitioners won.[49]

Another issue related to the judiciary is the implementation of the new *Xinfang* Regulations. It is anticipated that, due to the timing requirement provided for in the Regulations, administrative litigations would increase tremendously if the relevant administrative organs could not resolve the *xinfang* problems within the prescribed time. However, it is doubtful whether the court is ready for this challenge, particularly when its judicial authority is not yet fully established.[50]

The fourth dilemma rests with the fact that the rate of success for *xinfang* is very low. It is said that only 0.2 per cent of petitioners resolved their problems directly through the *xinfang* system.[51] Then why are there so many people craving for the *xinfang* system for remedies? A survey reveals that the petitioners knew there was little hope of having their problems solved by several visits or more visits; 90.5 per cent of them wanted the Central Government to "know their situation"; 88.5 per cent did the visits in order to put pressure on the relevant local governments; and 81.2 per cent "knew that the Central Government cannot solve the problems directly, but they were hoping to obtain an official directive".[52]

The fifth dilemma is the position of the *xinfang* system in a market economy environment. It is interesting to note that the increasing number of petition cases has been straining the national *xinfang* system since 1993.[53] This was the year just after Deng Xiaoping's trip to Southern China, when China began to implement its market-oriented economy policy.

It shows that most of the *xinfang* cases are related to the encroachment of the relevant government or its personnel upon the interests and rights of ordinary citizens, as in the failure to grant adequate compensation for land appropriation or house demolishing. These two matters are the result of urbanization or city construction, all reflecting the economic development in China. It is a challenge to the current Chinese leadership to know how to guarantee the legitimate rights and interests of ordinary Chinese citizens in the course of rapid economic development.

Despite the revision of the *Xinfang* Regulations and the improvement of its implementation, there is still a debate in China on whether the *xinfang* system should be kept or abolished. Some scholars advocate its total abolishment, while others argue that the system can still play a role in solving problems and disputes in Chinese society.

The scholars who favour the first option take the view that, although the *xinfang* system played a role in the planned economy era, it cannot cope with the current market economy environment due to its inherent weaknesses. It is, therefore, suggested that *xinfang* offices at all levels be abolished, and the *xinfang* work be transferred to the people's congress which acts as a supervisory body.[54] Another view to advocate the abolishment of the *xinfang* system is from a legal perspective in that the *xinfang* system does more harm than good in solving legal disputes because people can resort to the right to petition to overthrow an unfavourable court ruling.[55]

Nevertheless, the view that the *xinfang* system should be retained prevails, at least for the present time, as the Chinese government not only retains the *xinfang* system, but has also strengthened it by introducing a series of administrative and legal measures since 2005. Clearly, these efforts have been made under Hu Jintao's recent instruction to "create a new *xinfang* system".[56] It is well perceived that the *xinfang* system will not be abolished until China has reached the realm of the rule of law.

Yet, it is strongly suggested that China should improve its *xinfang* system by introducing useful elements from the long-practiced "ombudsman" system[57] in Western countries. The ombudsman system is similar to, but also different from, the *xinfang* system: similar in the sense that both allow people to make complaints about government organizations; both can investigate these complaints and make recommendations to resolve the relevant problems; but different in the sense that the ombudsman cannot investigate complaints outside his jurisdiction, but the office of the ombudsman is impartial and independent.[58] The last aspect is a most important one for the improvement of the *xinfang* system.

Conclusion

The purpose of establishing the *xinfang* system at the very beginning was to enhance the connections of the Party to the masses, the so-called "blood and flesh" relationship. At that time, the Communist Party regarded itself as part of the masses and the vanguard of the workers and peasants. However, with the passing of time, the nature of the *xinfang* system has changed from a means of enhancing the connections of the Party to the masses to a means of controlling society and the people. This is because of the change in the nature of the Party and the masses: one becomes the ruler and the other, the ruled, despite the fact that the Chinese Constitution still contains the wording, "vanguard of the workers and peasants". Thus, the *xinfang* system has become a governing instrument of the ruling party in China.

With the implementation of the new *Xinfang* Regulations, it seems the *xinfang* flood peak has been receding, though still remaining a headache for the Chinese Government. According to the State Bureau of Letters and Calls, the number of *xinfang* decreased 6.5 per cent in 2005 and 14 per cent in 2006.[59]

There is an even more headache-inducing societal problem which the Chinese government and the CCP have to deal with, i.e. the so-called collective cases (群体性案件), which occur in situations such as land acquisition, housing demolition, resettlement from areas affected by dam projects, enterprise downsizing, environmental pollution and the rights and interests of rural migrant workers. According to a figure released by the Chinese Ministry of Public Security, there were 87,000 social unrests (public disturbances) in 2005.[60] These cases may bring more severe societal repercussions than *xinfang* cases, affecting the course of China's development and reforms. Particularly so when unemployed college graduates as well as retired soldiers are involved in *shangfang* cases.

On the other hand, the transition from *xinfang* or *shangfang* to rights protection movements has well indicated that the ordinary people no longer believe modern *Bao Qing Tian* (包青天). Instead, they organize themselves to seek and safeguard their legitimate rights and interests prescribed under the law. In this sense, the effect of the *xinfang* system to solve social conflicts has to some extent been diminished, while it continues to play a significant role in this respect in today's China.

Notes

* Harris Professor of International Law, School of Law, University of Central Lancashire, Preston, UK.

1 "Party plenum to focus on social harmony", *China Daily*, 9 October 2006.

2 On 19 September 2004 the Chinese Communist Party officially put forward a historical goal to "build a harmonious society" on the 4th Plenary Session of its 16th Central Committee. The concept was enunciated by Hu Jintao in his speech to the NPC in March 2005. See "Harmonious Society", available at http://en.wikipedia.org/wiki/Harmonious_society (accessed 14 March 2006).

3 "Party plenum to focus on social harmony", *China Daily*, 9 October 2006.

4 See "State Council held a special conference on strengthening and improving the *xinfang* work and emphasized the legalization of the *xinfang* work without delay", *People's Daily* (in Chinese), 5 November 2005, p. 4.

5 Article 1 of the 2005 *Xinfang* Regulations. Text is available in *People's Daily* (in Chinese), 18 January 2005, p. 8.

6 Liu Wujun, "Government enacts new rule to regulate petitioning", *China Daily*, 24 February 2005, p. 6.

7 See Chen Bofeng, "Excessive Litigation, *Xinfang* and Legal Traditions of New China", *Peking University Law Journal* (*zhongwai faxue*), 16:2, 2004, p. 230.

8 See Chen Bofeng, ibid., p. 230.

9 See Diao Jiechen, *Brief History of People's Xinfang*, Beijing: Beijing College of Economics Press, 1996; cited in Ying Xing, "The Remedy of Xinfang: A Special Administrative Remedy", *Chinese Journal of Law* (*faxue yanjiu*), 26:3, 2004, p. 59.

10 See "Judicial Independence Should Come First", *Beijing Review*, 10 November 2005, p. 24.

11 See Li Jianguo, "Protect the Right to Petition", *Beijing Review*, 10 November 2005, p. 2.

12 See Yu Jianrong, "Xinfang System Reform and Constitutional Construction", *Twenty-First Century* (in Chinese), no. 89, 2005, p. 71.

13 "Petition cases rise 23.6 per cent last year in China", *China Daily*, 9 March 2005.

14 Zhao Ling, "The First Democratic Report on '*Xinfang*' Receives High Level Attention", *Southern Weekend* (*nanfang zhoumo*), 4 November 2004.

15 State Bureau for Letters and Calls, available at www.gjxfj.gov.cn/2005–01/13/content_3556739.htm (accessed 16 November 2005).
16 For details, see the Beijing Office website, available at www.bjxfb.gov.cn/Web_framework.asp (accessed 16 November 2005).
17 Article 6 of the *Xinfang* Regulations.
18 Article 36 of the *Xinfang* Regulations.
19 Article 7 of the *Xinfang* Regulations.
20 "Reply must be given to the petitioner within 15 days", *People's Daily* (in Chinese), 27 December 2006, p. 14.
21 Article 40 of the *Xinfang* Regulations.
22 Article 4 of the *Xinfang* Regulations.
23 See Yang Liu, "Sunshine Operations' Break though the Conundrum of Petitions to the Higher Authorities (*shangfang*)", *Outlook Weekly* (*liaowang zhoukan*), no. 46, 15 November 2005, p. 33.
24 Article 13 of the *Xinfang* Regulations.
25 Article 31 of the *Xinfang* Regulations.
26 See "Zhejiang first uses the *xinfang* hearing mechanism", *People's Daily* (in Chinese), 11 October 2005, p. 10.
27 For example, Kunming has introduced this mechanism, as well. See "New mechanism in Kunming to deal with misconducts of civil servants", *People's Daily* (in Chinese), 29 November 2005, p. 10.
28 Article 25 of the Intra-Party Supervision Regulations (Trial). Text is available at www.people.com.cn/GB/shizheng/1026/2344222.html (accessed 29 November 2005).
29 See Shao Daosheng, "The Intra-Party Supervision Regulations (Trial) which takes high regard to the handling of *xinfang*", available at www.peopledaily.com.cn/GB/guandian/1036/2463332.html (accessed 23 April 2004).
30 See Gu Ruizhen and Yu Jian, "Legalization and regularization is the only way for *xinfang*", *People's Daily* (in Chinese), 3 August 2005, p. 4.
31 Article 14 of the *Xinfang* Regulations.
32 Articles 17 and 18 of the *Xinfang* Regulations.
33 Article 20 of the *Xinfang* Regulations.
34 See Article 47 of the *Xinfang* Regulations.
35 The texts of the circular and the draft regulations are available at www.peacehall.com/news/gb/china/2005/11/200511220853.shtml (accessed 22 November 2005).
36 "Xi'an issued the measure to govern *shangfang* order", available at www.peacehall.com/news/gb/china/2004/06/200406191522.shtml (accessed 19 June 2004).
37 See "Central Military Committee: military persons organizing or involving demonstrations or visits to the higher authorities (*shangfang*) will be severely punishment", available at www.peacehall.com/news/gb/china/2005/08/200508161526.shtml (accessed 17 August 2005).
38 See "Comprehensively grasping the basic spirits of the *Xinfang* Regulations and earnestly strengthening and improving the *xinfang* work under the new circumstances", *People's Daily* (in Chinese), 27 February 2005, p. 4; and "Constantly creating a new prospect by implementing the *Xinfang* Regulations", *People's Daily* (in Chinese), 2 March 2005, p. 4.
39 Zhang Zhengyu, "People's congress's *xinfang* should not be 'transfer station'", *People's Daily* (in Chinese), 4 August 2004, p. 15.
40 The Law was adopted on 27 August 2006 and came into force on 1 January 2007. In Article 9 of the Law, it is provided that the Standing Committee of the people's congress can identify issues from various channels including people's letters and visits.
41 See "The First Explanation: Maintaining the *Xinfang* Order and People's Interests in Accordance with Law", available at http://legal.people.com.cn/GB/42731/3586018.html (accessed 2 August 2005).

42 Amnesty International, *People's Republic of China: Human Rights Defenders at Risk – Update*, March 2005, p. 7.
43 Liu Wujun, "Government enacts new rule to regulate petitioning", *China Daily*, 24 February 2005, p. 6.
44 Zheng was arrested in June 2003 while handling a lawsuit involving local property tycoon Zhou Zhengyi who was suspected by authorities of illegal financial dealings. See Xiao Yu, "Lawyer to appeal verdict", *China Daily*, 31 October 2003.
45 See *Yazhou Zhoukan*, 30 September 2006.
46 For details, see Bao Yonghui and Lü Guoqing, "Why do they believe in 'petition', but not 'law'?" *Outlook News Weekly* (*liaowang xinwen zhoukan*), no. 44, 1 November 2004, pp. 34–6.
47 There is a case in 2002 regarding the pollution from a chemical factory which poisoned hundreds of *mu* vegetables in an adjacent village. The farmers intended to resort to a judicial settlement, but when they came to know that the collection of pollution evidence needed more than 100 thousand RMB, they were stunned. See Bao Yonghui and Lü Guoqing, ibid., p. 34.
48 Bao Yonghui and Lü Guoqing, ibid., p. 36.
49 See "*Xinfang* during the first half were related to law enforcement and litigations", *People's Daily* (in Chinese), 26 September 2005, p. 10.
50 See Huang Jiabo, "The Main Spirits of the *Xinfang* Regulations and Their Impact on the Court's Work", available at www.hicourt.gov.cn/theory/artilce_list.asp?id=2748&1_class=4 (accessed 16 November 2005).
51 Li Li, "Life in a Struggle", *Beijing Review*, 10 November 2005, p. 23.
52 See Zhao Ling, "The First Democratic Report on '*Xinfang*' Receives High Level Attention", *Southern Weekend* (*nanfang zhoumo*), 4 November 2004 and Li Li, "Life in a Struggle", *Beijing Review*, 10 November 2005, p. 23.
53 Li Li, "Life in a Struggle", *Beijing Review*, 10 November 2005, p. 21.
54 Yu Jianrong, 2005, *supra* note 12, p. 73.
55 "Judicial Independence Should Come First", *supra* note 10, p. 25.
56 See "Premier Wen approves the new *Xinfang* Regulations", *Mingpao* (Hong Kong), 6 January 2005.
57 The word *ombudsman* is a Swedish word meaning "agent" or "representative" of the people, at Office of the Ombudsman Ireland, available at http://ombudsman.gov.ie/en/AboutUs/Introduction/ (accessed 6 December 2005).
58 For example, in Ontario, Canada, some types of complaints that cannot be investigated include, *inter alia*, police; decisions of judges or courts; and decisions of Cabinet. See Ombudsman Ontario website, available at www.ombudsman.on.ca/what.asp (accessed 6 December 2005).
59 See "*Shangfang* number began to decrease after 12 years", *Mingpao* (Hong Kong), 3 October 2006.
60 "Public unrest increasing in China" (A ministry spokesman said the figure did not refer just to mass protests, but to all criminal cases linked to public disorder, including mob gatherings, obstruction of justice, fighting, and trouble-making), 19 January 2006, available at http://news.bbc.co.uk/2/hi/asia-pacific/4627602.stm (accessed 29 June 2006).

9 The diffusion of legal institutions in China

Pierre F. Landry

It should not be surprising that authoritarian regimes seek to establish courts. The victims of the Moscow trials of the 1930s, political opponents in fascist Italy, Argentina, and Brazil in the 1970s, or in China, the famous "gang of four" were all tried in formal courts, with the explicit support of their respective regimes. Authoritarian systems rely on courts because formal legal institutions are expected to bring legitimacy to decisions that may not be fair or equitable. These courts are not limited to criminal or political cases. Courts handling cases in civil, economic, and administrative cases exist in many authoritarian regimes, as well.

What *is* surprising is the development of genuinely active and popular courts within an otherwise authoritarian system. Tate and Haynie (1993) are rather pessimistic about courts in authoritarian regimes, but others show that view is not always warranted. Argentinean judges tended to sympathize with the dictatorship, but their Brazilian counterparts did not, and used their position to undermine military rule (Osiel 1995). Spanish courts played an active role in the transformation of the Francoist dictatorship and the eventual democratization of the regime (Toharia 1975; Giles 1989; Pinkele 1992). Without claiming that an authoritarian regime can establish a genuine "rule-of-law", as the term is widely understood in democratic societies, the diffusion of formal legal institutions within authoritarian regimes compels legal scholars and social scientists to explain how (and preferably why) these courts do – in some instances – develop into credible institutions.[1]

Few cross-national studies on the impact of legal innovations in authoritarian regimes exist, but it appears that the degree to which they approach a meaningful rule of law has impacts on their prospect for survival. Using the global governance indicators (GGI) compiled by Kaufman *et al.* (2005) and the updated dataset on regimes by Cheibub (2004), we find that autocracies that rate highly on the rule of law dimension also appear more stable politically (Figure 9.1). It is less clear *how* autocracies successfully introduce reforms that strengthen the rule of law.

The case of the People's Republic of China since 1978 presents us with a remarkable case in order to unpack the process by which legal innovations are diffused in an authoritarian regime. It is a truism among comparativists that China has never been a democracy, regardless of the specific coding rules that are used to categorize regimes in political science; but the persistence of authoritarianism in

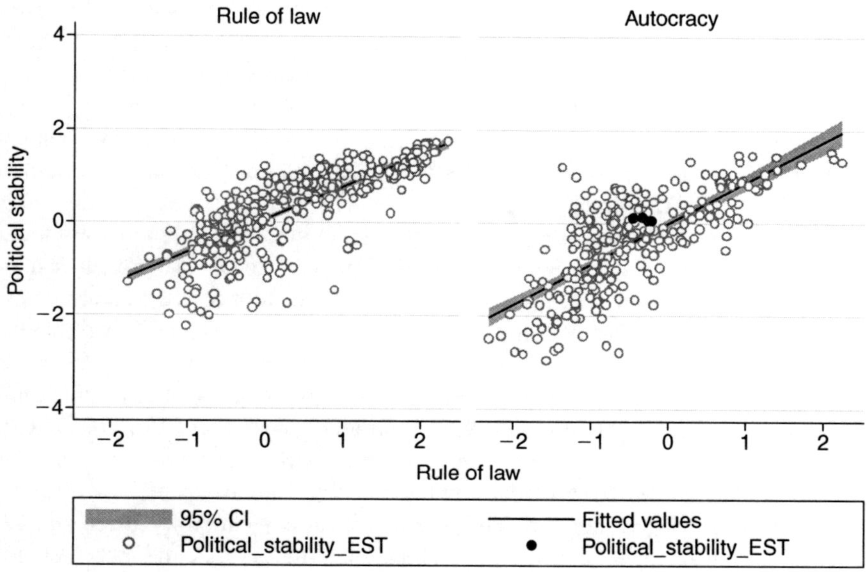

Figure 9.1 Rule of law versus political stability indicators among democracies and autocracies (1994–2002).

China allows us to rule out any possibility of institutional contamination by which new authoritarian regimes "inherit" legal institutions from the democracy that they overthrow. Historical Chinese regimes may have developed distinctive legal systems (Bernhardt *et al.* 1994; Huang 2001), but one cannot reasonably claim that Qing, Republican (Xu 1997), or PRC courts under Mao operated in a manner consistent with modern principles of the rule of law.

The regime's self-proclaimed goal of building the "rule of law" in China (以法治国) is a large-scale social experiment in a "hard" case: formal institutions have been introduced by the state on a social terrain that seems highly unfavourable to the development of the rule of law. The contradiction of the Chinese legal reforms has been widely noted. There is no pretense of judicial independence: Judges – who are almost always members of the Communist Party – are appointed by the state and vetted by Party Organization Departments set up within the judiciary and must in practice answer to bureaucratic superiors within local governments (Cohen 1997; Zhao 2003). Rule of law "with Chinese characteristics" requires Party control over the judiciary (Lubman 1996; Peerenboom 2002). Though appeals are possible, there is no proper judicial review, and the execution of civil judgments uncertain (Clarke 1995). Furthermore, information flows are heavily controlled, and social activists and lawyers who engage judicial institutions are routinely harassed, or worse. Going to court – particularly if one challenges state actors or seeks to sue the state – remains a highly charged political affair (O'Brien and Li 2005; Gallagher 2005).

If the Chinese experiment were to succeed under these adverse conditions, we should stand on less precarious ground, arguing that authoritarian regimes *can* build something approaching a meaningful rule of law. Indeed, despite the vast shortcomings of the Chinese legal system, the progressive trend is unmistakable: the Party is publicly committed to modernize the legal system and building more autonomous judicial and legal institutions than is typically the case in Leninist regimes (Potter 2003; Diamant *et al.* 2005; US Congressional-Executive Commission on China 2002; Peerenboom 2002).

The political dynamics behind these institutional innovations remain obscured by disciplinary and methodological differences between legal scholars and social scientists. The legal scholarship has focused on the institutional development of the past 20 years, but has not emphasized how these innovations affect different elements of Chinese society. Sociologists, economists, and political scientists on the other hand have developed an extensive literature on social stratification and inequality (Nee 1996; Zhou *et al.* 1998; Bian and Logan 1996; Wu 2002), and political participation (Shi 1996, 1999) – particularly the urban rural divide (Jennings 1997) – but have hardly emphasized the relationship of legal institutions with this divide. There are studies on political contention (O'Brien and Li 2005) on conflict dynamics in rural China, but the authors did not seek to compare the behaviour of their subjects with those of non-farmers.

The political and sociological divide between urban and rural China is also epistemological: rural China is often treated as a *sui generis* category and is rarely explicitly compared with the urban sphere. The dearth of systematic comparisons between urban and rural China is related in part to the difficulty and cost of research designs that are truly national in scope and are conducive to systematic comparisons between sup-populations. As a result, probability samples that include both urban and rural respondents are still a rarity (Walder *et al.* 2000; Walder 2002).

This chapter does not seek to argue whether China is or is not a rule-of-law society. A process that has taken centuries to mature in many countries cannot possibly be compressed into a few years, even by elites that are prone to social and institutional engineering. More modestly, my goal is to take Chinese legal institutions as they are perceived and utilized by ordinary Chinese citizens and to specify how and why these seemingly incongruous institutional innovations in an authoritarian regime are or are not taking root. I argue that understanding the initial phase of the diffusion of institutions (here, courts) is a necessary, but not a sufficient step to establish the basic conditions for the development of the rule of law in the long run. The long march towards *fazhi* requires at least courts that are reasonably trustworthy and render meaningful judgments that increase the appeal of the institution among potential adopters.

Data: the survey on the institutionalization of legal reforms in China

Quantitative evidence on Chinese legal reforms is scarce. Pioneering empirical work has taken place (Michelson 2002, 2006), but, to our knowledge, the national survey on the Institutionalization of Legal Reforms in China (ILRC) is the first national sample of its kind. We collected data on the types and extent of civil, economic, and administrative disputes on a national scale in order to examine in detail the multiple mechanisms by which grievances evolve.

The survey is based on a multi-stage stratified sample in which each province, municipality, or autonomous region of the Chinese mainland is taken as a stratum. Within each stratum, counties (or urban districts) were selected at random by PPS. Within each county, two townships (or their street committee counterparts in urban areas) were also selected at random. We used 2000 census data in order to develop measures of size at the township level. Below townships, a spatial sampling design was used in order to avoid the problem of coverage errors caused by imprecise household registration lists that exclude internal migrants and temporary residents (Landry and Shen 2005). Thus, the survey provides a solid foundation for testing the validity of prior case-study findings and also allows the making of point predictions and generalizable propositions about the behaviour of ordinary citizens. In summary, the sample is conveniently large enough that it captures rare events (such as disputes), conforms to the principle of equal probability selection, and is representative of China's varied geographic, demographic, social, and economic environment.

Institutional diffusion in an authoritarian setting

Trust

A great deal of the literature on institutional innovation stresses the role of trustworthiness as a key determinant of the success of institutional innovations, or of their failure when it is lacking. If, under conditions that need to be specified, people trust a given institution, they are likely to rely on it should the need arise. If they do not, they will instead turn to reasonable alternatives. Trust is also a condition of their endurance in the long run (Hetherington 1998; Levi 1999; Levi and Stoker 2000; Ulbig 2002).

In the case of China, many scholars have demonstrated empirically that both inter-personal trust and system-based trust are comparatively high (Inglehart 1997; Shi 2001; Tang and Parish 2000). However, generalized trust may not be as reliable a predictor of success or failure of a specific institution. Just as trust between individuals can be generalized or particularistic (Uslaner 2002), Jennings (1998) has shown that individual trust in government institutions can be highly differentiated (Levi 1998). Li Lianjiang (2004) has found that rural Chinese exhibit highly differentiated levels of trust regarding central and local institutions.

The ILRC survey results demonstrate that these broad findings also hold with respect to legal institutions. Political correctness probably accounts for the high score of the Communist Party in absolute terms, but the CCP provides at least a useful benchmark against which to gauge trust in other relevant institutions. We find that trust is institution-specific: whereas organizations that are frequently

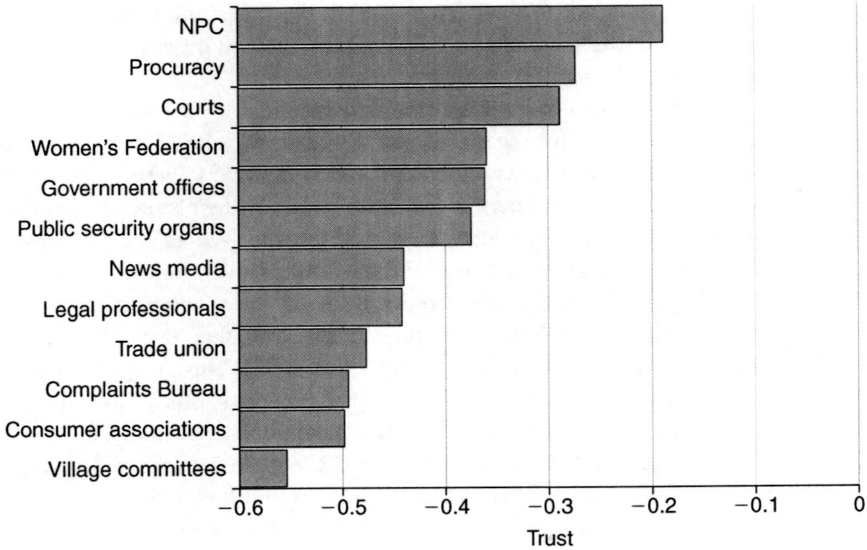

Figure 9.2 Relative measures of trust in public and legal institutions.

involved in dispute mediation (such as village committees), faired especially poorly, the courts and the procuracy are held in relatively high regard. Furthermore, most respondents trust institutions that are closely associated with the state to a far greater extent than non-bureaucratic actors: legal professionals are less trusted than public security organs, while village committees fair the worst of all institutions listed on the survey instrument (Figure 9.2).

Popular trust is overwhelmingly tilted in favour of central political and judicial institutions. As a follow-up to a general measure of trust (for instance, courts), we asked respondents to reveal whether they trust the supreme people's court, the local court, or neither. We also asked similar central/local comparisons of People's Congresses, the Communist Party and general government agencies. Although party members tend to be more trusting than non-Party members, central institutions enjoy a considerable degree of support in either group (Table 9.1).

These high-levels of trust in legal institutions bode well for the capacity of Chinese citizens to adopt institutional innovations. If Margaret Levi is correct that "trust is, in fact, a holding word for the phenomenon that enable individuals to take risks" (Levi 1998:1), the large segment of trusting Chinese citizens must be eager to test legal institutions, especially the courts, even if they have little personal experience in them.

Courts are an institutional novelty in China. Although they have existed throughout the history of the People's Republic, they did not play a significant role in dispute resolution during the Mao era. Their functions expanded in the 1980s and 1990s with a breathtaking series of reforms, the promulgation of numerous laws and regulations, as well as sheer physical institutional construction. In contrast with

Table 9.1 Relative trust in central political and judicial institutions, contrasted with local equivalents

	Non CCP members (%)	*CCP members (%)*
Supreme People's Court (versus local courts or neither)	90.5	94.9
National People Congress (versus local People's Congress or neither)	90.9	95.3
Central CCP Organizations (versus local or neither)	90.7	95.0
Central government institutions (versus local or neither)	90.8	93.0

Note
All measures are estimates that account for design effect.

the situation in 1978, virtually every Chinese county (or district) now has a functioning court.

The aggregate statistical evidence strongly suggests the diffusion of this institutional innovation: while the act of going to court was virtually unheard of in 1978, the ratio of court users has now reached approximately four per thousand (Figure 9.3). If we make the assumption that citizens use an institution because they trust it, trust in Chinese courts is decidedly on the rise. The changing mechanisms of dispute resolution provide further evidence of the rising popularity of the courts. A much larger proportion of disputes are settled in court rather than being "mediated" in quasi-governmental organizations (*tiaojie weiyuanhui*/调解委员会), as was the norm during the Mao era. Since 2001, the number of civil and administrative cases settled in court has reached about 4.6 million per annum, on par with the number of mediated disputes (Figure 9.4).

Surely, the popularity of the courts cannot be explained by a long record of openness and fairness of Chinese judicial institutions. Nor can we invoke institutional developments that predate the Communist regime to argue that popular trust in courts was acquired before the reform era, and that citizens are eager to use them now that they have the opportunity to do so. Introducing (or reforming) courts may be a necessary component of legal reforms, but the supply side is not a convincing explanation of sustained innovation. State propaganda may persuade citizens to become first-time users of the court system, but if they encounter abuse, corruption or unfair treatment, disappointed litigants are unlikely to maintain their trust in the institution and adopt it in the long run. Without the trust and tangible benefits of end-users, we expect the introduction of courts in authoritarian systems to be short-lived. After an initial fad, disillusioned first-time users would not only personally turn to more efficient alternatives, but they would also probably discourage relatives, friends, and acquaintances from following their path. Under such conditions, courts should see a steady stream of users only among citizens with small social networks or those who are poorly informed about the practical realities of legal institutions. Over time, the number of court cases would dwindle, leading to the gradual failure of the innovation.

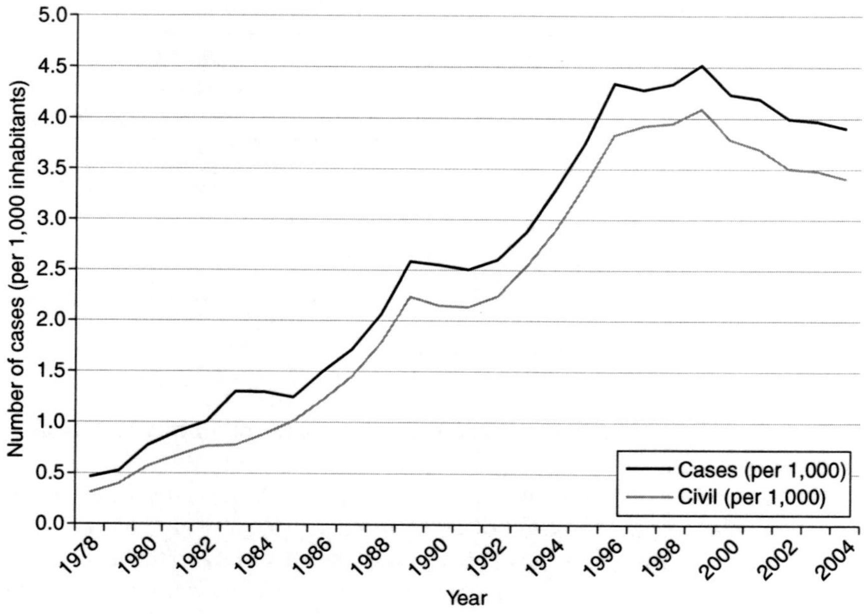

Figure 9.3 Number of cases per capita accepted by Chinese courts.

Networks

Explaining institutional diffusion: Social networks are central to theories of diffusion, and the problem of the adoption of institutions like courts in authoritarian regimes can be better understood by examining in detail the social structure of the regimes that innovate. The number of actors, the structure and the density of their networks, as well as the distribution of adopter and non-adopters within a network have been used in formal modelling and computer simulations to explain not only the rate of diffusion of innovations, but also patterns of partial diffusion within networks (Hägerstrand 1967; Mahajan and Peterson 1985; Hall and National Bureau of Economic Research 2004). Bandwagoning is more likely to occur when potential adopters learn from actual adopters with whom they are networked that an innovation is worthwhile, or not. Computer simulations have uncovered counter-intuitive results: even among networks that were seemingly small, the idiosyncrasies of their structure sometimes allow for rapid diffusion (Abrahamson and Rosenkopf 1997).

Court users in transitional regimes fit this description quite well. In societies where the rule of law is not well developed, the proportion of court users is likely to be very low. Furthermore, in authoritarian regimes that control information flows, rapid diffusion is likely to be concentrated among small clusters of individuals who enjoy privileged access to information. The patterns of diffusion should closely match the ways in which citizens are tied to the regime,

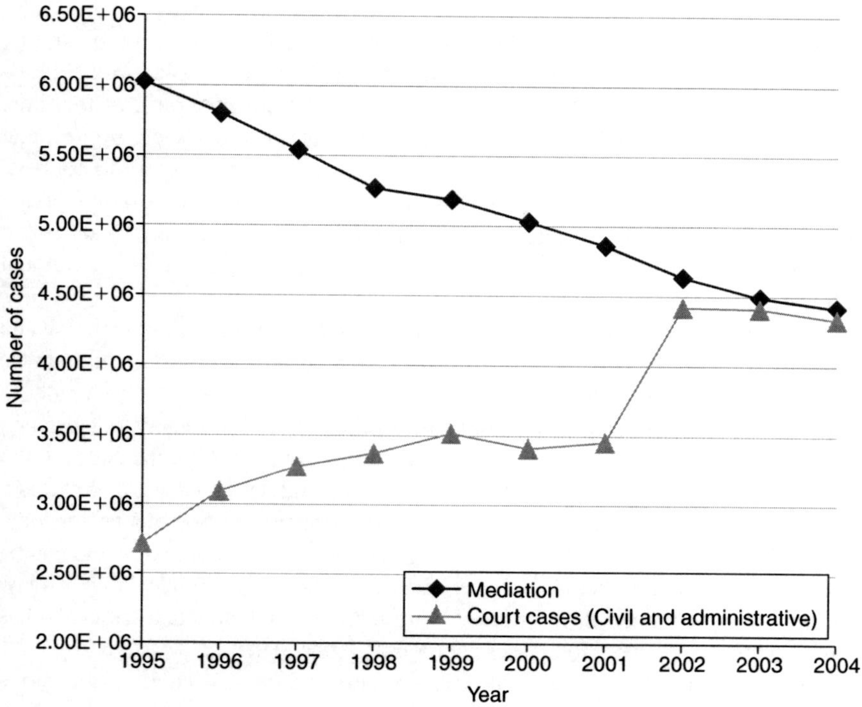

Figure 9.4 Evolution of court cases and cases handled by mediation committees.

both in terms of individual attributes (for instance, membership in the ruling party) and in terms of his social network (having friends in high places never hurts). Furthermore, when the performance of the courts is uncertain, the ways in which satisfied and dissatisfied users are clustered in the population may have a considerable impact on the behaviour of potential adopters.

The role of social networks is especially intriguing given the nature of Chinese society and the structure of the post-Maoist state. Considerable research in anthropology (Kipnis 1997; Yang 1994; Ku 2003), sociology (Bian 1999; Guthrie 1999; Gold *et al.* 2002), economics (Luo 2000; Wong 2001; Krug 2004; So 2006), as well as political science and law (Oi 1986; Lee 1997) has been devoted to the study of *guanxi*, its extent and its impact on individual behaviour. If the importance of *guanxi* has indeed endured in the contemporary period, Chinese society should therefore be more prone to the quick adoption (or rejection) of an innovation once it becomes known to members of a tightly-knit social network. Dense ties facilitate information flows and the rapid diffusion of the benefits and shortcomings of innovations among connected individuals. In the past few years, we have indeed witnessed extraordinary rates of diffusion of several innovations among Chinese consumers, innovations such as electric appliances, cellular phones, and internet usage. The same logic applies to institutional diffusion.

When we are concerned with the innovation and the diffusion of an institution, it is more difficult to specify when saturation occurs. Unlike cheap consumer products, courts are not devised for persistent use by most citizens, most of the time. Principles of fairness and the ideas that underpin a rule-of-law society suggest that access to courts ought to be universal, but the decision to actually go to court is, for most individuals, a rare event. A dispute resolution mechanism is only relevant when a dispute actually occurs, and only a subset of disputes ever reaches the judicial stage. We should not be overly surprised that the process of institutional diffusion is a slow one.

The aggregate statistical data on court cases for China seems to match the S-shaped pattern that theorists of diffusion have identified in other disciplines. During the 1980s and 1990s, the use of judicial institutions grew very rapidly, a reflection not only of rising demand for such institutions within society, but also and more prosaically because judicial institutions were a novelty: After the chaos of the Cultural Revolution, existing courts were re-opened and new ones were built down at the county level, while a host of innovations (such as the creation of a professional corps of lawyers) and specific laws and regulations facilitated access to the courts. However, the picture seems to have changed since 2000. While "rule of law reforms" have continued, the number of judicial cases – both civil and criminal – has reached a plateau of about four cases per thousand inhabitants.

Supply constraints may explain this plateau to some extent: the time-series data presented in Figure 9.3 only reflects cases *accepted* by the courts. Overburdened courts may simply not be able to cope with the demand for the institutions. The state may also limit access to the courts for fear that unbridled access to legal institutions may become politically destabilizing. A third explanation is that social heterogeneity produces idiosyncratic networks that are only conducive to partial diffusion. If access to the courts and initial successes are clustered within a narrow social elite (or specific geographical regions), the lack of connectivity between the beneficiaries of the courts and the general population may have slowed or even interrupted the diffusion process. It is possible that even ordinary citizens with close ties to somebody who was victorious in court will not emulate him if they infer that it is the particular characteristics of the winner – and not the choice of institutional venue – that explain the outcome. For instance, non-Party members may believe that only Party members can win court cases. If the sole winner of a court case in a given community happens to be a Party member, non-members do not have enough information to sort out whether Party membership or the decision to go to court is the decisive factor of their success. Diffusion would occur only among Party members.

Sample Design and Diffusion

The ILRC sample is uniquely suited to test the impact of the small community networks due to it special design. Below the township level, respondents were selected from micro-spatial communities in which all households were interviewed in order to ensure equal probability of inclusion (Landry and Shen, 2005). Though I aggregate the results by township in this article, a sampled township is in fact composed of two "half square miles" (equivalent to a natural village) in which clusters of about 90 × 90 metres were drawn. Thus, the probability that respondents know each other is very high.

I hypothesize that two parameters are jointly conducive to rapid institutional diffusion. The trustworthiness of the court and presence of individuals within small communities who have engaged courts successfully are conducive to the acceptance of the court as the proper dispute resolution venue. We cannot directly observe social networks, but it is reasonable to make the assumption that if the community is small enough, its members interact with each other frequently and learn quickly about unusual events. Given its rarity, victory in court certainly qualifies as the kind of news that is likely to spread fast in small communities. Rapid diffusion is likely to occur when a high proportion of satisfied and trusting end-users propagate their behaviour through dense social networks.

If only one of these factors is present, the process will be more gradual. If neither is present, we should see little or no diffusion. Note that the absence of diffusion does not imply that the number of court users will not rise: it simply means that individuals who use the courts will not be emulated in their communities. However, if individual-level variables that predict this behaviour change over time, a greater proportion of the population will still adopt the institution.

Community experiences and institutional diffusion

The ILCR survey allows use to identify respondents in their specific communities who were directly involved in legal disputes, went to court, and are, therefore, in the position to influence their network, based on their experiences with the courts. For each dispute category covered by the instrument – civil, economic, and administrative – we inquired whether the choice of going to court was decisive in the resolution of their dispute. If so, we further asked whether they would be willing to use the same method should a similar dispute occur in the future. We can thus identify the specific communities with which adopters (defined here as past disputants who would use the courts in the future) are present.

Table 9.2 Conditions for institutional diffusion

Density of adopters	*Trustworthiness of the institution*	
	Low	*High*
High	Gradual diffusion	Rapid diffusion
Low	No/very slow diffusion	Gradual diffusion

For each community, we can compute the mean share of respondents $\bar{x}$ who are "decisive adopters" in each kind of dispute. For additional precision, the computation of s_i excludes the respondent herself, and necessary correction since the clusters of respondents are relatively small.

$$s_i = \frac{(\bar{x} \cdot N) - x_i}{N - 1}$$

where x is the variable of interest and N the total of respondents sampled in the community. These shares are theoretically specific to each community member, though any pair of individuals who share the same behaviour has the same share. Since the variable of interest occurs rarely, $s = 0$ in most cases, and has a maximum value of one.

Although diffusion theory assumes that "adopters" are local opinion-makers, it must be emphasized that these experienced individuals constitute only a small fraction of a community. Using the township as the level of analysis, we encountered very few localities where more than one respondent has actually experienced a dispute that was decisively resolved in court. Furthermore, we could not identify any experienced users in the majority of the communities: we only found 69 townships (out of 200 surveyed) where civil disputes were resolved in court, 47 for economic disputes, and only 16 for administrative ones.

However, the lack of clustering among adopters does not mean that adopters have no measurable impact in their respective communities. As rare as they may be, diffusion research suggests that they may have a substantial impact on the behaviour of others if they happen to have strong links with "ordinary" community members.

The aggregate data suggest that adopters out-number non-adopters among respondents who have successfully engaged formal legal institutions. We estimate that 90 per cent of the citizens who have settled an economic dispute in court would do so again and 78 per cent in the case of civil disputes (Table 9.3). The odds are more even among administrative disputants, most likely because

Table 9.3 Distribution of actual court users who claim that the court was decisive in the disposition of their dispute

Dispute category	*Would you use the same method again?*			*Design-based estimated probability of using courts in the future*
	Yes	No	No answer	
Civil	72	17	7	0.78
Economic	56	6	1	0.90
Administrative	9	7	0	0.54

Notes
Table C13 C18 if C13=3.
Table C31 C36 if C31=3.
Table C49 C54 if C49=3.

the scope of the law and the odds of success in administrative litigation remain limited. Overall, these proportions are consistent with the diffusion hypothesis: very few people ever go to court, but since those who did express the desire to use the institution in the future, they are likely to diffuse their behaviour within their social network. This would explain the rising proportion of court-users among citizens who are engaged in a legal dispute for the first time.

We can gauge the potential impact of these adopters by comparing the propensity of inexperienced respondents who go to court across communities with varying densities of actual adopters. Specifically, we asked respondents who had not experienced a dispute whether they would be inclined to go to court based on a hypothetical situation presented in a vignette for each dispute category. If the diffusion hypothesis is correct, we should observe a greater propensity to go to court among respondents who happen to live in communities where one (or more) of their neighbours has "adopted" the institution.

The preliminary evidence is again encouraging for the diffusion hypothesis: when using townships as the unit of analysis, two of the three simple bivariate regressions show that in townships where residents who have been to court in civil and administrative dispute and are willing to use the institution against their neighbours who were never engaged in a dispute are more prone to go to court than residents of communities where no one has any experience with courts (Table 9.4). However, this does not seem to be the case for economic disputants. In order to be certain of the net impact of these "adopters" on institutional diffusion, we require a fully specified model that captures both the impact of individual characteristics of the respondents and the impact of institution adopters in their community. Such models allow proper measures of the magnitude of these diffusion effects.

Individual characteristics

Social networks

The kind of diffusion that we have considered so far does not account for the more direct and personal ties that citizens may have with legal institutions. The diffusion theory assumes that people learn from the direct experiences

Table 9.4 Impact of court adopters on the mean propensity to go to court

	Civil	*Economic*	*Administrative*
N	200	200	200
F(1, 198)	5.86	0.08	3.85
Model Prob > F	0.02	0.78	0.05
	Coef.	*Coef.*	*Coef.*
Share of court adopters in township	1.662	0.345	4.43
Constant	0.419	0.492	0.30

of their peers, but social networks can affect behaviour in other ways. This is particularly true in authoritarian systems where information flows are controlled and where connections with political and legal institutions of the regime can confer a decisive advantage over those who lack the requisite connections to "work" the system, particularly if a well-connected citizen is engaged in a dispute with a less connected one. In a society like contemporary China where social relations (*guanxi*) are highly valued (Bian 1997, 1999), these ties are likely to have powerful cognitive and behavioural consequences.

We attempted to capture the density of ties to key political and legal institutions by asking ILRC respondents whether they have regular contact with persons holding jobs in organizations that require (or are likely to result in) specialized legal knowledge (Table 9.5). Such ties with "experts" may have differentiated impacts depending on the specific problem that respondents encounter: an acquaintance in the official trade union may be helpful in resolving economic disputes, whereas contact with a Party cadre may be particularly useful in case of administrative disputes. The point is that well-connected citizens can gain specific knowledge and engage legal institutions more effectively, thanks to their social interactions with the political and legal elite in their community. These include Party and government cadres, members of people's congresses (at any level), employees of the courts or the procuracy, as well as lawyers and legal aid bureau personnel, and trade union officials. Most – but not all – of these professionals are likely to be CCP members.

Not surprisingly, Party members have a considerable networking advantage over ordinary citizens. These ties have even stronger effects among government employees, but even ordinary CCP membership confers a clear advantage. The empirical question is whether 36 per cent of ordinary citizens who interact regularly with the political, legal, and administrative elite do in fact capitalize on these ties by gaining greater access to the courts.

Table 9.5 Density of social ties with political and legal professionals

	All respondents	*Non-government employees*	*Government employees*	*CCP members*
Party and government leaders	24.7	23.9	71.1	50.1
Court and procuracy cadres	13.9	13.2	53.1	33.5
People's Congress representative	9.5	9.0	41.4	25.0
Labor union cadre	11.6	10.9	48.4	30.3
Legal aid bureau officials	4.5	4.0	29.7	12.9
Lawyers	6.9	6.6	29.7	17.2
Any of the above	36.8	36.0	85.9	64.5

Note
All estimates account for design effect.

Political institutions and the acquisition of legal knowledge

A successful rule-of-law programme requires at minimum a basic understanding of the institutions and norms that help sustain it. Ordinary social actors need not be legal experts, but they must at least have sufficient practical knowledge of the system in order to know where to turn and what basic choices are available to them when legal issues arise. Superior knowledge and information can also help end-users reduce the transaction costs of using an institution. In the Chinese context, these costs are high because many legal institutions – such as administrative litigation or private law firms – are still a novelty. Learning how to use them effectively while they evolve so rapidly is particularly challenging.

Membership in political institutions like the Youth League, and more importantly, the Communist Party, can help reduce these costs. CCP membership has direct benefits (Walder 1995; Walder *et al.* 2000; Dickson and Rublee 2000; Bian *et al.* 2001). It confers a competitive edge and offers various shortcuts that facilitate access to valuable information. For example, the policy diffusion process favours party activists because all important policy changes are announced through the CCP document system ahead of their dissemination to the general public. Information that is transmitted through Party channels is also less likely to be distorted than what is available through the general media. Party members have access to specific media that discuss issues that are otherwise censored and are theoretically reserved to members. Some of these have higher levels of classification and are reserved to cadres. Thus, both the timing and the quality of information confer a substantial advantage to CCP members. If they are in conflict with non-members, they can use such information strategically as they seek to resolve their disputes.

In order to test the proposition that Party members are more knowledgeable about the law than ordinary citizens, I rely on an additive knowledge score that is designed to capture the underlying variation in basic legal cognition within the population (Table 9.6). The ILRC survey asked each respondent 11 questions with varying levels of difficulty. This methodology is similar to efforts in public opinion research to measure the political knowledge of mass publics (Zaller 1991).

The indicators are aggregated into a simple additive index that ranges from 0 (no correct answers) to 11 (all correct answers). We obtain an index that is very close to a normally distributed variable, with a slight tilt to the left: 262 respondents scored 0, while only two persons have a perfect score. Design based estimates clearly show that this score is tied to membership in political institutions (Figure 9.2). Non-CCP members who never joined the Communist Youth League (who represent 80.9 per cent of the population) have a mean score of 4.2, in contrast to the elite of CYL members who later joined to CCP (1.1 per cent of the population) whose average score is 6.0. Current or past CYL members who never joined the Party (11.8 per cent of the sample) and Party

Table 9.6 Items used to test basic legal knowledge

Item	*Correct answers (estimated percentage)*
It is illegal to cohabit prior to marriage	26.04
Our laws explicitly prohibit extramarital affairs	24.07
Citizens can have permanent land ownership	42.02
Firms can employ 15 year old workers	12.11
All financial contracts signed by both parties are legal	30.56
A married woman does not have the duty to support her parents	71.70
Criminal suspects have a right to not answer when questioned by law enforcement agencies	27.44
Married daughters do not have inheritance rights	59.08
Courts have a legislative function	36.80
The procuracy cannot file a civil lawsuit	25.72
Local governments can put forward suggestions about court decisions	6.01

Note
Percentages account for design effect (N=7,714).

members who never joined the League (6.2 per cent of the population) have identical knowledge scores of 5.2 (see Figure 9.5). To some extent, the diffusion of legal knowledge among CCP members reflects the increasing importance of educational attainment as a criterion for membership. In this sense, membership may not result in additional knowledge after entry. Since legal knowledge and educational attainment are positively correlated, the Party's recruitment policy in the 1980s and 1990s that favour the well-educated may indirectly select out people with poor working knowledge of the law.[2]

Since many Party members are cadres, the command of administrative and political resources gives them a first-hand understanding of the concrete operations and shortcomings of the legal system. The CCP is also actively promoting legal awareness to the cadre corps. Most officials must attend training courses in Party schools at various levels, where law is becoming an explicit part of the curriculum.[3] These courses target cadres who are either being groomed for future promotion (Zhong 2003) or, having been promoted, are sent for training before actually taking up new assignments. Cadres who receive legal training in Party schools as part of their professional development can easily apply this knowledge for private gain.

Beyond the Communist Party, other political institutions can also help diffuse legal cognition. The CYL is less exclusive than the CCP, but a filtering mechanism similar to the CCP's is also in place in the League (Bian *et al.* 2001). Education is also a very important criterion for membership: it is now virtually impossible for somebody with a mere primary school education to join the League. Membership in the League exceeds 70 per cent in the current cohort of middle and high school graduates, a major increase from past generations. The

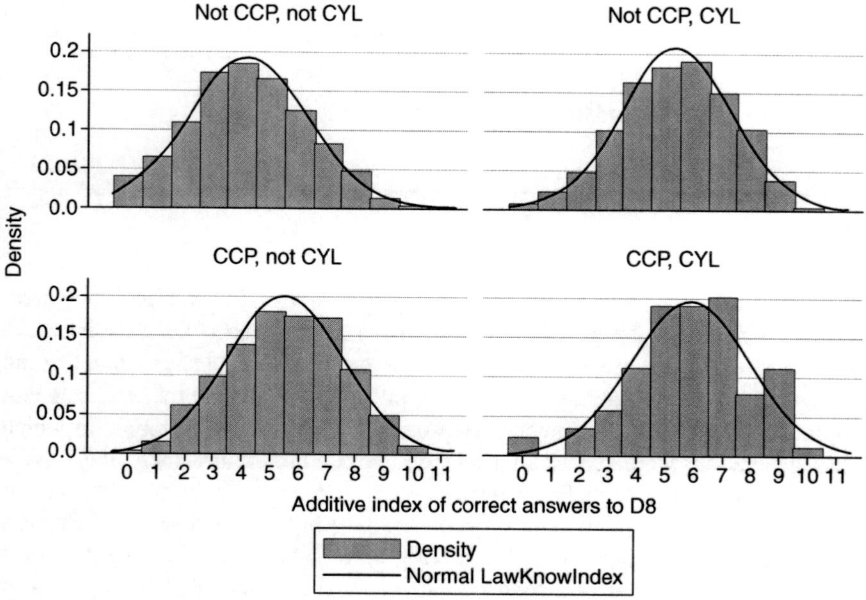

Figure 9.5 Distribution of basic legal knowledge score, by membership in the CCP and the CYL (0–11 scale).

CYL has traditionally been a vehicle of policy diffusion (Ngai 1997), and has been very active in recent efforts to publicize legal reforms in rural areas. CYL members who are mobilized for such campaigns are likely to learn about these reforms, probably better than the public they are supposed to reach.

Media consumption

Even without access to or connection with political and legal institutions, ordinary citizens can indirectly improve their legal knowledge. In recent years, the government has deployed considerable efforts to spread legal education and information through the media. Television stations carry numerous shows and mini-series depicting all kinds of legal disputes and their resolution. The book industry has seen an explosion of handbooks and guides designed to help ordinary citizens navigate China's evolving legal system. We observe considerable variation in the level of media consumption, which is now dominated by television. Only 5 per cent of the sample claims to never watch it. In contrast, printed media reaches a narrower group of wealthier, better educated, and usually urban, residents (Table 9.7).

We anticipate that much of knowledge of the law is acquired through the consumption of media, particularly among the subset of older adults who were not exposed to formal legal education in the school system.

Table 9.7 Frequency of media consumption

	Newspapers	*Magazines*	*TV*	*Radio*
Often	1,223	615	5,076	874
Sometimes	1,245	1,045	1,394	1,150
Very rarely	1,652	1,587	808	1,637
Never	3,463	4,272	386	3,889

Education

Education is another obvious channel through which legal knowledge is acquired. In today's middle and high schools, compulsory politics and civics classes weave new legal concepts into traditional political teaching. The lessons taught (and presumably learned) naturally reflect the priorities of the regime, yet standard politics textbooks are now much more sophisticated than the materials to which older generations were exposed during their youth. Furthermore, the young have a strong incentive to internalize new legal norms, because politics is a required subject on the college entrance examination. Entire generations of Chinese teenagers are now being exposed to a body of knowledge to which their parents simply never had access. In a context where general educational attainment is also rising rapidly, we expect a large generation gap in substantive command of basic legal issues. Our instrument captures this effect well: younger age groups clearly have higher mean scores than older ones (Table 9.8).

Multivariate analysis

"Urban" and "rural" subpopulations

Both household registration and occupation can help classify respondents as "rural" or not. If we use the nature of the *hukou* alone to make this determination, only 24.3 per cent of the sample could be considered "urban". However, this categorization exaggerates the size of the rural sector because a large proportion of "agricultural" *hukou* holders do not primarily work in agriculture. This category includes migrants who have moved out to urban areas and not adjusted their registration, as well as non-migrants who happen to live in areas classified as rural, but do little or no agricultural work. This category is large, amounting to 19.5 per cent of the entire sample. The most restrictive categorization of the rural population consists in extracting the subset of respondents among agriculture *hukou* holders who are full-time farmers. Such farmers are defined as respondents who engage in traditional farming work, but have no sideline business or who seek outside employment (*dagong*). Using this benchmark, 42.8 per cent of the sample consists of full-time farmers.

I hypothesize that institutional diffusion is more likely among groups whose activities place them at greater risk of conflict. Citizens who have successfully engaged the courts are more likely to convince neighbours with similar socio-

Table 9.8 Legal knowledge score, by age group

Age group	*Estimated mean*	*SD*
18–24	5.2	2.0
25–29	4.9	2.1
30–34	4.5	2.0
35–39	4.4	2.1
40–44	4.5	2.0
45–49	4.2	2.1
50–54	4.1	2.1
55–59	3.9	2.2
60–66	3.9	2.2

Note
All measures are estimates that account for design effect.

economic characteristics to make use of the institution. Since ordinary farmers rarely share the individual characteristics that tend to favour the use of legal institutions in the first place, the popularity of the institution is more likely to spread among the (smaller) social categories that share the characteristics of these judicial activists: namely, those whose more complex economic activities are more likely to experience conflict in the first place, and whose higher level of education, working knowledge of the law, and exposure to the media, make them more likely to actively seek to resolve conflicts when they occur.

Thus, the key contrast need not be between "rural" and "urban" Chinese, categorized in distinct geographical spheres, but instead between traditional farmers, rural residents who do not farm, and urbanites. The third (32.9 per cent) of the active population that has a rural *hukou* but no longer farms for a living is more likely to behave like urban residents, quite simply because they live, or at least work, in small towns and county seats where the bulk of non-agricultural jobs are located.

Modelling the propensity to go to court

The propensity to go to court is modelled as a probit equation that takes into account the multi-stage stratified nature of the sample design, and uses probability weights. Separate estimates were computed for each class of dispute that was covered in LIRC project. We asked all respondents whether they had been involved in civil, economic or governmental disputes in the past 20 years, and whether they chose to go to court in order to resolve it. The dependent variable is coded 1 if the respondent went to court, and 0 otherwise. Those who did not experience disputes were asked to react to a simple vignette and describe the actions they would likely take under such circumstances. This technique is more reliable than asking unstructured questions, particularly since we do not have the problem of cross-cultural comparisons in a single country study (King *et al.* 2003). The translation of each vignette is provided in Table 9.9. If respondents never encountered a civil (respectively economic or administrative) dispute, the dependent variable is also coded 1 if

Table 9.9 Sub-populations by household registration and main occupation

	Main occupation is agriculture	
	No (%)	*Yes (%)*
Urban *hukou*	23.9	0.4
Agricultural *hukou*	19.5	56.2
	Farmer	
	No (%)	*Yes (%)*
Urban *hukou*	24.3	0
Agricultural *hukou*	32.9	42.8

Note
Percentages are cell proportions and account for design effect.

they asserted that they would use the courts in their evaluations of hypothetical civil, economic, and administrative cases presented as vignettes.

The model accounts for the disparity between respondents who actually experienced disputes and those who responded to these hypothetical situations on the left hand-side.

$prob(Court)_{d=0} = \Phi(X\beta) + \varepsilon$ for individuals who did not experience a dispute of type d

and,

$prob(Court)_{d=1} = \Phi(X\beta + d) + \varepsilon$ for individuals who did.

The respondents who answered the "costless" hypothetical questions after a vignette were more likely to state that they would go to court: their expressed preferences were costless. However, disputants who actually chose to go to court faced tangible transaction costs. It is not too surprising that all else being equal, their propensity to go to court under such circumstances would be lower. I interpret the magnitude of the coefficients associated with these dispute-specific dummy variables as markers of the transaction costs of going to court.

Civil dispute

C2. Since you have not had such experiences, let's use a hypothetical case to understand your views. The labour contractor of a construction site has been embezzling the workers' wages, and the workers were denied their demands for payment numerous times. If you were one of the workers, what would you do? Would you take action to settle the dispute, or would you not do anything?

Economic dispute

C20. Since you have not had such experiences, let's use a hypothetical case to understand your views. To help a township business through some financial difficulties, a township government borrows 100,000 yuan from villager Wang Lin. The agreement specifies that this amount should be repaid in two years. But two years go by, and the amount has still not been repaid. If you were Wang Lin, what would you do? Would you take action to settle the dispute, or would you not do anything?

Administrative dispute

C38. Since you have not had such experiences, let's use a hypothetical case to understand your views. Zhang Jie is an individual industrial household with a licence to set up his stall. But the City Management Department found his stall detrimental to the aesthetics of the city, and thus confiscated his goods and fined him. If you were Zhang Jie, what would you do? Would you take action to settle the dispute, or would you not do anything?

Institutional diffusion

Since the diffusion hypothesis rests on the impact of two variables (the trustworthiness of courts and the density of adopters in the community) we need to test whether adding these variables to a baseline model actually improves the predictive power and the statistical significance of the model. The standard likelihood-ratio test cannot be performed on probit regressions for complex survey design. We must rely instead on a more indirect approach based on unweighted probits with the same set of independent variables. Furthermore, due to missing data when these two variables "trust in court" are added to the baseline model, we need to further restrict the LR-test to a subset of observations that are observed in both the saturated model and the nested model.

Whether we consider civil, economic or administrative disputes, these LR-tests are all consistent with diffusion hypothesis. The saturated models are always superior to the nested ones. However, the specific significance of the variable that captures the presence of adopters in the community varies by dispute category: it is considerable in the case of civil disputes; less so for economic ones; while it is not significant for administrative disputes. Since the coefficients are always positive (in the expected direction) for both variables, the dynamics of diffusion presented in Table 9.2 seem to hold very well for civil disputes. The propensity to go to court varies across individuals and communities as a function of these parameters. Varying these parameters and holding all other variables at their sample mean yields a more intuitive picture of the substantive impact of these variables (Figure 9.6). The findings of diffusion research through simulations that small idiosyncrasies of a network can have

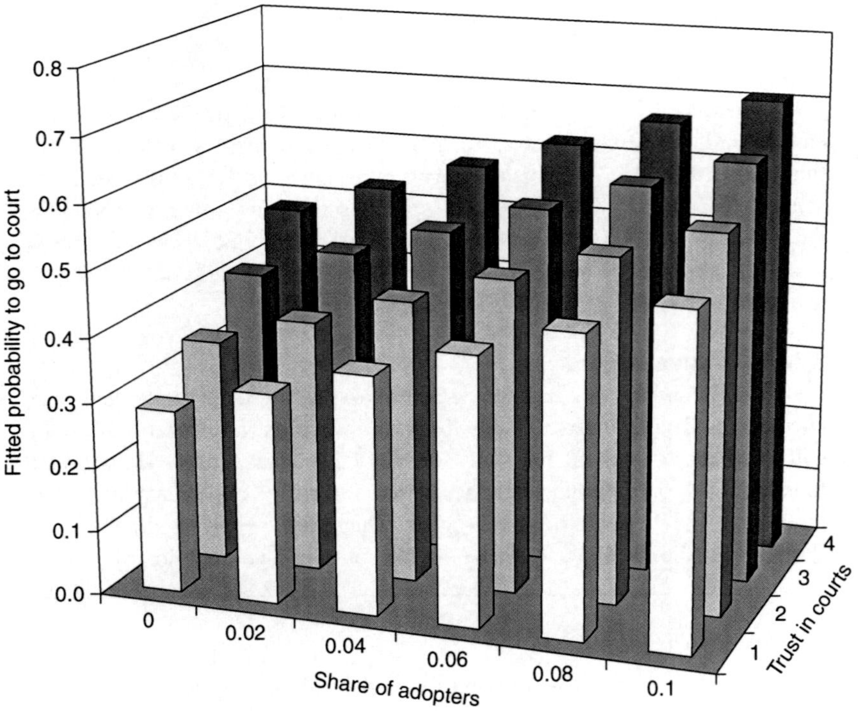

Figure 9.6 Fitted probability of adopting the court in future civil disputes.

large behavioural consequences apply here as well: even a small share of court adopters in a community greatly increases the likelihood that other members of the same community will also adopt the same behaviour.

Diffusion effects may not be homogenous across social groups, because the presence of adopters in a community is itself not random. Since court adopters belong to privileged social groups, and if these groups tend to be geographically segregated from other subpopulations, the diffusion process will be limited. While the results in Table 9.10 indicate that the propensity to go to court is much higher among holders of an urban registration, they do no tell us whether specific groups are particularly influenced by the presence of successful adopters in their community. We could specify a set of interaction terms in order to capture these effects, but such models rarely have an intuitive interpretation. It is also cumbersome to specify complex interactions across a wide range of independent variables that may also be sensitive to group heterogeneity. Since the number of observations in the sample is large, a simpler solution consists in estimating separate models for each sub-population and comparing the coefficients of interest directly.

Given the heterogeneity of the rural population, Table 9.10 tests whether the diffusion effect varies between urban and rural residents, as well as within subgroups of the rural population. Although the overall regression shows that urban

Table 9.10 Probit estimates of going to court in civil, economic, and administrative cases

	Civil	*Economic*	*Administrative*
Number of strata (24)	24	24	24
Number of PSUs (counties)	100	100	100
Number of observations	7,160	7,160	7,160
Estimated population size	850	850	850
Prob > χ^2	0.0000	0.0000	0.0000
Control for actual disputes			
Civil	–0.841	–	–
Civil dispute	–	–0.862	–
Economic dispute	–	–	–1.062
Human capital and information			
Formal education (years)	0.023	0.030	0.020
Legal knowledge score	0.061	0.044	0.056
Television	0.119	0.052	0.076
Political and social capital			
CYL member	0.172	0.130	0.005
CCP member	0.229	0.189	0.102
Contact w/Party or gov. cadre	0.055	0.091	0.063
Contact w/legal or public security official	0.225	0.174	0.162
Contact w/People's Congress	0.084	0.050	–0.001
Contact w/lawyer	0.131	0.191	0.017
Contact w/legal aid bureau	0.038	–0.181	–0.176
Contact w/Labour Union	0.030	0.129	0.047
Diffusion variables			
Trustworthiness of courts	0.177	0.252	0.208
Share of court adopters in township			
Civil cases	5.903	–	–
Economic cases	–	5.845!	–
Administrative cases	–	–	3.717
Demographic variables			
Age	0.006	0.008	–0.024
Age-squared	0.000	0.000	0.000
Female	–0.019	–0.026	0.105
Han nationality	–0.016	0.008	–0.102
Urban Registration	0.334	0.123	0.148
Full-time farmer	–0.040	–0.098	–0.041
Constant	–1.548	–1.356	–1.133
LR-test of full versus nested model without diffusion variables (unweighted probit with 7160 observations)			
LR $\chi^2_{(2)}$	102.61	131.33	112.15
Prob > χ^2	0.000	0.000	0.000

Note

Because only one PSU was drawn in small provinces, the original strata are grouped in 24 post-estimation strata. !=significant at the 0.108 level. Insignificant coefficients are shaded in gray. Linearized variance estimates account for complex multi-stage survey design effects, with stratification, first-stage selection of PSUs (counties) and second stage selection of SSUs (townships). These calculations ignore design effects at and below the third stage. Coefficients and standard errors shaded in grey are not significant at the 0.1 level.

Table 9. 10a Sub-population analysis for civil disputes

	Farmer	*AG*hukou	*Non-farmers*	*Non-farmers+ AG*hukou	*Non-farmers+ non-AG*Hukou
Control for actual disputes					
Civil dispute	–0.701 (0.111)	–0.814 (0.119)	–0.933 (0.157)	–0.937 (0.168)	–0.934 (0.258)
Diffusion variables					
Trustworthiness of courts	0.193 (0.045)	0.173 (0.047)	0.151 (0.056)	0.164 (0.076)	0.200 (0.070)
Share of court adopters in township	3.465 (2.752)	6.155 (2.908)	7.594 (3.354)	8.185 (3.724)	5.350 (3.527)
Human capital and information					
Formal education (years)	0.029 (0.011)	0.026 (0.011)	0.035 (0.014)	0.019 (0.017)	0.016 (0.016)
Legal knowledge score	0.049 (0.021)	0.053 (0.016)	0.080 (0.016)	0.059 (0.022)	0.098 (0.023)
Television	0.137 (0.033)	0.125 (0.031)	0.097 (0.047)	0.108 (0.051)	0.077 (0.069)
Political and social capital					
CYL member	0.113 (0.140)	0.068 (0.073)	0.226 (0.067)	0.054 (0.089)	0.340 (0.122)
CCP member	0.432 (0.157)	0.379 (0.106)	0.177 (0.094)	0.278 (0.140)	0.077 (0.116)
Contact w/Party or gov. cadre	0.029 (0.090)	0.083 (0.072)	0.080 (0.073)	0.145 (0.084)	0.016 (0.101)
Contact w/legal or public security official	0.069 (0.085)	0.082 (0.063)	0.308 (0.073)	0.100 (0.100)	0.473 (0.098)
Contact w/People's Congress	0.093 (0.148)	0.060 (0.108)	0.056 (0.104)	0.030 (0.125)	0.108 (0.155)
Contact w/lawyer	0.267 (0.164)	0.139 (0.108)	0.092 (0.112)	0.053 (0.150)	0.073 (0.128)
Contact w/legal aid bureau	–0.224 (0.183)	–0.034 (0.123)	0.143 (0.124)	0.158 (0.146)	0.080 (0.183)
Contact w/labour union	0.183 (0.128)	0.095 (0.092)	0.023 (0.074)	0.014 (0.115)	–0.062 (0.087)
Demographic variables					
Age	–0.005 (0.019)	0.015 (0.013)	0.013 (0.013)	0.036 (0.018)	–0.020 (0.022)
Age squard	0.000 (0.000)	0.000 (0.000)	0.000 (0.000)	–0.001 (0.000)	0.000 (0.000)
Female	–0.099 (0.052)	–0.047 (0.051)	0.085 (0.075)	0.028 (0.083)	0.077 (0.110)
Han	0.029 (0.131)	–0.009 (0.093)	–0.047 (0.142)	–0.065 (0.120)	0.021 (0.287)
Constant	–1.379 (0.489)	–1.674 (0.307)	–1.748 (0.355)	–1.911 (0.387)	–1.021 (0.618)

residents are more prone to go to court, the analysis by sub-population shows that urban residents (non-farmers, non-agricultural *hukou*) are *not* influenced by community events. In their case, going to court is driven purely by individual factors. In contrast, the diffusion effect that we detected for civil disputes is positive and significant among non-farmers, regardless of their registration status (β = 0.759). However, it is even more pronounced only among agricultural *hukou* holders who are not farmers themselves (β = 8.185).

It is also obvious that the rate of diffusion (measured as the fitted probability of going to court in a civil dispute) varies across communities systematically. Since the ILRC is a national sample stratified by province, it is legitimate to compare findings across provinces where the number of primary sampling units is not too small, though of course variance estimates within provinces are larger than the sampling variance of indicators measured at the national level: we forecast more rapid diffusion in Beijing in the case of civil disputes than anywhere else in the country, but this finding should be interpreted with caution because Beijing's contribution to the national sample is small, as it should be, given the size of the municipality.

If we separate the points on the scatter plot of average levels of trust and shares of court adopters in civil cases in four quadrants, the upper right corner of the figure represents the set of provinces where we expect rapid diffusion, since both the level of trust and the share of court adopters is higher than the national average. With the exception of Liaoning, all of the cases in the quadrant represent relatively poor, hinterland provinces. Most coastal provinces that have benefited the most from economic reforms since 1978 belong instead to the intermediate quadrants, where one of the two factors conducive to diffusion takes a low value. Three large interior provinces (Henan, Anhui, and Jiangxi) are especially noteworthy for their low values of both scores. Overall, there seems to be no systematic relationship between the level of economic development and the likelihood of diffusion of judicial institutions.

The rarity of court adopters in economic and administrative cases relative to civil ones also suggests that the institutionalization of the courts is likely to occur only through the process of civil dispute resolution. The novelty of administrative litigation which only began in earnest in the 1990s (the administrative litigation law was passed in 1989) and the low rate of success of citizens who sue government agencies will defer the diffusion of the habit of "suing the state" in court to the more distant future. Currently, the odds of finding satisfied ALL litigants in a given community is simply too remote to have any detectable impact on community behaviour.

The impact of individual-level variables

One variable alone cannot explain the popularity of the courts in China. The individual characteristics of the respondents also play an important role in the decision to adopt or reject an institutional innovation. Some of these factors are not specific to authoritarian regimes: the importance of education and legal knowledge is often cited as an important condition of access to the legal system in democracies, as well. Others are more regime-specific, such as membership in the Communist League or the Communist Party.

Social ties

The diffusion process that we examined so far focuses on networks linking actual adopters of an innovation to potential adopters. However, other types of social ties can also have an impact on the propensity to adopt an innovation, such as *guanxi* ties. Citizens with privileged access to the political and administrative elite can gain valuable information and perhaps even use these ties to manipulate the institution to their advantage. There is indeed evidence that the value of ties with employees of the judiciary varies systematically with the nature of the disputes. As is true with the effect of adopters in the community, the substantive impact of these ties is larger when the disputes are less likely to involve state institutions (i.e. civil disputes), but one's social network is less decisive in administrative cases than in civil disputes where state interests are not threatened.

It may seem surprising at first glance that the variables that capture *guanxi* ties have virtually no effect on the rural sub-population's propensity to go to court, in contrast to the largely positive coefficients among non-farmers. The importance of interpersonal ties in rural communities has been well documented, but one should keep in mind that the types of *guanxi* being tested here are quite specific. In a rural setting, these ties may have little impact, not because they are inherently unhelpful, but simply because such professionals live and work in urban areas: thus, only

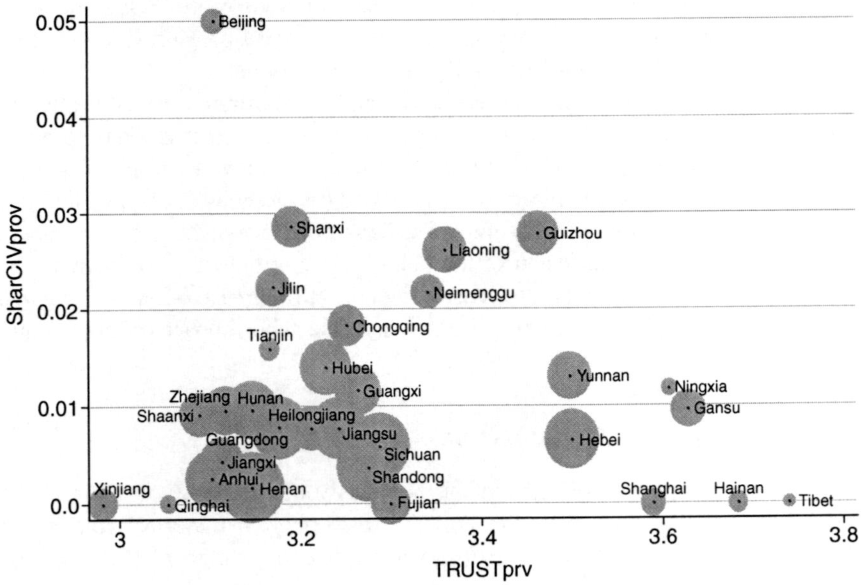

Figure 9.7 Trustworthiness of courts and share of adopters, by province.

a handful of mobile and well-connected rural residents – for instance, village leaders – are likely to make contact with these privileged social categories, and even when they do, these ties are unlikely to be close. Such processes are especially striking with respect to ties with the legal and public security officials: their impact is strong and positive for every dispute category, but not among non-farmers.

Party and youth league membership

Political connections magnify the impact of social ties: when the estimate models for the entire population, CCP membership systematically increases individual propensities to go to court. In addition, the effects of Party seniority are stronger when the issue is less politically charged. Both Youth League and Party members are more likely to go to court in civil disputes than non-members, but only Party members – whose political credentials are stronger than mere youth League members – are willing to go to court in economic and governmental disputes to a lesser extent than for civil disputes. Party members may be reluctant to bring their disputes to court, because such a drastic action may be construed as a breach of Party discipline if it involves a conflict with CCP or government officials. However, in economic and – even more so – in civil disputes, the political costs of going to court are likely to be lower and the benefits large: in conflicts against non-Party members, it is to the Party member's advantage to rely on courts that are institutionally dependent on the CCP, in order to seek redress against a non-Party member.

The importance of Party membership varies between farmers and non-farmers. The coefficient for CCP membership is twice as large for farmers than non-farmers in case of civil disputes. However, for economic disputes, urban CCP members are prone to court action, while the coefficient is not significant for farmers. Membership has no impact for the behaviour of either group in case of administrative disputes.

Media exposure, education, and legal knowledge

Unlike Chen and Shi (2001) who found no evidence of a relationship between media usage and general political trust in China, television viewers in the ILRC sample are more prone to use the court than non-viewers, regardless of the nature of the dispute. This difference may be due to the specificity of the institution considered: contemporary Chinese media broadcast very pointed educational or fictional programmes that convey clear messages that propaganda departments are eager to disseminate during legal education campaigns (*pufa jiaoyu*/普法教育). Judges and lawyers embody a stylized modern society that citizens are encouraged to join, and a host of soap operas include characters that see their disputes adjudicated in invariably well-organized and corruption-free courts staffed by righteous judges. Post-Leninist regimes are better equipped than other authoritarian regimes to use the media to their advantage. Once the state has decided to innovate, as the Chinese state has in the area of judicial institutions, its propaganda apparatus can be a highly effective agent of institutional change. Propaganda alone may not be sufficient to convince litigants to return to the courts if they are disappointed after a first experience, but it can at least prime the population of potential first-time users to be favourably predisposed towards judicial institutions. Furthermore, many media organizations test the boundaries of political correctness and do report on legal affairs in a far less stereotypical fashion than in the past, which may further increase the popularity of lawyers, judges, and the courts. Television programmes are particularly important because broadcasts originally intended for provincial audiences are watched nationwide. Satellite dishes usually carry a large bundle of (if not all) provincial stations, in addition to CCTV channels. A farmer from Yunnan can seamlessly learn from documentaries on Shanghai Television, and apply what he has learned on TV in his local community. Of course, formal education and legal knowledge strongly complement the impact of the media in the promotion of the courts. The impact of these factors is large and statistically highly significant across all dispute categories.

Concluding remarks

China's effort to build the rule of law seems paradoxical given the nature of Party control over judicial institutions in a post-Leninist state. Stanley Lubman's metaphor of the "bird in a cage" is a powerful reminder of the limits of this enterprise. Indeed, the sceptics could point to several empirical findings of this chapter and forecast doom, because key individual-level factors that explain the propensity to use the courts are closely related to the nature of Chinese authoritarianism: exposure to state-owned media, ties to the judicial elite, as well as membership in the Youth League and in the Communist Party all explain why citizens would (and in some cases did) solve their disputes in court. If access to the legal system is restricted to the regime's elite, the legitimacy of Chinese courts could be seriously eroded.

On the other hand, the Party facilitates the diffusion of legal knowledge as well as access to the courts among its members. Party and, to a lesser extent, Youth League membership have a direct and positive impact on the likelihood of going to court in civil and economic cases. To the extent that one of the key goals of Chinese legal reformers is to shift the traditional burden of dispute adjudication away from the Party and government agencies to more autonomous courts, Party and League members seem to be a positive force for change. A reform sequence in which non-Party members would be incited to use the courts while Party members would rely on other institutions to solve their disputes would almost certainly weaken the legitimacy of legal institutions among non-Party members. We find no evidence that this is the case. Instead, the CCP enhances access to legal institutions among its members. This is good politics, and is likely to strengthen China's reform effort: if Party members receive selective benefits from these institutions, they are more likely to support them in the long run.

The diffusion effects that are noticeable in the ILRC sample are a cause for further optimism. The transaction costs of going to court are high, and a fair amount of social, political, and human capital is required in order to overcome these costs at this early stage of Chinese legal reform. If ordinary citizens – who are often deprived of these capitals – were to suddenly engage the courts in large numbers, most would lose or give up, and probably turn into cynical and embittered opponents of legal innovations. We are instead witnessing a gradual diffusion process in which rare but satisfied users who probably owe a great deal of their success to their social and political capitals help diffuse their experience in the communities in which they live. Local elites may well be one step ahead of the general population, but the benefits that they derive from their close ties to the regime and, with that, increased odds of success in court, allows the public to learn from positive rather than negative experience, and ensure the gradual but steady diffusion of the institution.

Notes

1 For a detailed discussion of the underlying theories of institutional diffusion and its application to China, see Tang and Holzner (2006).
2 See Gerber (2000) and Rona-Tas and Guseva (2001) for the debate about the inherent benefits of membership versus selection effects among members of the Communist Party of the Soviet Union.
3 We estimate that 65 per cent of government employees are CCP members, against 5.9 per cent in the rest of the adult population aged 18–65.

References

Abrahamson, Eric and Lori Rosenkopf, "Social Network Effects on the Extent of Innovation Diffusion: A Computer Simulation", *Organization Science* 8:3, May–June 1997, pp. 289–309.

Bernhardt, Kathryn, Philip C. Huang, and Mark A. Allee, *Civil Law in Qing and Republican China, Law, Society, and Culture in China*, Stanford: Stanford University Press, 1994.

Bian, Yanjie, "Bringing Strong Ties Back In: Indirect Ties, Network Bridges, and Job Searches in China", *American Sociological Review* 62:3, 1997, pp. 366–85.

——, "Getting a Job Through a Web of *Guanxi* in China", in B. Wellman (ed.) *Networks in the Global Village: Life in Contemporary Communities*, Boulder: Westview Press, 1999.

—— and John R. Logan, "Market Transition and the Persistence of Power: The Changing Stratification System in Urban China", *American Sociological Review* 61:5, October 1996, pp. 739–58.

——, Xiaoling Shu, and John R. Logan, "Communist Party Membership and Regime Dynamics in China", *Social Forces* 79:3, 2001, pp. 805–41.

Cheibub, J. A. and Gandhi, J., "Classifying Political Regimes: A Sixfold Classification of Democracies and Dictatorships", paper presented at the Annual Meeting of the American Political Science Association, 2004.

Cheibub, José Antonio, *Political Institutions*, New Haven: Yale University, 2004.

Chen, Xueyi and Tianjian Shi, "Media Effects on Political Confidence and Trust in the People's Republic of China in the Post-Tiananmen Period", *East Asia: An International Quarterly* 19, Fall 2001, pp. 84–118.

Clarke, Donald C., "The Execution of Civil Judgments in China", *China Quarterly* 141, March 1995, pp. 65–81.

Cohen, Jerome A., "Reforming China's Civil Procedure: Judging the Courts", *American Journal of Comparative Law* 45:4, Autumn 1997, pp. 793–804.

Diamant, Neil Jeffrey, Stanley B. Lubman, and Kevin J. O'Brien, *Engaging the Law in China: State, Society, and Possibilities for Justice*, Stanford: Stanford University Press, 2005.

Dickson, Bruce J. and Maria Rost Rublee, "Membership Has Its Privileges: The Socioeconomic Characteristics of Communist Party Members in Urban China", *Comparative Political Studies* 33:1, 2000, pp. 87–113.

Gallagher, Mary E., "'Use the Law as Your Weapon!' The Rule of Law and Labor Conflict in the PRC", in N. J. Diamant, S. B. Lubman, and K. J. O'Brien (eds) *Engaging the Law in China: State, Society, and Possibilities for Justice*, Stanford: Stanford University Press, 2005.

Gerber, T. P., "Membership benefits or selection effects? Why former Communist Party Members do Better in Post-Soviet Russia", *Social Science Research* 29, 2000, pp. 25–50.

Giles, Michael W. and Thomas D. Lancaster, "Political Transition, Social Development, and Legal Mobilization in Spain", *American Political Science Review* 83:3, September 1989, pp. 817–33.

Gold, Thomas, Doug Guthrie, and David L. Wank, *Social Connections in China: Institutions, Culture, and the Changing Nature of Guanxi: Structural Analysis in the Social Sciences; 21*, Cambridge, New York: Cambridge University Press, 2002.

Guthrie, Doug, *Dragon in a Three-Piece Suit: The Emergence of Capitalism in China*, Princeton: Princeton University Press, 1999.

Hägerstrand, Torsten, *Innovation Diffusion as a Spatial Process*, Chicago: University of Chicago Press, 1967.

Hall, Bronwyn H. and National Bureau of Economic Research, *Innovation and Diffusion* National Bureau of Economic Research, 2004 [cited]. Available from http://papers.nber.org/papers/W10212.

Hetherington, M. J., "The Political Relevance of Political Trust", *American Political Science Review* 92:4, 1998, pp. 791–808.

Huang, Philip C., *Code, Custom, and Legal Practice in China: The Qing and the Republic Compared, Law, Society, and Culture in China*, Stanford: Stanford University Press, 2001.

Inglehart, Ronald, *Modernization and Postmodernization: Cultural, Economic, and Political Change in 43 Societies*, Princeton: Princeton University Press, 1997.

Jennings, M. Kent, "Political Participation in the Chinese Countryside", *The American Political Science Review* 91:2, June 1997, pp. 361–72.

——, "Political Trust and the Roots of Devolution", in V. A. Braithwaite and M. Levi (eds) *Trust and Governance*, New York: Russell Sage Foundation, 1998.

Kaufmann, Daniel, Aart Kraa, and Massimo Mastruzzi, "Governance Matters IV: Governance Indicators for 1996–2004", World Bank, 2005.

King, Gary, C. J. L. Murray, J. A. Salomon, and A. Tandon, "Enhancing the Validity and Cross-Cultural Comparability of Measurement in Survey Research", *American Political Science Review* 97:4, 2003, pp. 567–83.

Kipnis, Andrew B., *Producing Guanxi: Sentiment, Self, and Subculture in a North China Village*, Durham: Duke University Press, 1997.

Krug, Barbara, *China's Rational Entrepreneurs: The Development of the New Private Business Sector, RoutledgeCurzon Studies on China in Transition; 20*, London; New York: RoutledgeCurzon, 2004.

Ku, Hok Bun, *Moral Politics in a South Chinese Village: Responsibility, Reciprocity, and Resistance*, Lanham: Rowman and Littlefield, 2003.

Landry, Pierre F. and Mingming Shen, "Reaching Migrants in Survey Research: The Use of the Global Positioning System to Reduce Coverage Bias in China", *Political Analysis* 13:1, 2005, pp. 1–22.

Lee, Tahirih V., *Contract, Guanxi, and Dispute Resolution in China, Chinese Law; 3*, New York: Garland Pub, 1997.

Levi, Margaret, "A State of Trust", in V. A. Braithwaite and M. Levi (eds) *Trust and Governance*, New York: Russell Sage Foundation, 1998.

——, "The Problem of Trust", *American Journal of Sociology* 104:4, 1999, pp. 1245–6.

—— and L. Stoker, "Political Trust and Trustworthiness", *Annual Review of Political Science* (3), 2000, pp. 475–507.

Li, Lianjiang, "Political Trust in Rural China", *Modern China* 30:2, 2004, pp. 228–58.

Lubman, Stanley B., *China's Legal Reforms*, Oxford; New York: Oxford University Press, 1996.

Luo, Yadong, *Guanxi and Business, Asia-Pacific Business Series; v. 1*. Singapore; River Edge: World Scientific, 2000.

Mahajan, Vijay and Robert A. Peterson, *Models for Innovation Diffusion, Sage University Papers Series. Quantitative Applications in the Social Sciences; 07–048*, Beverly Hills: Sage Publications, 1985.

Michelson, Ethan, "How Much Does Law Matter in Beijing?", *Manuscript*, 2002.

——, "The Practice of Law as an Obstacle to Justice: Chinese Lawyers at Work", *Law and Society Review* 40:1, 2006, pp. 1–38.

Nee, Victor, "The Emergence of a Market Society: Changing Mechanisms of Stratification in China", *The American Journal of Sociology* 101:4, January 1996, pp. 908–49.

Ngai, N. P., "China's Youth Work in Rural Areas: Some Reflections on a Town and Two Villages", *International Social Work* 40:1, 1997, 27sq.

O'Brien, Kevin J. and Lianjiang Li, "Suing the Local State: Administrative Litigation in Rural China", in N. J. Diamant, S. B. Lubman, and K. J. O'Brien (eds) *Engaging the Law in China: State, Society, and Possibilities for Justice*, Stanford: Stanford University Press, 2005.

Oi, Jean, "Commercializing China's Rural Cadres", *Problems of Communism*, September–October 1986, pp. 1–15.

Osiel, Mark J., "Dialogue with Dictators: Judicial Resistance in Argentina and Brazil", *Law and Social Inquiry* 20:2, Spring 1995, pp. 481–560.

Peerenboom, R. P., *China's Long March Toward Rule of Law*, Cambridge; New York: Cambridge University Press, 2002.

Pinkele, Carl F., "Plus ça change: The Interaction between the Legal System and Political Change in Francoist Spain", *International Political Science Review* 13:3, July 1992, pp. 285–300.

Potter, Pitman B., *From Leninist Discipline to Socialist Legalism: Peng Zhen on Law and Political Authority in the PRC*, Stanford: Stanford University Press, 2003.

Rona-Tas, Akos and Alya Guseva, "The Privileges of Past Communist Party Membership in Russia and Endogenous Switching Regression", *Social Science Research* 30: 4, December 2001, pp. 641–52.

Shi Tianjian, *Political Participation in Beijing: A Survey Study*, Cambridge: Harvard University Press, 1996.

——, "Voting and Nonvoting in China: Voting Behaviour in Plebiscitary and Limited-Choice Elections", *The Journal of Politics* 61:4, November 1999, pp. 1115–39.

——, "Cultural values and political trust – A comparison of the People's Republic of China and Taiwan", *Comparative Politics* 33:4, 2001, 401sq.

So, Ying Lun and Anthony Walker, *Explaining Guanxi: The Chinese Business Network*, New York: Routledge, 2006.

Tang, Wenfang and Burkart Holzner,, *Social Change in Contemporary China: C.K. Yang and the Concept of Institutional Diffusion*, Pittsburgh: University of Pittsburgh Press, 2006.

—— and William L. Parish, *Chinese Urban Life under Reform: The Changing Social Contract, Cambridge Modern China Series*, Cambridge; New York: Cambridge University Press, 2000.

Tate, C. Neal and Stacia L. Haynie, "Authoritarianism and the Functions of Courts: A Time Series Analysis of the Philippine Supreme Court, 1961–1987", *Law and Society Review* 27:4, 1993, 707–40.

Toharia, José J., "Judicial Independence in an Authoritarian Regime: The Case of Contemporary Spain", *Law and Society Review* 9:3, Spring 1975, pp. 475–96.

Ulbig, S. G., "Policies, Procedures, and People: Sources of Support for Government?", *Social Science Quarterly* 83:3, 2002, pp. 789–809.

United States, Congressional-Executive Commission on China, *Taming the Dragon: Can Legal Reform Foster Respect for Human Rights in China? Hearing before the Congressional-Executive Commission on China, 107th Congress, 2nd session, 11 April 2002*, Washington DC: US GPO, 2002.

Uslaner, Eric, *The Moral Foundations of Trust*, New York: Cambridge University Press, 2002.

Walder, Andrew G., "Career Mobility and the Communist Political Order", *American Sociological Review* 60:3, 1995, pp. 309–28.

——, "Markets and Income Inequality in Rural China: Political Advantage in an Expanding Economy", *American Sociological Review* 67:2, April 2002, pp. 231–53.

——, Bolai Li, and Donald J. Treiman, "Politics and Life Chances in a State Socialist Regime: Dual Career Paths into the Urban Chinese Elite, 1949 to 1996", *American Sociological Review* 65:3, 2000, pp. 191–209.

Wong, Y. H. and Thomas K. Leung, *Guanxi: Relationship Marketing in a Chinese Context*, New York: International Business Press, 2001.

Wu, Xiaogang, "Work Units and Income Inequality: The Effect of Market Transition in Urban China", *Social Forces* 80:3, March 2002, pp. 1069–99.

Xu, Xiaoqun, "The Fate of Judicial Independence in Republican China, 1912–37", *The China Quarterly* 149, March 1997, pp. 1–28.

Yang, Mayfair Mei-hui, *Gifts, Favours, and Banquets: The Art of Social Relationships in China*, Ithaca: Cornell University Press, 1994.

Zaller, John, "Information, Values, and Opinion", *American Political Science Review* 85:4, 1991, pp. 1215–37.

Zhao, Yi, "The Expansion of Judicial Power in China", *Political Science*, New Haven: Yale University, 2003.

Zhong, Y., *Local Government and Politics in China: Challenges from Below*, Armonk: M. E. Sharpe, 2003.

Zhou, Xueguang, Phyllis Moen, and Nancy Brandon Tuma, "Educational Stratification in Urban China: 1949–94", *Sociology of Education* 71:3, July 1998, pp. 199–222.

10 Would democratization help remedy China's corruption problem?

Comparative insights on China and India

Yan Sun

Implicit in the theme of this volume is the assumption that China's political institutions, which draw strength from economic globalization but refuse to go beyond that, form the fundamental political constraints for settling the social problems facing China. Corruption is among the most acute of those social-political problems and at the core of China's governance deficit. How China is doing on corruption, not surprisingly, has become a focal point of contention among some leading scholars in the field. Has China already significantly reformed its institutional framework for economic governance, including the control of corruption?[1] Or is China's lack of political liberalization the very cause of runaway corruption and the regime's failure to contain it?[2] Or, to echo the theme of this book, are the contradictions of China's "capitalist communist" system indeed the cause of rampant corruption and, as well, the chief obstacle to its effective remedy?

In this context, it is useful to look at Chinese corruption comparatively: have comparable countries, without China's systemic contradictions, done better on corruption? Most relevantly, China and India make good comparative cases. The two have many important similarities, in their vast territorial size, their severe "principal–agent" problems arising from the attendant complexity, the particularistic cultures that buttress nepotism, the legacies of a centralized economy, and their recent economic liberalization. Because state intervention and economic liberalization are both associated with greater corruption,[3] China should be expected to do worse on corruption, as it has had both a more centralized economy to begin with and more extensive liberalization subsequently. Among the key differences that may affect their relative performance on corruption are the level of development and the type of regime. The level of development affects corruption by helping to shape incentives and alternative avenues to seeking wealth,[4] a factor that favours China. Those incentives also need to interact with the opportunities and constraints provided by the polity. Controlling for the level of development, this is where the two cases should have the greatest potential to diverge: the nature of the polity and how it affects the capacity of political elites to resist private seeking incentives or to exert control over the extent and direction of rent-seeking activities.[5]

Based on the salient similarities and differences assessed above, one can pinpoint the most important factors that may differentiate corruption in the two cases: the level of development and the regime type. These two factors, I argue, interact to provide key explanations for the variation of corruption in the two cases. Specifically, thanks to a combination of greater economic pressures, open politics and lesser state strengths (defined as elite autonomy), India, as a poor democracy, may not do better on corruption than China. Conversely, thanks to greater economic development, political constraints and state strengths, China as a developmental autocracy may not do worse. In other words, my argument is that democracy per se has made little difference when the two cases are contrasted. At the very least, democracy alone, in the absence of attendant economic development and its social fallout, will not suffice to restrain corruption.

The rest of the chapter will present the theoretical framework and empirical evidence for my argument. Section one will discuss the theoretical framework. Section two will assess the evidence for the levels of corruption in the cases, relative both to each other and as measured in their developmental and regional contexts. The next three sections will turn to the qualitative evidence for my argument, from a variety of angles. Section three will discuss economic distress as a cause of corruption in the two cases by drawing on existing literature. Section four will compare the structural conditions for corruption in the two cases. Section five will compare corruption's impact on regime legitimacy in each case. I shall conclude by highlighting the implications of my findings for improving governance and fighting corruption in contemporary China.

State strength and corruption

The nature of the state is a strong determinant of corruption because the relative autonomy of political elites is critical for shaping the corruption scenario in a political setting. Corruption takes many forms, and the dominant patterns in modern political and economic systems take the form of illicit exchange between state power and societal interests. If democracy or the lack thereof is characterized by different relationships between the state and society (aside from institutional differences), then these different relationships should have an important impact on the types of corruption which result.[6]

According to Robert Wade, the shortest answer to why the abuse of public power is limited in East Asia is that the region's states are relatively "hard". That is, the position of a state in relation to its society can be thought of as varying along a continuum from decentralized and constrained by social groups – or "soft", to centralized and relatively insulated from society – or "hard". Because hard states have the capacity to resist private demands, they are able to exert control over the direction of the society and economy.[7] That continuum is characterized by Michael Johnston as a dynamic balance between the accessibility and autonomy of political elites. Where political elites are significantly more accessible than autonomous, they are vulnerable to private influence (legitimate or not) and find it difficult to resist private demands. Where political elites are more autonomous than accessible, they may exploit private interests with relative ease. Where the political and societal forces are well-balanced, private interests have significant political influence but officials can formulate and carry out policies authoritatively.[8]

Compounding the balance between political accessibility and autonomy is a second set, one between political opportunities (positions of power) and economic ones (poverty or wealth). Samuel Huntington has pointed to imbalances here as a major source of corruption. According to this line of argument, where opportunities for positions of political power exceed those for accumulation of wealth, individuals are likely to use the former to achieve the latter. Where economic opportunities exceed political ones, however, people will tend to use wealth to pursue political power. The first scenario is frequent in modernizing societies while the second, is seen in mature democracies such as the United States.[9] In alternative scenarios, where political and economic paths to advancement are both numerous and open enough, temptations for the exchange of public power and private wealth can be reduced. Here officials and private interests can influence each other but also can resist exploitation by one or the other. Neither end of the resources, moreover, must chase the other, thus more control of corruption. Where one or both sets of imbalances are present, a variety of corruption scenarios will result.[10]

Variations in state strengths and available opportunities in different polities result in the dominance of different state and societal interests in the political process. In Type 1, interest groups are strong while political elites are vulnerable. The result is the use of economic resources (campaign financing and such) by business interests to influence political elites. Limited elite autonomy and plentiful economic opportunities, meanwhile, help contain rent-seeking by political elites. In Type 2, entrenched elites dominate, and are able to influence the direction of economic activities, as well as the extent of rent-seeking, among political and economic actors. In Type 3, elite accessibility, political opportunities, and economic scarcities, combine to produce insecure elites vulnerable to rent-seeking and patronage politics.[11] In Type 4, political elites and a few private interests share rent extraction, through a monopoly over patronage. Both groups are oligarchs in the sense that much of the most significant competition for power and wealth takes place among relatively few players.[12]

Parallel arguments by other students of Asian states reinforce the point about the strength and orientation of the state vis-à-vis society in determining corruption outcomes. In David Kang's analysis, the more balanced competition between the political and economic elite in South Korea was the reason why corruption there did not spiral out of control as it did in the Philippines.[13] In Paul Hutchcroft's topology of capitalist systems, based on the relative strength of the state and society and the motivational logic of elites, the developmental state of East Asia has produced a "statist capitalism" more production-oriented than the "bureaucratic capitalism" or "booty capitalism" of the patrimonial administrative or oligarchic states of South East Asia.[14]

Does the autonomy of the Chinese state entail relatively more restrained corruption? Existing studies offer a mixed assessment. Closed political processes ensure that political elites need not depend on business interests for political support, "making it possible for the state to fend off, insulate itself from powerful social forces".[15] Greater economic opportunities also ensure that ambitious individuals have more alternative avenues for pursuing wealth in the economic sector than in the non-competitive, one-party system.[16] More centralized rent-seeking also tends to produce less wasteful rent-seeking.[17] On the negative side, decentralization has allowed the chief executive office to become the main locus of favour exchanges at the local government level, with little supervision from above or below.[18] In less developed regions and more rural areas, such political monopolies can contribute to "local predatory states".[19]

Does the accessibility of the Indian state entail less restrained corruption? Existing literature offers a more negative assessment. The Indian state is said to lack autonomy from groups involved in so-called zero-sum activities (speculation, corruption, landlordism, usury, etc.).[20] Indian politicians are said to have presided over a dominant coalition with three main elements: the industrial bourgeoisie, the rich farmers and the bureaucracy, which place serious limits on state autonomy. Each group strives to maximize the benefits from state policies and the state is unable to rise above their interests or to work for society as a whole. The result is a state long on regulatory law and weak on enforcement,[21] or a democracy long on rhetoric and weak on controlling self-seeking politicians.[22]

The above discussion on state strength and corruption reveals important tradeoffs among different institutional features. Lack of curbs on state autonomy renders the Chinese state less susceptible to capture by private interests yet more vulnerable to unaccountability. Lack of state autonomy, or elite dependence on societal groups for political survival, on the other hand, renders the Indian state more vulnerable to capture by private interests.

Relative levels of corruption

This section will assess the relative levels of corruption in my two cases. The most authoritative cross-national data on corruption provides slightly more favourable evidence for China. Table 10.1 shows their Corruption Perception Index (CPI) scores from 1995–2006. The CPI is a robust index that combines the measurements of leading surveys and ratings by consultancies based outside the relevant countries.

The differences shown below may be statistically insignificant and could signify little difference at the baseline of corruption levels. But they are significant in one important sense: the scores do not indicate China to be more corrupt than India over a similar period. China's scores were poorer in the mid-1990s, a likely result of the cumulative effects of intensified liberalization since the early 1990s. As enforcement efforts caught up, China's scores have improved since the late 1990s. Similarly, India's scores worsened since the late 1990s, a likely cumulative effect of economic reform since the early 1990s. As in China, enforcement efforts could yet catch up and narrow the difference with China.

Table 10.1 CPI scores for China and India, 1995–2006 (perfect score = 10)

Year	*China*	*India*
1995	2.16	2.78
1996	2.43	2.63
1997	2.88	2.75
1998	3.5	2.9
1999	3.4	2.9
2000	3.1	2.8
2001	3.5	2.7
2002	3.5	2.7
2003	3.4	2.8
2004	3.4	2.8
2005	3.2	2.9
2006	3.3	3.3
Average	3.14	2.83

Source: Transparency International, 1995–2006.

Does the CPI, based essentially on surveys of foreign business executives, realistically reflect corruption in the domestic sector? On balance, it does so more in China's case than in India's. Thanks to the much larger presence and variety of foreign executives in China, both the size and types of business these executives represent matter. Diaspora executives, who oversee the bulk of China's FDI, are often from China's vicinities and are familiar with the informal practices of Chinese cultural surroundings. They tend to be both vulnerable and adaptable to illicit exchanges with local Chinese officials.[23] China's foreign executives, by the size and variety of their businesses and investments, also reach beyond industrial zones and into the larger Chinese society. In other words, they have more encounter with real Chinese society. In India's case, the offshoring sector is limited to a few industrial enclaves and is less exposed to routine illicit exchanges of the larger society, thus creating a more amenable – yet less typical – business environment for foreign and diaspora executives doing business in India.[24]

Does a lower level of development account for India's somewhat poorer scores? An affirmative answer is highly plausible. The level of corruption is closely associated with the level of development because the latter affects individual incentives, alternative avenues for wealth-seeking, modernization of the government apparatus and the educational level of the population. A contrast of CPI scores with GDP per capital (PPP) for 20 Asian states, indeed, bears out the close correspondence between corruption and development levels both for our two countries and for Asia as a whole. Placing the contrast in the regional context, as shown on Figure 10.1, also raises the larger question of why Indian democracy, as well as other poor democracies of the region, have, on the whole, not done well, despite the promised strength of their regime types?

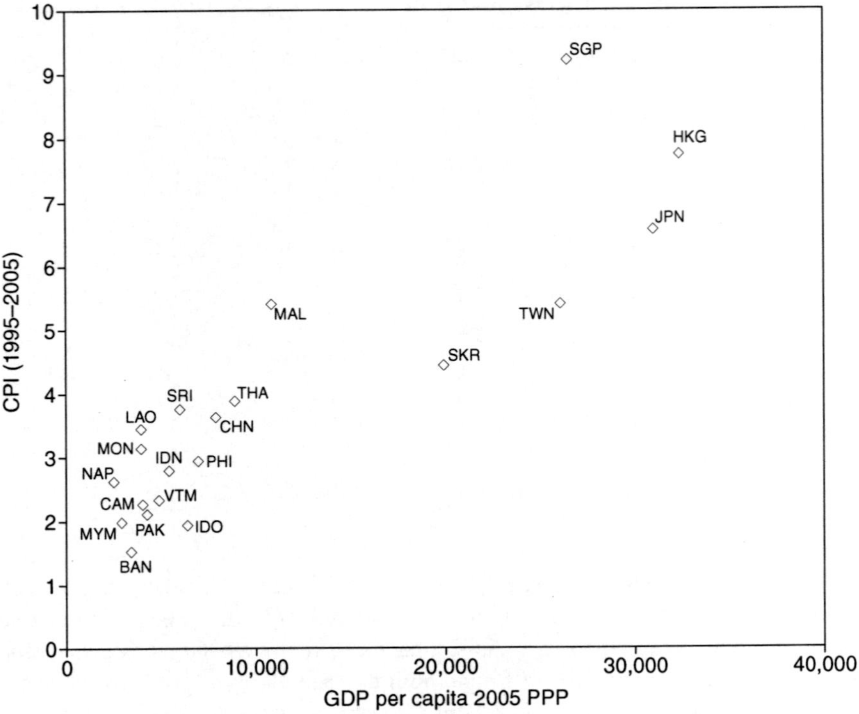

Figure 10.1 TI CPI scores and economic development: Asia.

Three general patterns are notable from Figure 10.1, all of which force us to rethink economic and regime dynamics underlying corruption. First, states with lower levels of corruption tend to be associated with higher levels of economic development. Conversely, states with higher levels of corruption tend to be associated with lower levels of development. Second, democracy per se does not appear to be a strong indicator of the level of corruption in Asia. Democracies with low levels of development are just as likely to be among the more corrupt countries as other poorer countries: India, the Philippines, Bangladesh, and the intermittently democratic Pakistan. Bangladesh has been ranked the most corrupt country in the world between 2001 and 2005. Third, strong states, rather than democracy per se, are generally associated with low levels of corruption. The top CPI scorers, mostly East Asian developmental states, have successfully reduced corruption under what Fareed Zakaria calls "liberal autocracies". The "liberal" part includes especially the rule of law, which term may come with or without democracy. The illiberal democracies, which may be used to describe Asia's poor democracies, perform uniformly worse. So do the illiberal autocracies, Indonesia and Myanmar. The type of strong states makes a difference. While the strong states of East Asia have managed to limit corruption, the strong states of

Southeast and South Asia have not. That is, liberal autocracies appear to have out-performed both illiberal democracies and illiberal autocracies in Asia.

Placing my two cases in the context of the region, in short, indicates that overall, poor democracies of Asia, including India, have not done as well as the pack of developmental or liberal autocracies. This collective deficit points to the twin dynamics of underdevelopment and political regime as key variables for corruption in those societies. In the next section I shall turn to the issue of underdevelopment and corruption.

Economic wants and corruption

This section will assess the link between underdevelopment and corruption in our two cases, by surveying scholarly evidence on the issue. From Huntington's perspective, described earlier, underdevelopment is an important source of corruption because it entails scarce economic opportunities and exerts pressures on individuals to (ab)use the political to achieve the economic.

One reason for the correlation between poverty and corruption is the "make ends meet" argument. Students of corruption in developing countries regularly cite conditions of poverty as a key incentive and stimulus. Leslie Palmier's observation is classic,

> Poor pay is a powerful pressure towards corrupt gains, if only to make ends meet. ... Public servants not paid enough to fulfill their usual obligations are only too likely to take advantage of whatever opportunities may arise for unauthorized gains.[25]

One study of corruption in the Philippines is appropriately titled, "What are we in power for?"[26] Jeffrey Sachs, adviser to the UN Millennium Development Goals, proposes that corruption in poor countries be measured against their poverty levels. This leads to his idea of "relative corruption" for Africa.[27] Corruption and poverty also feed on each other, causing a cycle of underdevelopment.[28] Another reason for the link between poverty and corruption is inequality in a society. Income inequality increases corruption, Jong-Sung You and Sanjeev Khagram argue, because the rich are likely to have greater motivation and opportunities to engage in graft as one means to preserve and advance their privileges and interests, while the poor are more vulnerable to extortion at higher levels of inequality. They find that, while authoritarian countries are likely to have greater levels of corruption on average, the effect of greater inequality on corruption will be higher in democracies.[29] Corruption, moreover, widens the inequality between those with access to power and those without, and leads those placed low in the stratification system to justify deviant means to attain their goals, as well.[30]

Empirical studies of India confirm the central role of these economic incentives. Gunnar Myrdal writes of "the low real wages of officials, especially those at the lower and middle levels" as conducive to pervasive corruption in post-colonial

India.[31] The Third Pay Commission in India (1970–73) recognized the link between low salaries and corruption by concluding that while high salaries would not in themselves guarantee officials' honesty and integrity, "it can be confidently stated that the payment of a salary which does not satisfy the minimum reasonable needs of a government servant is a direct invitation to corruption".[32] Robert Wade places "acute scarcities" on the top of his list of causes for India's bureaucratic graft.[33] Leslie Palmier ranks poverty among his three top causes for India's corruption, the other two being ample opportunities for abuse and ineffective policing. Singaporean scholar Jon Quah lends support to this argument with a comparison of salary levels for top politicians in several Asian countries, with India being the lowest.[34] Indian scholar Vinod Pavarala, in his survey of Indian elites in the 1990s, suggests that a majority of bureaucrats, industrialists, and judges he interviewed blame economic compulsion of people for corruption in the political and bureaucratic strata, especially at the lower levels.[35] Above all, Hans Schenk points to the uniquely corrosive nature of India's poverty: "the embedding of scarcity in a system of morally based inequality and in a set of tight dependency relations." This embedding helps to sanction and perpetuate patrimonial relations.[36]

Economic scarcities rooted in central planning did constitute a major incentive for bureaucratic abuse in the spartan era of Mao. But corruption then was relatively insignificant compared with that of the reform era.[37] For the reform period, most studies emphasize structural causes of Chinese corruption.[38] Poverty remains a leading source of corruption in poor regions, thanks to the same incentives that drive corruption in other poverty-ridden contexts: a lack of developmental opportunities, or alternative avenues to seeking wealth. While corruption in more developed regions involves interaction between officials and businesses, the dominant types of corruption in poor regions, by contrast, rely on interaction with the state. Perpetrators either prey on developmental and other public funds, or on public office posts as a source of black income. The effects are non-developmental and anti-developmental, creating a vicious cycle for poor regions.[39] These incentives and forms are echoed in the Indian case.

There is significant scholarly evidence, then, to support a meaningful correlation between the level of development and corruption, more generally in India and more regionally in China. India's democracy per se, thus, has not been sufficient to overcome the impact of underdevelopment in the matter of corruption. Why? In the next section I shall turn to the political dynamics.

Structural conditions and corruption

This section will contrast the structural conditions for corruption in my two cases. It will look at three structural dimensions that differentiate their regime features on the one hand and the resulting corruption patterns on the other, including the availability of political versus economic opportunities, access to decision-making by private interests, and collusion between politicians and bureaucrats.

Political versus economic opportunities

The type of opportunities available helps determine the incentives for, as well as the alternative avenues to, wealth seeking. As a developmental autocracy, China offers more economic opportunities than political ones, while India, as a poor democracy, provides more political opportunities than economic ones. The imbalances in each case generate their own logic for corruption and the resulting patterns.

China has liberalized its economy earlier and more extensively, creating a larger and more vibrant non-state, and non-agricultural, sector. Waves of Chinese officials have quit their official posts to "jump into the sea of business". Those remaining in official posts seek shares and other forms of participation in business ventures. India's liberalization, in addition to its later start, has been limited by strong unions, lower classes, and a large agrarian sector. In contrast to the plethora of Chinese township and village enterprises (TVEs), FDI-invested firms, and other non-state enterprises, India's private enterprises are often owned by cliques of upper classes and castes.[40] India's famed IT and other offshoring industries employ a small fraction of its total labour force, with a huge contribution to overall economic growth.[41]

Politically, India's myriad of government institutions (executive, legislative, judicial and bureaucratic), electoral processes, and political parties – each at federal, state, and local levels – provide far more open and extensive political opportunities than China's one-party state. While the Indian bureaucracy draws its members from the urban, upper-caste, and middle professional classes, those from lower classes, lower-middle classes, and lower castes occupy clerical and other lower-level jobs in the administrative hierarchy. The electoral process has opened the political path to rural elites more recently, transforming the class character and social base of Indian politicians from upper and upper-middle classes, and professional backgrounds during the pre-Independence and early post-Independence days to rural and agricultural backgrounds. Big landlords constitute nearly 50–60 per cent of the members of Parliament at state levels, who bring their feudal mores of favour exchanging into the Parliament.[42] A constant and open "market for public office" has existed among bureaucrats and politicians eyeing official posts and promotions, which are available at fixed rates.[43]

In China, far fewer desirable political opportunities exist than economic ones. The electoral process is only available at the local level and opens the political path at that level only. Access to higher-level positions is more closed and depends much on steady promotion, careful cultivation, and (real or manipulated) performance evaluation. For ambitious individuals, state offices and managerial posts in state firms are still desired, thanks to the substantive economic decision powers (and thus material stakes and rents) involved. The Party positions, meanwhile, have become less attractive to professionally trained people.[44] The ruling party has stumbled into major difficulties in retaining and recruiting talented people for Party positions (such as branch Party secretaries), because these positions now have to compete with far more prestigious and lucrative professional and technocratic jobs in the expanding new economy. Many, or even most, non-state businesses do not have enough willing Party members to form Party branches or conduct regular Party activities, because Party identification has become irrelevant to their professional advancement. A "market for public office" does exist, but more in poor and inland regions with fewer economic alternatives than in developed regions, where multiple attractive alternatives are available for ambitious individuals and public office is but one of many career options and economically not the most attractive.[45]

The combination of elite accessibility and meagre economic opportunity can contribute to a fragmented patronage system in a poor democracy. The clientelism literature establishes a causal relation between democracy and corruption by suggesting that clients or voters desire patronage politics because it supplies extra-bureaucratic material benefits.[46] In such a political setting, as Johnston notes, political elites are not only accessible but seek power amid weak institutions, intense political competition, and scarce economic opportunities. They therefore depend on building personal patronage systems to secure and maintain power. Yet because material rewards are scarce and political opportunities more plentiful, patronage politics is fragmented. Elites build personal followings, rather than broad-based parties, and find them hard to control due to a chronic shortage of material rewards. Such patronage politics may also involve more sinister groups that resort to intimidation and violence.[47]

These characteristics have afflicted India's political system. Efforts by politicians to create broad organizational support have often failed because "the ordinary voter has an extremely narrow view of public responsibility and is not willing to give time and effort without the promise of immediate material reward".[48] Robert Wade finds the Indian electorate "primarily swayed by material and particularistic inducements" and "people vote for whom they think can give them the most favour, in a particularistic way". A cohesive, policy-oriented political party would be unlikely to survive in this type of electorate.[49] Material rewards can also purchase stability for government or alter the arithmetic of elected representatives, by engineering defections in Parliament through monetary payoffs. Money can even recruit "muscle", i.e. violent or criminal groups that extort contributions, scare off opponents, and intimidate voters, a process that has "criminalized" Indian politics at the local level.[50] The result is referred to as the "criminalization" of politics or even as "bandit democracy".[51]

China's centralized and non-competitive structures tend to produce joint monopolies in the corruption process. The Chinese system has been decentralized by devolving power to local levels, yet decision-making at each level remains centralized – usually in the chief executive of a state agency or public enterprise. Since this decentralization has come amid a retreat of hierarchal control from above and weak supervision from below, the result has been effectively localized centralization. This process has allowed the local chief executive office to become the main locus of favour exchanges at the local government level, especially in less developed and inland regions and at the county level and below, where central and outside monitoring is weakest. Such local political monopolies can constitute "local predatory states".[52] At the same time, centralized structures and processes of illicit exchange may also result in a relatively lesser degree of dissipation and with potentially less detrimental outcomes, from the standpoint of development.[53] That is, centralized corruption paradoxically produces two "efficiency" effects, relative to a fragmented patronage system. At one end, bidders for government favours, rather than having to squander resources on multiple state agencies or agents, need to bribe only the principal power holders. At the other end, officials in an authoritarian system do not depend on these favour bidders to seek and maintain power, therefore, they have control over who gets access and benefits, and on what terms.

Chinese corruption, however, does not just consist of illicit activities involving exchanges between officials and societal groups. It also involves a variety of kinds of theft from the public coffer. Because many public projects and a few key sectors remain in the ownership and/or administration of the state, they are ready targets for bureaucratic predators through a variety of government projects: privatization programmes, land allocation, developmental assistance, relocation funds, infrastructure projects, administrative funding, banking, transportation, etc. In activities involving effective theft of public resources, local political monopolies can cause far more detriment and dissipation, since key officials have unchecked control over the dispersal of those resources.[54] Centralized corruption, thus, has both "efficiency" and inefficiency effects. In this sense, the lack of political opportunities, or the lack of contending groups in the political process to ensure accountability, is a structural liability of the Chinese case.

Decision-making access

Another difference in the patterns of corruption in our two cases is the access to policy-making by private interests. Elite accessibility entails greater influence by private interests than does elite autonomy, with some paradoxical consequences.

Typical of a democracy, in India, politicians depend on campaign financing from the business world, both to fund elections and tighten their grip on constituencies.[55] Changing technologies of the mobilization of political support have intensified this financial dependence. Whereas in the "old days" mobilization through public sector patronage (e.g. jobs) might have been effective, when parties operated as political machines, the increasing importance in the contemporary world of mobilization through electronic technologies (television commercials, etc.) and the use of pollsters, has made financial contributions more important. The degree to which campaign finance contributes to corruption, of course, depends more on the nature of the institutional regime regulating it than on democracy itself or even the nature of a poor democracy. But the combination of weak institutions, insecure elites, and scarce economic resources make a poor democracy all the more vulnerable to the problem of campaign finance as a source of corruption.

The sources of campaign funds, as a former Central Vigilance Commissioner of India writes, "greatly affect the motivations and actions of the politicians who benefit from them".[56] Before economic liberalization, the business sector contributed out of "its dependence on government for licenses and permits to establish and operate its businesses and also for patronage and protection", exercising influence through formal lobbying efforts and informal and decentralized contacts with the state machinery and political parties, and receiving huge returns by way of favourable and exclusive fiscal and industrial benefits and policies.[57] Though economic liberalization since the early 1990s has shrunk the administrative base of corruption by cutting regulatory controls at higher levels, it has not affected corruption in policy-making at all levels or regulatory roles at lower levels. In fact, it has expanded corruption at policy-making levels by marrying economic liberalization and the democratic process. Economic liberalization has opened new opportunities for India's exclusive cliques of tycoons and contractors to influence economic decision-making at key junctures of power from the highest levels: policy decisions on divestment of government investment in public enterprises, preferred buyout of state assets, provision of subsidized finance, selective termination of government monopoly on service sectors, government investment in new public projects and other lucrative business deals and contacts.[58]

In China, the lack of fund-raising pressure on elites or political access for business groups at higher decision levels ensures that corruption occurs mainly at the implementation and local levels, after central decisions have been already made. Even in China, it has become common for localities and sectors to have offices in the capital to lobby central ministries for projects and financing, and industrial lobbying groups have increasingly sought and won national policy advantages.[59] The dynamic is, however, fundamentally different. Whereas in India every politician and political party needs to raise campaign funds (and most will pocket some personally, as well), out of the twin pressures of the political and personal, in China it is the illicit officials who accept kickbacks out of personal motives. Whereas in India business groups can demand policy patronage from politicians at the national level through large-scale bribery or contribution, in China it is as yet impossible for businesses to induce politburo members, top state executives, or national legislators this way. In China a different institutional pressure for corruption has been on the rise: corruption carried out collectively by a public agency. For example, a state agency may accept a kickback from the recipients of its fund allocation. It is an effective strategy to avoid individual culpability. The loci of institutional corruption, however, remain at the implementation level and the objective is often personal. Usually, the spoils are shared as welfare benefits within the agency.[60]

One paradoxical consequence of political access to central policy-making, or the lack thereof, may be the impact on a key issue in current debates about the potential and prospects of China and India as emerging economies. Thanks to influence-peddled lobbying (in part or in major part), Indian businesses have been able to demand "a level playing field" and fend off policies favouring foreign investors. Some Indian analysts view this as a negative consequence, because the real dynamics of the policy is patronage politics, available to both

Indian or foreign industrialists for a price.[61] Others blame the fallout of such corruption for the country's failure to attract more foreign investment. Nonetheless, the political access of India's domestic industries must be surely envied by their Chinese counterpart. Although Chinese industries have lobbied for levelling the playing field with foreign investors, they have not been successful. Pending changes in FDI policies have come mainly from changing national needs and interests, rather than from industry pressures.[62]

If indeed, India's indigenously-led growth holds long-term advantages over China's FDI-led growth,[63] and if China's FDI policies have privileged foreign firms at the detriment of domestic private enterprise,[64] then corruption at higher decision levels in India would seem to bear out one important benefit of elite accessibility and an open political system.

Politician–bureaucrat nexus

Another comparable dimension of corruption in the two cases is the collusion of politicians and bureaucrats in the Indian case, and the unintended consequences of separating the Party and state in the Chinese case.

In the wrangling between the political and administrative, India's democracy should start with inherent structural advantages: periodic elections should keep politicians in check, who should in turn keep bureaucrats in check. India's long tradition of a sharp separation between politicians who formulate policies and bureaucrats who implement them should be an added advantage. Nonetheless, as a major locus of political power, accumulated from India's imperial, colonial, and socialist legacies, the Indian bureaucracy has become a major source of corruption. The root problem is the collusive ties between bureaucrats and politicians. Wade's earlier observation still rings true today: Indian politicians compel the bureaucracy to acquiesce in their nefarious activities by controlling a system of rewards and punishments (appointments to or transfer out of "cushy jobs").[65]

Bureaucrats, in turn, seek political patronage "to escape unwanted places and unpopular posts" as well as to share spoils. A relationship of quid pro quo thus exists between them: politicians supply opportunities and protection while bureaucrats dispense official favours and patronage.[66] These motives and ties are unabated, though reoriented, under economic liberalization. Instead of the myriad of regulatory controls at the discretion of bureaucrats, favour dispensing now manifests through "arbitrary award of contracts, sanctioning of deals and investment projects without competitive bidding or transparency. The 'license permit raj' has been replaced by the 'tender raj.' "[67]

In the Chinese case, reforms have been introduced to separate Party and state functions in local governments and public firms. Rather than ending the over-concentration of power, however, the reforms have led to unintended consequences leading to new over-concentration of power.[68] Under the separation, Party organizations and officials exit from routine administrative and managerial functions but retain control over key personnel matters and perform oversight functions. However, Party oversight has become ineffective in most cases, while

Party-bureaucratic collusion results in other cases. One problem is that the appointment of personnel below the top ranks now falls under the prerogatives of the administrative/managerial strata, as do routine decision powers. Party officials are usually not involved in decision-making at administrative and managerial levels, where substantive power lies and engenders more occasions for illicit deals. Second, in public enterprises, Party posts are no longer desired by the best and brightest individuals, who prefer professional and technocratic career paths. In small state firms where Party officials are appointed within the firm, they may even face job dismissal by managers. Thus Party posts are often concurrently held by key administrative or managerial personnel, a practice that renders Party oversight impossible.

In less developed and rural regions of China, collusion between Party officials and administrative chiefs is similar to India's case. As the former offers "sale of office" and protection for cronies, the latter engages in "purchase of office" and favour dispersion. The collusion has contributed to local "corruption networks" wherein layers of officials and private bribers are directly or indirectly linked in "cluster cases". The last decade has seen a surge of such cases in China, especially in poor counties and provinces.[69]

The qualitative differences between the two cases, as identified in the contrast of structural conditions for corruption in this section, again bolster the argument that India's democracy has not outperformed China in corruption. A weak state (elite accessibility), with political opportunities but economic scarcities, has simply produced different types of corruption, not less of it, than a stronger state (elite autonomy) with less political opportunities but greater economic opportunities.

Corruption and regime legitimacy

Finally, this section looks at whether regime types make a difference in terms of corruption's impact on political legitimacy. Have the essential elements of a democracy, i.e. competitive elections, an independent judiciary, a parliamentary opposition, and a free press, served to undermine corrupt regimes in India, thus potentially deterring corruption more effectively than China could?

In reality, corruption has made little difference on regime legitimacy in either case. In India, corruption has served as an issue in delegitimizing a particular regime, but not in bringing about a cleaner one. Incumbent politicians and parties are often vulnerable to "anti-incumbency" sentiments in the country's electoral politics. Yet the electorate often ousts corrupt governments only to have no option but to bring in another corrupt government. The futility of anti-incumbency voting highlights again the importance of structural and institutional factors facilitating corruption in the Indian system. Consequently, the public has a low level of trust in the government no matter who or which party is in power, with the net impact of corruption on legitimacy of particular parties in power being inconsequential.[70] As one finance bureaucrat observes, "corruption does not adversely affect the legitimacy of particular governments", because

> there does not seem to be any difference from one party to the other. Whoever comes to power indulges in corruption, people feel. There is a total apathy towards the political system among the public. The general opinion is that there is no difference between Tweedledum and Tweedledee.[71]

A highly fractured society such as India's also renders "rational public opinion" difficult, as group identities, educational disparities and other socioeconomic factors influence political awareness.[72]

Still another neutralizing factor is the cooptation and incorporation of the political opposition into the collusive and sharing network of political and bureaucratic corruption. Like ruling parties, opposition parties, too, depend on private capital for campaign funds and self-seeking.[73] Since members of these parties are often readily available for defection at a price, they are also easily persuaded to look the other way on corruption matters. The judiciary, though independent, has increasingly lost its effect as an instrument against corruption since the end of the Nehru era. Besides the general erosion of good leadership, a key reason is that the power of sanctioning discipline and prosecution rests with the executive branch, which has authorized few cases for prosecution. Long delays, manipulation of judicial processes, and corrosion of judicial appointments, further compound the problem. In such a political environment, the media and civil critics have also found it difficult to have their criticisms taken seriously or to demand accountability.[74]

Ironically, the monopoly of the Chinese Communist Party (CCP) also means it has to take the blame for the corruption of its rank and file, with attendant liabilities. The CCP may tolerate few political and media critics at home, but it constantly faces comparative assessment against two alternative models: the relatively clean and egalitarian Mao era on the one hand and the example of mature democracies on the other. The former helps to undermine the CCP's legitimacy from the left, and the latter, from the right. Farmers and workers of down-sized state enterprises have expressed pent-up frustration through riots and surveys over their deplorable transformation – from being the core social base of the CCP during the Mao era to being the prime victims of inequality and corruption in the era of economic liberalization.[75] Indeed, land grab from farmers has become a major form of contemporary corruption in the Chinese countryside, while mismanagement and insider privatization are frequent causes of bankrupt state enterprises. On the right, critics abroad and some intellectuals at home see one-party monopoly as the root cause of corruption and look to a multiparty system and parliamentary democracy as fundamental solutions.

Compounding the liabilities for the CCP is the public awareness of the corruption problem, despite a dearth of transparent politics. Word of mouth is a potent channel of communication in a communal culture. Corruption stories are also reinforced by first-hand experiences with state agencies, most of which nowadays charge excessive fees for routine services. Both the Party and the media also publicize details of major corruption cases once they are exposed.[76] The media increasingly reports ongoing abuses by local cadres, a practice sanctioned by the

CCP.[77] Criticizing corruption is not itself equated with attacking the Party and remains morally and historically legitimated in Chinese society. It was the Chinese people, after all, who staged the famous Tiananmen protests against corruption long before the "colourful" revolutions of post-Soviet republics. The judiciary is a further liability for the Party's legitimacy, being politically dependent but increasingly compromised by its concern with commercial interests.

Nevertheless, regime legitimacy has not been critically undermined by widespread corruption in post-Mao China.[78] One major reason may resemble the neutralizing effect of corruption's ubiquity, as in India's case. As corruption becomes mostly materially based, it is now more accessible, less exclusive and less inflammatory than in the early years of economic reform. Contemporary corruption, moreover, is no longer seen as directly caused by central policies, as was the case during the earlier years of reform. Rather, it is now viewed more as the errant behaviour of officials at local levels. In fact, when local protesters and rioters complain about localized injustices, they are more likely to demand that central policies be upheld and not deviated from and distorted. Another key reason may be that the top national leadership remains clean and devoted to national development. The "princeling party", or children of top leaders, including those of Deng Xiaoping and Party head Zhao Ziyang, was tarnished during the "official profiteering" of the 1980s, a main complaint of Tiananmen protesters. The leaders themselves were credibly clean and firmly willing to ban family members from doing business. The children of many top leaders remain prominently engaged in business, but the success of many other ordinary individuals has diffused this as a politically explosive issue. Below the top leadership, a few provincial governors and party secretaries, several deputy central ministers, and an increasing number of deputy provincial governors have been brought down by corruption scandals, but the effect of such high-level exposure on regime legitimacy remains ambiguous, as they seem to undermine the Party's credibility as much as they repair it, if only temporarily. Finally, harsh crackdowns, though erratic, are still frequent reminders of the limits of wanton transgression.

In short, the Chinese state is not itself organized for rent capture, nor is it dependent upon the exchange of official favours for political survival. Both conditions would likely pose serious legitimacy problems for a one-party authoritarian regime. Whether these two conditions exist in the Indian system may be a point of debate, but either way, they have made no significant impact on regime legitimacy, in reality. In other words, regime type once again has made little difference.

Conclusion

Both the quantitative and qualitative evidence reported in this chapter has lent sufficient support for my argument: democracy in the poor, developing, country of India has not proven to be more successful at tackling corruption than the authoritarian, developmental, state of China. While it may not have done significantly worse, it has not done meaningfully better.

This basic finding contributes to our understanding how regime types interact with the dynamics of corruption in transitional and developing settings. Thanks to a combination of the sources of corruption that characteristically affect weak democracies, on the one hand, and those that typically afflict transitional economies on the other, liberalization of politics without essential institutional or economic foundations will not reduce corruption, but rather increase it. Thus, driven by political openness but economic compulsion (both personally and politically), India is affected by both political and bureaucratic corruption, and at both national and local levels. Yet constrained by closed politics, institutional continuity and tempered economic pressures (i.e. politically), China is more shielded from political corruption at the national level and is mainly afflicted with bureaucratic corruption at sub-national levels.

The Indian case offers some important lessons for China's political liberalization. In India's case, the primary fact of corruption is that politically and economically ambitious elites are insecure. This insecurity is fuelled by poorly institutionalized opportunities and by contention. In such a setting of weak institutions and intense competition, elites rely on building personal support or patronage systems from which they exploit the state and the economy. Moreover, where political and legal institutions increasingly deteriorate and civil society fragments, elites resort to "money and muscle" to secure and pursue power – and then wealth – resulting in a "criminalization of politics" or even a "bandit democracy". Pervasive insecurity also ensures that corruption and violence are too tempting as alternatives to institutional means. In such contexts, further liberalization in the name of reform "may well make things worse, erasing the feeble boundaries between wealth and power, state and society, and adding insecurity at all levels of society".[79]

Institutional continuity and partial reform, as in China's case, have thus served to lessen insecurity or the stakes of contention for elites in a period of rapid transition, easing the pressures for out-of-control abuse and violence. China's partial reform strategy, in other words, has served to prevent a worse scenario of corruption by building economic opportunities and market institutions before firing up political competition. The main advantage is to have reduced elite insecurity and institutional uncertainty while expanding legitimate alternatives to corrupt ways of pursuing and defending economic self-interest. The short- and middle-term reforms should be to build or further strengthen institutions that serve to guarantee legitimate economic deals and political rights. Economically, these include property rights, market oversight bodies, sound banks and currency, reliable and fair capital markets, and codes of business practices backed by rewards and sanctions.[80] Politically, legally, and socially, the priority should be to build the "liberal" part of liberal democracy: rule of law, constitutionalism, separated power, professional bureaucracy, protection of property, and other basic rights, and media openness.

Given the widening social inequalities under China's economic liberalization, any discussion of political liberalization should also consider the political fallout of procedural democracy too quickly, too soon. By opening up political opportunities and elite accessibility, it is likely to enhance the influence and interest peddling of already privileged nouveau rich groups, thereby contributing to new forms of corruption. These new forms, moreover, will be most likely at the policy and legislative levels, nationally, provincially, and locally. To the extent that corruption itself is undemocratic, as it limits political access for less powerful groups, increased corruption at the policy and law-making levels will simply create new forms of tyranny. As my comparative cases illustrate, an unstructured and unruly democracy can undermine genuine liberty and rule of law, while serving the interests of a few.

Notes

1 Dali Yang, *Breaking the Chinese Leviathan: Market Transition and the Politics and Governance in China*, Stanford: Stanford University Press, 2004.
2 Minxin Pei, *China's Trapped Transition: The Limits of Developmental Autocracy*, Cambridge: Harvard University Press, 2006.
3 For the association between economic liberalization and corruption, see for example, Yan Sun, *Corruption and Market in Contemporary China*, Ithaca: Cornell 2004; Marshall Goldman, *The Piratization of Russia: Russian Reform Goes Awry*, New York and London: Routledge, 2003; and Vadim Volkov, *Violent Entrepreneurs: The Use of Force in the Making of Russian Capitalism*, Ithaca: Cornell University Press, 2002. This is the case even in liberalizing societies not of the post-socialist kind. See e.g. Kurt Weyland, "The Politics of Corruption in Latin America", *Journal of Democracy* 9, April 1998, pp. 108–21; Robero Pablo Saba and Luigi Manzetti, "Privatization in Argentina: The implications for corruption", *Crime, Law and Social Change* 25, 1997, pp. 353–69; David Watt, Rachel Flanary, and Robin Theobald, "Democratization or the Democratization of corruption? The Case of Uganda", in Alan Doig and Robin Theobald (eds), *Corruption and Democratization*, London: Frank Cass, 1999, pp. 37–63; Moises Naim, "The Corruption Eruption", *Brown Journal of World Affairs* II/2, Summer 1995, pp. 245–61; and Raymond A. Hinnebush, "The Political Economy of Economic Liberalization in Syria", *International Journal of Middle East Studies* 27, 1995, pp. 305–20.
4 Robin Theobald, *Development, Underdevelopment and Corruption*, Durham: Duke University, 1990.
5 Robert Wade, *Governing the Market*, Princeton: Princeton University, 1990, pp. 333–42; Paul Hutchcroft, "Booty Capitalism in the Philippines", in Andrew MacIntyre (ed.), *Business and Government in Industrializing Asia*, Ithaca: Cornell University Press, 1995, p. 221; and Hutchcroft, *Booty Capitalism: The Politics of Banking in the Philippines*, Ithaca: Cornell University Press, 1998.
6 Michael Johnston, "Public Officials, Private Interests and Sustainable Democracy: When Politics and Corruption Meet", in Kimberly Ann Elliott (ed.), *Corruption and the Global Economy*, Washington DC: Institute of International Economics, 1997, p. 73.
7 Wade, *Governing the Market*, pp. 333–42.
8 Johnston, "Public Officials", pp. 68–9.
9 Samuel Huntington, *Political Order in Changing Societies*, New Haven: Yale University Press, 1968, pp. 59–71.
10 Johnston, "Public Officials", 68–74.
11 The forgoing discussion is mainly based on Johnston, "Public Officials", 70–3.
12 Johnston, *Syndromes of Corruption: Wealth, Power, and Democracy*, London and New York: Cambridge University Press, 2005, p. 44.
13 David Kang, *Crony Capitalism: Corruption and Development in South Korea and the Philippines*, London and New York: Cambridge University Press, 2002.

14 Hutchcroft, "Booty Capitalism in the Philippines", p. 221.
15 Cited in Georg Sorensen, "Democracy, Authoritarianism and State Strength", *European Journal of Development Research* 5:1, 1993, p. 9.
16 Chai and Roy's comparative study suggests that the Indian economy is about ten years behind China's; see Joseph C. H. Chai and Kartik C. Roy, *Economic Reform in China and India: Development Experience in a Comparative Perspective*, Northampton: Edward Elgar Publishing, 2006.
17 Andei Shleifer and Robert W. Vishny, "Corruption", *Quarterly Journal of Economics* 58:3, 1993, p. 599. Under joint monopoly, one may need to bribe only the chief official, rather than numerous ones as under independent monopoly.
18 Sun, *Corruption and Market*, chapters 4 and 5.
19 Pei, *China's Trapped Transition*, in his chapter 4, sees the "local predatory state" as a more general and widespread problem than Sun, *Corruption and Market*, in her chapters 4–5.
20 J. Bhagwati, "Directly Unproductive Profit Seeking Activity", *Journal of Political Economy* 76, 1982, pp. 169–217.
21 P. K. Bardhan, *Political Economy of Development in India*, Oxford: Basil Blackwell, 1984.
22 Fareed Zakaria, *The Future of Freedom: Illiberal Democracies at Home and Abroad*, New York and London: W. W. Norton, 2004, p. 109.
23 For the role of Taiwanese and Hong Kong businesspeople in China's corruption, see Sun, *Corruption and Market*, pp. 105–6.
24 Interviews of Chinese IT executives in Silicon Valley, California.
25 Leslie Palmier, *The Control of Bureaucratic Corruption: Case Studies in Asia*, New Delhi: Allied Publishers 1985, p. 271.
26 J. V. Abueva, "What are We in Power for? The Sociology of Graft and Corruption", *Philippine Sociological Review* 18:3–4, July–October 1970, pp. 203–8.
27 Jeffrey Sachs, *The End of Poverty*, New York: Penguin Press, 2005.
28 Shahid M. Alam, "Anatomy of Corruption: An Approach to the Political Economy of Underdevelopment", *American Journal of Economics and Sociology*, 48:4, October 1989, pp. 441–56 and Peter Ward (ed.), *Corruption, Development and Inequality*, New York and London: Routledge, 1989.
29 Jong-sung You and Sanjeev Khagram, "A Comparative Study of Inequality and Corruption", *American Sociological Review* 70, 2005, pp. 136–57.
30 Colin Leys, "What is the Problem with Corruption?" *Journal of Modern African Studies* 3:2, 1967 and S. K. Dash, *Public Office, Private Interest: Bureaucracy and Corruption in India*, New Delhi: Oxford University Press, 2001, p. 110.
31 Gunnar Myrdal, "Corruption as a Hindrance to Modernization in South Asia", in Arnold J. Heidenheimer, Michael Johnston, and Victor T. LeVine (eds), *Political Corruption: A Hand Book*, New Brunswick: Transaction Books, 1989, pp. 414–15.
32 Cited in Das, *Public Office, Private Interest*, p. 105.
33 Robert Wade, "The Market for Public Office: Why the Indian State is not Better at Development", *World Development* 13, 1985, p. 486.
34 Jon S. T. Quah, *Curbing Corruption in Asia: A Comparative Study of Six Countries*, Singapore: Eastern University Press, 2003, pp. 58–77.
35 Vinod Pavarala, *Interpreting Corruption: Elite Perspectives in India*, New Delhi: Sage Publications, 1996, pp. 110–11.
36 Hans Schenk, "Corruption … What Corruption? Notes on Bribery and Dependency in Urban India", in Ward, *Corruption, Development and Inequality*, pp. 110–23.
37 Julie Kwong, *The Political Economy of Corruption in China*, Armonk: M. E. Sharpe, 1997 and Alan Liu, "The Politics of Corruption in the People's Republic of China", *American Political Science Review* 77:2, 1983, pp. 602–21.

38 Most notably, see Sun, *Corruption and Market*; Pei, *Trapped Transition*; and Melanie Manion, *Corruption by Design: Building Clean Government in Hong Kong and China*, Cambridge: Harvard University Press, 2004.
39 Sun, *Corruption and Market*, chapter 4.
40 Pavarala puts the per cent of local enterprises owned by upper castes in Andhra Pradesh at nearly 80 per cent, in Pavarala, *Interpreting Corruption*, p. 33.
41 Stephen Cohen, *India as Emerging Power*, Washington DC: Brookings: 2001, p. 105.
42 Pavarala, *Interpreting Corruption*, p. 100.
43 Robert Wade, "System of Administrative and Political Corruption: Canal Irrigation in South India", *Journal of Development Studies* 18, April 1982, pp. 287–328.
44 Information for much of the rest of the paragraph is based on surveys and investigations by various organizational departments of the Chinese Communist Party at central and local levels, collected in Li Huibin and Xue Xiaoyuan (eds), *Investigative Reports on China: Changing Socioeconomic Relations and the Building of the Party*, Beijing: Social Science Documents Press, 2003.
45 For the problem of office for sale, see Sun, *Corruption and Market*, pp. 145–7 and Pei, *China's Trapped Transition*, pp. 145–6.
46 Cited in Oskar Kurer, "Why do Voters Support Corrupt Politicians?", in Jain, *The Political Economy of Corruption*, p. 68.
47 Johnston, "Public Officials", p. 73.
48 Cited in Kurer, "Why do Voters Support Corrupt Politicians?", pp. 68–9.
49 Wade, "The Market for Public Office", pp. 479, 486–7.
50 Robert Hardgrave and Stanley Kochanek, *India: Government and Politics in a Developing Nation*, New York: Wadsworth Publishing, 1999, chapter 7.
51 Zakaria, *The Future of Freedom*, p. 109.
52 Pei, *China's Trapped Transition*, Chapter 4.
53 Shleifer and Vishny, "Corruption", p. 599 and Andrew Wedeman, "Looters, Rent-scrappers, and Dividend-collectors: Corruption and Growth in Zaire, South Korea, and the Philippines", *Journal of Developing Areas* 31, Summer 1997, pp. 457–78.
54 For a detailed treatment of transaction and non-transaction types of corruption and their consequences in the Chinese case, see Sun, *Corruption and Market*, chapters 2 and 3.
55 Lal, *Corruption: Functional Anarchy in Governance*, New Delhi: Siddharth Publications, 2002, p. 144.
56 Nagarajan Vittal, "Corruption and the State: India, Technology, and Transparency", *Harvard International Review* Fall 2001, p. 22.
57 Pavarala, *Interpreting Corruption*, p. 31 and Lal, *Corruption*, p. 144.
58 Vittal, *Corruption in India*, pp. 38–9.
59 Scott Kennedy, *The Business of Lobbying in China*, Cambridge: Harvard University Press, 2005.
60 See Sun, *Corruption and Market*, chapters. 3 and 4 and Xiaobo Lu, "Booty Socialism, Bureau-preneurs, and the State in Transition: Organizational Corruption in China", *Comparative Politics* 32:3, 2000, pp. 273–94.
61 Lal, *Corruption*, p. 184.
62 The Chinese National People's Congress is set to pass a new enterprise tax law in March 2007, which will phase out preferential tax rates for foreign investors. The implementation is expected to take place before 2008. The move is due to a combination of issues, including China's already high capital reserve and economic security concerns associated with foreign takeover of major industrial and commercial sectors through increasing buyout.
63 See Yasheng Huang and Tarun Khanna, "Can India Overtake China?", *Foreign Policy* July–August 2003.
64 Yasheng Huang, "A Tale of Two Provinces: Private Sector Investment, Growth and FDI", available at www.info.worldbank.org/etools/docs/library/86421/.

65 Wade, "System of Administrative and Political Corruption", pp. 286–321 and "The Market for Public Office", pp. 467–89.
66 P. C. Alexander, *The Perils of Democracy*, Bombay: Somaiya Publications, 1995.
67 Lal, *Corruption*, pp. 184–91.
68 Information in this paragraph is based on surveys carried out by the party's personnel department in various localities, in Li and Xue, *Investigative Reports on China.*
69 Principal–agent problems entailed by the separation of party and state are best described in Sun, *Corruption and Market*, chapter 5; and local corruption networks in her chapter 4. See also Pei, *China's Trapped Transition*, chapter 4.
70 Pavarala, *Interpreting Corruption*, p. 151.
71 From an Indian Administrative Service officer in the finance ministry, cited in Pavarala, *Interpreting Corruption*, p. 151.
72 Lal, *Corruption*, pp. 145–6 and Pavarala, *Interpreting Corruption*, pp. 151–2.
73 Das, *Public Office, Private Interest*, p. 194 and Lal, *Corruption*, pp. 144–5.
74 Das, *Public Office, Private Interest*, pp. 174–5, 192–5 and Zakaria, *The Future of Freedom*, pp. 109–10.
75 Li and Xue, *Investigative Reports on China.*
76 See the list of national and local periodicals related to corruption matters, in Sun, *Corruption and Market*, pp. 219–22.
77 "The CCP Issues Document to Promote the Media's Oversight Power", *Qiao Bao*, 20 April 2005.
78 Information in this paragraph is based on Sun, "Corruption, Growth and Reform: The Chinese Enigma", *Current History* September 2004, p. 262.
79 Johnston, *Syndromes of Corruption*, p. 207.
80 Johnston recommends these reforms to deal with Russian-type oligarchic corruption, and different reforms for China. I feel that his suggestions for Russia are more appropriate for China. See Johnston, *Syndromes of Corruption*, p. 208.

11 Conclusion

Social tension and political adaptation under globalization

Guoguang Wu

As the material wealth of China has been fast accumulating with double digits of economic growth for about three decades, social tensions and unrest have grown remarkably to a degree that the nation has never seen before in its contemporary history under communist rule. This volume has presented a collective endeavour to examine some major issues that fuel social tensions, which range widely from the rise of unemployment and rural–urban migrants, to the decline both of healthcare and state capacity to administrate citizens' spiritual life. It also attempts to look at how political institutions of authoritarian China work to accommodate the conflicts via various possible means, including policy adjustments, legal reforms, and political institutional adaptation. Moreover, the individual chapters, as one can easily sense when reading them, more or less point to a grand question for comprehending the big picture of transitional China. This can be summarized as how the convergence of the Leninist party-state and the market mechanisms shapes today's Chinese social landscape and how the combination, acclaimed by some as a success of so-called "Beijing consensus", addresses human development and deals with the social challenges that affect the quality of life of China's citizens.

Drawing conclusions from the preceding chapters, this chapter suggests the following arguments: (1) both the political and institutional legacies of Maoist socialism as once practiced in China prior to reforms and the introduction of capitalist market mechanisms into such a political and institutional environment greatly contribute to the rise of social problems; (2) this unique institutional combination featuring the embracing of capitalist globalization by the authoritarian Chinese party-state is impotent to address the social conflicts, although it has made efforts to do so; (3) today's China, though favoured by Leftists because of its claimed socialism and international power to check the United States, and also by Western capital for its contribution to the global causes of profit-making, actually has neither capitalist nor socialist merit, particularly in terms of managing social issues. Rather, the combination negates the ability of either socialism, even the Leninist kind, or capitalism to govern social transformations. With the embracing of marketization and globalization, China has betrayed the socialist principles of egalitarianism and humanism; with the still dogmatic attachment to so-called "socialism with Chinese characteristics", the

Chinese authorities repress and contain the social forces, often arising with the development of a capitalist economy, which lead to the gaining of social benefits for citizens.

To be sure, China has achieved astonishing economic prosperity with this hybrid of Leninist political institutions of socialism with the marketization strategy of developmental capitalism. This simply makes the situation more perplexed than otherwise, however. Why is economic development accompanied by social unrest in China? Is social tension an inevitable by-product of fast economic growth? How does the Chinese authoritarian regime respond to the social problems? Will the regime successfully deal with the problems as it did with the post-Tiananmen crisis? How does the rise of social unrest affect state-society relations in transitional China? Is there any possibility of political transition from authoritarianism taking place under growing social pressure?

Based on the analyses of the proceeding chapters, this concluding chapter attempts an examination of these questions, while focusing on the interactions between the rise of social problems and the state strategies to deal with them. In the pages that follow, we shall first look at why social tensions and unrest arise against the background of China's successful economic development, inquiring into the patterns and characters of the social problems that trouble the authoritarian regime and the nation in general. The chapter then turns to an analysis of strategies taken by the state to deal with the problems, with the emphasis on those measures in regard to social policy adjustments and political institutional adaptation. In the last section before the concluding remarks, the chapter will discuss the implications of the spreading of social unrest and the rise of social forces to China's long-impending political transition.

Why social tensions with economic prosperity? Developmental and institutional causes

Public protests have been rising at a time when the party-state proclaims the prosperity (*shengshi*) of today's China, as shown by many chapters of this volume, particularly Chapter 2 by Jay Chen. This observation is based on the official statistics released by the Chinese national government, which reveal that public protests, or "mass incidents" (*quntixing shijian*), in the governmental terminology, have dramatically escalated tenfold from 1993, the year immediately following the beginning of China's post-Tiananmen marketization waves in 1992, to 2005, the latest year with such governmental statistics available. Yes, a few defences occurred here or there to argue that this is nothing, or nothing deserving special attention, as such tensions were more severe in seventeenth- or eighteenth-century's Europe of industrialization, or, in a more sophisticated line of reasoning, that this is actually an achievement of good governance, as protests indicate the trust of protesters in the government to resolve the problems. Most people, including Chinese party-state leaders, however, do not deny this trend of increasing social turmoil and its negative implications for the nation. As social tensions mean massive human suffering, they also doubtlessly present tremendous challenges to both the governance of China and the model of development that China has claimed to be successful.

Various sources fuel the rise of social protests in contemporary China, widely ranging from workers' wage problems to resistance by suppressed religious groups. The underlying causes, however, can be roughly divided into two major categories: developmental and institutional. The first refers to those issues brought about by fast growth of the economy, by overspent material and social costs of such growth, and by ineffective transferring of economic wealth to social sectors during such growth. The second is rooted in the existing political economic institutions that govern China's development. Together, they have intensified those concrete issues which cause social unrest. Empirical evidence strongly supports this analysis, as exemplified in the dramatic increase of petitioners who seek assistance from the national government to alleviate their sufferings. According to Keyuan Zou (Chapter 8), while the year of 1993, namely, the year just after Deng Xiaoping's trip to Southern China revitalized the marketization reform, clearly marked the coming peak of petitions, most of the petition cases being related to the encroachment of the relevant government or its personnel upon the interests and rights of ordinary citizens in the name of promoting economic development.

Land dispute stands out as the foremost type around which social tensions increase between the state and capital, on the one hand, and urban and rural residents, on the other. Such disputes mainly take the form of citizen protests over the terms and inadequate compensation offered for their requisitioned houses for urban development, and, in rural areas, of farmers' resistance to seizure of their lands by local government and developers with the underpaying of their compensations (Chen, Chapter 2). A minor yet rising problem in this category is with the private homeowners who already have moved in the newly developed real estate struggling for their legitimate terms of rights and services. The disputes are prevailing everywhere in China, as Chen points out, because the "forced demolition and eviction" (*qiangzhi chaiqian*) ignite the resistance and collective action of poor people, while the discontents over post-development deliveries of services are causing homeowners to protest.

It is apparent that rapid development causes such problems. Economic development, however, always takes place under a kind of institutional arrangement. The marketization of real estate, on the one hand, leads to the overturn of socialist principles in housing affairs by the state that still claims itself "socialist", as Chen argues in Chapter 2, and to the termination of welfare housing and transformation of publicly-owned homes into private homes. On the other hand, while China has been marching towards a market society since the late 1970s, state power still takes a lead, and even expands, in some dimensions with economic development, while at the same time it shrinks in terms of intervening in the daily life of citizens, in comparison with Mao's politics.[1] Specifically speaking on the issue of land, the Chinese state, as it has been constructed since 1949 as a Leninist socialist state, still monopolizes this indispensable and irreplaceable resource of development. With the marketization of productive means, the state, consisting of various levels of authorities and a huge number of bureaucrats, now tries to make use of this monopolized resource for its organizational, departmental, and individual benefit. Political institutions of China that lack popular supervision and citizens' checks over state power allow huge space for governments and bureaucrats to manipulate the opportunities provided by urban development and rural industrialization for their private benefit, at the cost of the public interest, as demonstrated by their management of land seizures.

Another instance is the *hukou* system, or the Chinese household registration system, as it is investigated by Xiaogang Wu in Chapter 3, which demonstrates how the institutional arrangements established during Maoist socialism are now joined by marketization to create social inequality, while working well to promote economic development. In Mao's China, the *hukou* system had an economic function as a tool of political control, as it was designed to exclude the rural populace from access to opportunities and benefits conferred by the socialist state upon urbanites. The current Party-state that embraces capitalist globalization, however, does not rescind this institutional discrimination against rural residents. Rather, it easily takes advantage of it for a new purpose of capitalism, which is the ensuring of the supply of cheap labour, the most valuable source of support for China's competitiveness in the world and, therefore, for China's economic prosperity. In other words, this socialist institutional legacy, having once created a second class of citizen during Mao's years, retains this function under capitalist marketization, directly resulting in the discrimination suffered by the 79 million (a total greater than the population of either France or Britain, as Wu points out) of *mingong*, or rural–urban migrant workers. They are denied the rights and benefits of citizenship on the basis of local household registration status when they come to cities; certain occupations are not open to them. They are not entitled to job security and welfare benefits such as housing, pensions, and medicare plans; their children are not allowed to enrol in local public schools.

The socialist state also creates problems through its retreat from social responsibilities. If the above examples of land monopolization and *hukou* discrimination indicate the pitfalls of China's insisting on the legacies of the socialist state's omni-control of social resources, the privatization of SOEs, or state-owned enterprises, is a prominent example in which the reducing of such omnipresence of the state, or state withdrawal, is equally causing tensions and protests. The SOE workers, as Chen analyses, once the pride of Mao's China, now feel "betrayed, hopeless, and desperate" during the marketization reform, especially because they have no channels to influence the decision of those very issues concerning their jobs and benefits, and no way to express their discontent except by protesting against late pay-cheques and unreasonable layoffs. As the privatization of the huge state sector is perhaps a necessary step in China for promoting economic development, the policies, attitudes, and measures of the bureaucracy to manage the privatization do more to stir popular discontent than help the workers. The socialist state is now employed to serve the development of capitalism, so to speak, and the deprived are unable to find either political or economic cures for their problems.

The state's strategy towards unemployment, as examined by Feng Xu in Chapter 4, provides one more typical example of how the state retreats during the marketization without assuming necessary responsibilities for promoting citizens' wellbeing. Xu's observation is that unemployment is a policy area where the Chinese government mixes governance techniques of both neo-liberal and Chinese communist orientations. This "modernization" of governance lays the burden of employment on the individual citizens in giving them the freedom of selling their labour, as said by classic Marxism, while the state still draws its political legitimacy, with the absence of democracy, from the self-claim of representing the interests of the Chinese people. How the socialist legacies distort citizens' freedom, according to Xu, is also reflected in the paradox in which the government has felt itself obliged to intervene as the guarantor of self-steering individualism among China's unemployed, rather than allow the self-steering individualism of the market itself to exercise its own disciplining force alone.

The state's retreat and its negative impact are even more evident in social welfare and social services, among which healthcare is prominent along with education and the like. There were reform efforts, for example, in healthcare, but, as Yanzhong Huang observes (Chapter 5), the reform has failed to achieve improvements in terms of either decreasing cost or increasing access and equality, due to the buckpassing polity in which the government is unwilling and incapable of shouldering its responsibilities. The national leaders' economy-centred approach to development together with their concern for legitimacy also contribute to this failure, as they marginalize health issues on the national development agenda, significantly reducing government health spending.

It is evident that, with the existing developmental model and with institutional arrangements as they are in China, both state monopoly, the legacy of Maoist socialism, and state retreat, the intrusion of capitalism into the nation's political-economic life, have created pitfalls for Chinese society. Further, the state machine itself creates social tensions due to its poor regulation, widespread malfunction, and rampant corruption. Though Yan Sun (Chapter 10) argues that with democracy India does no better than China in curbing corruption, many other researches, including many chapters in this volume, have found that numerous issues caused by the government's arbitrary decisions without sufficient and substantive influence from citizens fuel social tensions and stir public protests. For example, arbitrary taxes and fees collected by local governments once powerfully pushed rural residents to rebel.[2] Based on the Chinese official statistics, Chen (Chapter 2) also lists cadres' corruption as the second most significant issue causing rural unrest. Now the epidemic has been quickly spreading to urban areas, as university students, taxi drivers, hospital patients, and various clients and consumers of state-owned utility companies have to struggle for their respective work rights or complain about specific regulations harmful to their benefits or income rights (Chapter 2). It is not difficult to find that behind such events there is the problem of the absence, inadequacy, or blockage of the channels through which citizens may, by any means possible, influence public policy-making and governmental behaviour. One may argue that those group actions are one way to effectively participate in the Chinese context,[3] but it is obvious that such un-institutionalized, often uncontrollable, and in nature, confrontational "participation" costs more economically, socially, and politically than the conventional and collaborative participation that a democracy allows. To be sure, democracy will not be able to address all the regulative problems, but this does not say that the Chinese governmental policy-making institutions beyond the reach of ordinary citizens are working well to reduce popular grievances or improve governance. Though people may dispute over the question of what political economic arrangements work better for realizing good governance, it is without argument that in the Chinese context, the existing institutions, despite their remarkable performance in promoting economic growth, are more making than remedying social tensions.

Double-edged globalization: from living conditions of the poor to the spiritual dimensions of social conflicts

Though the growing social tensions in China are caused by various problems and take various forms, it is easy, and without the possibility of mistake, to identify those who suffer from such social situations and those who rebel against the sufferings. They primarily include the industrial workers of the state-owned enterprises under privatization programmes, the rural–urban migrant workers in the construction industry and foreign-funded firms, and the farmers who are facing eviction from their lands and houses due to industrialization and urbanization (Chen, Chapter 2; Wu, Chapter 3; and Zou, Chapter 8). Moreover, the women and youth of the working class find themselves disadvantageously competitive in the employment market, little protected in terms of social welfare, and much more vulnerable as the nation becomes more prosperous (Xu, Chapter 4).

They are not the minority of the populace. Rather, they are the majority, though without the voice, let alone the social and political influence, that should rightly match their proportion in this populous nation. The hugeness of their numbers puts them at a disadvantage, while the massive pool of these working classes helps secure the supply of cheap labour to international capital that comes into China. This vast pool of low-paid workers is, of course, one of the major comparative advantages of China's competitiveness on the global market; it is also, therefore, the class-relation foundation of China's economic prosperity in the age of globalization. These social classes were not really privileged during Maoist socialism, but they were at least entitled "the leadership classes" as the foundation of the proletarian dictatorship. China's embracing of marketization has dissolved this political illusion, leaving all-too obvious the ugly, cold reality, in which the erstwhile masters of socialism are selling their cheap labour to an alliance between their former servants, namely, the Party-state cadres, and those whom the Party-state previously claimed were the enemy, domestic and international capitalists.

The dramatic increase of labour disputes provides a clue for comprehending this new type of class relations in China. As shown by Chen in Chapter 2, the number of labour disputes increased from 47,951 cases in 1996, to 135,206 in

2000, and skyrocketed to 313,773 in 2005, representing an average annual dispute growth rate of 24 per cent. What is revealing is that in terms of the number of cases or of workers involved, labour disputes occurring in state-owned enterprises (SOEs) and collective-owned enterprises (COEs) have remained significantly large, while those in the non-state sector has kept growing. This indicates how the insertion of market into the Maoist socialist institutions, more so than either market or socialism alone, erodes the living conditions of the industrial workers. Further, according to Wu (Chapter 3), when a labour dispute takes place, local governments are more aligned with the interests of the employers than with the protection of workers' rights, because local governments are competing with each other for investments in order to boost local economic development, and serious implementation of the labour law would drive investors away – one more piece of evidence supporting the argument that the current pattern of state-led development, as it has been practised in China for decades, is to blame for the intensification of social conflicts.

As the state stands together with capital for promoting economic development at the price of working-class rights and benefits, social inequality inevitably increases, providing a major, powerful source of social protest. Due to the unique combination of market and Chinese socialism, inequality in today's China is also manifested in a conceptual triplicity: residual institutional inequality of state socialism, the market-driven inequality, and the inequality caused by the institutional insertion of market to state socialism that brings about mutual distortions of socialism and market. Socialist institutions in today's China still matter for redistribution, as reflected in the case of the *hukou* system, which, according to Wu, continues to be used as the main criterion to allocate government subsidies, welfare, and employment opportunities to local urban permanent residents while excluding farmers and rural–urban migrant workers. As his chapter records, with this system, most government services are not available to the rural–urban migrant workers. They have to pay extra fees to go to hospital, to rent an apartment, to have their children attend local schools. Moreover, many city governments have instituted a set of local regulations requiring migrants to have specific documents for their stay to be considered legal.

Further, there are institutional barriers to prevent these have-nots from defending their own material and non-material rights. The socialist state forbids the workers to organize their own unions, while the government-sponsored workers' associations have recently been allowed by the regime in foreign-owned plants as a check over the business people's profit-making practice if it jeopardizes workers' income and working conditions. Farmers and rural–urban migrant workers, however, are left living totally without organizations, despite the self-celebration of the ruling party of its representing of all people's interests. Ironically, the proposing of the so-called "Three Represents" theory that claims the Communist Party's overall representation of the Chinese people was tightly linked with the Party's path-breaking action to open its doors to capitalists. This, in turn, may "represent" an answer to why the working people are left behind when the Chinese regime embraces the pursuit of fortunes.

The Communist Party also claims to "represent advanced culture", which in practice also means the monopolizing power of the single party over the citizens' choices, this time in the spiritual realm. The role of economic marketization and globalization in this regard, however, seems different in that it deals in material production. Here it helps enlarge space for diversity and individual choices, and thus is in confrontation with the Chinese state which still struggles to maintain its dominion over people's minds while, with tremendous difficulties, adapting itself to the growing diversity. As McCormick observes (Chapter 7), there has been a change from Leninist China, in which the communication media were a critical means by which the Party and state mobilized power, integrated into state hierarchies, and disseminated information and perspectives in accordance with the political correctness decided by party-state leaders, to contemporary China, in which the mass media are now expected to succeed in competitive markets while the Party-state remains powerful in managing public opinion. The market competition, in any event, has created new incentives for media entrepreneurs, and has led to importing global culture and disseminating critical news. This challenges China's still-authoritarian leaders.

The matters concerning beliefs are even more troublesome for Chinese society in general and, in particular, for an authoritarian regime "with totalistic aspirations", in Hamrin's words (Chapter 6). In analysing China's involvement with the global market of belief systems, Hamrin has found that, with the Chinese citizens' growing awareness of the necessity of individual options in beliefs rather than a blind following of the ruling Communist Party's ideology, "there is a wide spectrum of collaboration, compliance, and contention between state and society, and growing competition among old and new belief systems, with much diversity of outcome in different spaces of this more complex society". Globalization as a "cultural earthquake" intensifies this dynamic, making China's peculiar hybrid "market Leninism" in a dilemma of participation in the global economy and resistance against global cultures.

This tension yields a series of elements that help create China's social conflicts. As Chen observes, the protests of Falun Gong members against the state crackdown constitute a considerable portion of China's recent growing collective actions. Meanwhile, as indicated by Hamrin, Christian resistance to political repression is becoming a remarkable phenomenon in the Chinese populace's thriving spiritual pursuit. Moreover, ethnic tensions that widely exist in China are often related to the struggle between religious autonomy and state dominance. Hamrin is definitely correct in observing that "[t]he widespread worry about corruption and social tension is creating a search for new moral sources of personal and social ethics by which to live" which leads to the rise and resurgence of various religious beliefs in Chinese society. As this search will not abate as the nation becomes wealthier than before, the trend is clear that more and more conflicts will arise between the spiritual autonomy of Chinese society and state control of human minds. The single-minded welcome of economic globalization by the Chinese Communist Party will not work to handle the double-edged sword of a global flowing of materials and ideas that has tremendous ramifications in the realms beyond economics.

Governing social tensions: national policy adjustments and local governmental resistance

The Chinese Party-state has paid close attention to all the social problems, of course. Its ability to resolve the conflicts, however, has been for a long time under debate. There is no doubt that various governmental adaptations took place for governing the new China that has experienced three decades of market transition, but the social and political effectiveness of the regime adaptation has been in question.[4] Further, adaptation is only one side of the story. The post-Tiananmen Chinese authorities have never ceased repressive, sometimes violent, actions to put down social unrest when they feel threatened. State control of mass communication has been constantly strengthened, in response to the spreading of information high technology which enables more and more Chinese citizens to get access to wider and, often, freer, channels of information acquisition, as noticed by McCormick (Chapter 7). Our focus, however, is on one dimension of the politics of surviving of the authoritarian regime, namely, how the regime adaptation takes place and how it is constrained by various elements, leaving other aspects of state response, like repression, in the background.

Roughly speaking, the Chinese Party-state has made three not-exclusive kinds of efforts to strengthen its governance capability to make socio-economic changes in order to reduce, or, at least, relax, social tensions. They are adjustments of national policies, reforms of the legislative and legal systems, and adaptive changes of political institutions. In this section we shall discuss the first, as the next section turns to the other two measures.

In terms of policy adjustment, the Hu Jintao-Wen Jiabao leadership has initiated a cluster of platforms, programmes, and policy measures since 2002 when it came into office, all with backbones consisting of the "people-oriented" attitude (*yimin weiben*), perspective of "scientific development" (*kexue fezhan guan*), and the concept of "harmonious society" (*hexie shehui*). Some policy measures were devised to flesh out the platforms. These include the abolishing of agricultural taxes, the initiation of rural public health programmes, and tighter supervision by the central government over local land uses. The policies have had an impact, but they also have their constraints, of which the most fundamental comes from the heavy dependence of the regime's political legitimacy upon rapid economic growth.

In the contemporary Chinese context, political legitimacy can be analysed at two levels: government or state legitimacy, and leader or individual legitimacy. That is to say, not only the authoritarian Party-state relies on its good economic performance to maintain legitimacy of ruling China, as it has been doing in the past decades, but the individual leaders of the Communist Party also need to convince their comrades and organizations that they are qualified to occupy their current, if not higher, positions because they are able to promote economic development. With power transition from the revolutionary generation to technocrats, this issue of Chinese politics becomes prominent and even pressing, as the power/position competition within the Party elite goes on. Incumbents and aspirants to power have to cite their accomplishments of governance (*zhengji*) to support and promote their ascendance within the Party-state power hierarchy. At the same time, non-political, often illegitimate benefits that the individual Party-state cadres may draw from economic development of their jurisdictions are even greater, for them, than the political utilities of economic growth. Such benefits are more widespread than career benefits among Party-state cadres, as the opportunity to gain and improve them involves all cadres, including those who may have no further career ambitions. In other words, extremely strong incentives widely exist for the Chinese Party-state as a whole and for its cadres as individuals to promote economic growth for their own power and wealth. This "developmental mentality" constrains both the contents and implementation of those policy measures proposed by the Hu–Wen leadership, and it works in various ways to minimize the national policies' effectiveness.

Local governmental resistance to the national policy adjustments to reduce social tensions comes into prominence in this context. As many contributors to this volume have noticed, "there is a wide gap between what the central government promises and what local officials deliver" (Chen, Chapter 2), and the increasing discrepancy between the preferences of central and political leaders, on the one hand, and local and bureaucratic officials, on the other, always allows the latter to pursue, in a strategic manner, their departmental or personal interests at the expense of the public interest (Huang, Chapter 5). On the issue of rural–urban migrant workers, for example, Wu (Chapter 3) has observed the important role local governments play in generating rather than mitigating the problems, as local governments, for their better record of economic development, provide no help to the workers while counting the workers' contributions to local GDP. This incentive, rooted in the "developmental mentality", further accounts for local governmental resistance to reforms of the *hukou* system that disadvantage the migrant workers.

The *xinfang* or mass petition system, systematically examined by Zou in Chapter 8, is particularly relevant to this institutional dilemma of central-local relations vis-à-vis social discontent. Although the offices for *xinfang* exist at every level of Party committees and governments, the petitioners involved in *xinfang* activities still prefer overcoming various difficulties by personally visiting the national bureau in charge of *xinfang* to seeking ultimate help from central leaders for their grievances. This implies a distrust of local authorities. The system, to a large extent, is actually designed as a mechanism of Chinese authoritarianism for national leaders to monitor local authorities through a direct information flow to the national leadership from those citizens who suffer. A serious challenge has arisen to this system, according to Zou's report, as the number of petitioners is said to have reached a "flood peak" in recent years and is expected to continue climbing. This clearly illustrates the failure of local governance; as huge pressures mount over the national government, the tug of war between central and local authorities is intensified. The strategy the central leadership adopts, however, is simply to kick the ball back into the local government's court. Under the newly formulated guidelines, by which "who is in charge, is responsible [to remedy the problems that cause petitions]", mass petitioners get virtually no help from either Beijing or their local emperors. Furthermore, as Zou concludes, "local governments used the new Central regulations to control *xinfang* activities in their localities, rather than sincerely resolve the problems raised by the petitioners". It is, therefore, no surprise that the rate of success for *xinfang* is extremely low. It is said that only 0.2 per cent of petitioners resolved their problems directly through the *xinfang* system.

As local resistance to the regime's efforts to resolve social injustices becomes a growing obstacle to the building of a so-called "harmonious society", the imperatives for centralization and concentration of power is often recommended to the national leadership as an effective strategy for reforms.[5] In the Chinese context of post-reform, however, both practically and normatively, the recentralization of power is problematic, especially for the governance of social tensions. The feasibility problem mainly lies in the significant functions of local states in economic development, functions which, as emphasized before, bolster the political legitimacy of the whole authoritarian regime. A recentralization programme has to retreat when it undermines these functions. Moreover, the effective centralization of state power would leave local governments weak and sluggish in dealing with social unrest, something opposite to the assumed goals of social stability. Strong local power can help to govern localities, of course. As we have seen too often in China, on the other hand, such power with only supervision from above but no checks from below is inclined to create social tensions rather than remedy them, because the local cadres' discretionary power always comes to the bullying of ordinary citizens. As the 17th Party Congress wrote "harmonious society" into the Party constitution but proposed no way to resolve this dilemma, all the beautiful phrases and platforms aiming at a "harmonious society" are no more than empty rhetoric.

Beyond economics: institutional adaptation and its political constraints

Legislative innovations and legal reforms may create stronger institutional constraints than policy adjustments on cadres' misbehaviour that often cause social protests, but in Chinese politics this is truer in theory than in practice.[6] Zou, as an expert on Chinese law and the Chinese legal system, notices that the current legal system in China is not effective in resolving the social disputes within its mandate (Chapter 8). To build people's confidence in using legal means to defend their legitimate rights and interests, problems due to judicial corruption and litigation costs must be solved. His conclusion is that "The current legal aid system in China is far from enough to provide legal assistance for the needy people".

Trying to understand the process by which legal innovations are diffused in an authoritarian regime, political scientist Pierre Landry (Chapter 9) has found that the ruling party's control over the judiciary contradicts the regime's self-proclaimed goal of building the "rule of law". Under the conditions in which information flows are heavily controlled, and social activists and lawyers who engage judicial institutions are routinely harassed, going to court – particularly if one challenges state officials or seeks to sue the national or local government – remains a highly charged political affair and, therefore, extremely difficult, if it is ever possible. Following Stanley Lubman,[7] both Landry and Zou describe the system under their respective scrutiny as "a bird in a cage", which highlights the political inhibitions that confine both functions of the Chinese legal system and the efforts to reform them. Zou points out a series of dilemmas besetting the reforms of the *xinfang* system, and also other parts of the legal endeavour to govern social tensions. While the system allows ordinary people to exercise the right to petition, it gives priority to maintaining social stability; as a product of "rule of man", it contravenes the ongoing legal reform towards the rule of law and is detrimental to the building of the legal awareness of the Chinese citizens and of a rule-of-law society. Zou is correct to conclude that "the nature of the *xinfang* system has changed from a means of enhancing the connections of the Party to the masses to a means of controlling society and the people". This is also perfectly applicable to China's legal system and its reforms.

Many observers of Chinese reform share the point that political institutional reform can be the niche to reconstruct China's state-society relations in order to effectively address social tensions, although their views vary about how much China has carried out political reform and how effectively these reform measures have ameliorated social contradictions.[8] Many contributors to this volume hold a pessimistic view in this regard, emphasizing how administrative innovations are often paralysed by political constraints under the existing institutional framework. For example, though acknowledging the Hu–Wen leadership's post-SARS effort to improve China's healthcare, Huang (Chapter 5) finds that all the measures "fall short of addressing the fundamental problems in public financing, central-local relations, and bureaucratic incentive structure", and concludes that in the absence of fundamental changes in the polity, a policy shift alone is unlikely to bring to Chinese people affordable, accessible, equitable, and quality healthcare.

China's effort to "internationalize" its governance sometimes fools observers, however. Yes, the Chinese authorities have learnt much from international society in terms of public and social administrations, and knowledge and expertise in that regard pour into China from the outside through globalization. In particular, the Chinese authorities have adopted some neo-liberal measures of governance, though ideologically it decries neo-liberalism. This has no contradiction with the getting-rid-of social responsibilities by the Chinese state, as analysed by Xu on employment (Chapter 4), Huang on public healthcare (Chapter 5), and Wu on rural–urban migrant workers' living conditions (Chapter 3). Rather, it is actually a part of the "grand strategy" of the Chinese ruling party to trade social and economic functions of socialism for its political monopoly in the name of socialism. In other words, the Chinese regime keeps its nature of monopolizing political power by utilizing those things which can be utilized, including the market mechanisms. The world dominated by capitalist globalization often chooses to applaud social irresponsibility in the name of marketization, but ignores the political obsession of authoritarianism.

This mistake, for professional observers of China, is perhaps less because of the considerations of their own material or academic interests than their hidden Eurocentric approach when viewing the oriental nation. The approach often has two seemingly contradictory assumptions, as it either believes that any step China takes to follow globalization that spreads Western standards is laudable, or that anything reflecting China's uniqueness is valuable. With the conventional ideological spectrum, we may say that Rightists, or those in political and economic power, often follow the first assumption while the Left and generally the intellectuals incline to the second. Both are able to find reasons to favour today's China. For intellectuals, though they are, more often than not, able to reflect critically on the West, it seems they are less often able or willing to do the same thing with China. The sophistication of the Chinese regime in dealing with globalization is widely admired. This leads to a certain loss of intellectual sophistication in comprehending China, particularly as the Chinese Party-state has learnt, in Xu's incisive argument, to follow the West's way of framing freedom to steer citizens towards the government's desired policy goals. Xu is right in saying that China, as an authoritarian regime, is increasingly adopting international norms and standards. She is even more right in reminding us that adopting neo-liberal ways of governing does not necessarily mean China is giving up its political authoritarianism.

In the realms more political than administrative, the Party-state's adaptation is even more limited and hindered, and it has to turn to coercion and violence to maintain the single party's monopoly of political power. When China's commercialized media imitate their US counterparts to broadcast the hit television series *Super Voice Girls*, McCormick has found (Chapter 7) that the Chinese government can carefully distinguish between the public goods that are necessary for economic growth and those that are politically sensitive, and allows the former to prosper but represses the latter. Nevertheless, Chinese television has also imported foreign formats, and a limited space and strong financial incentives for critical journalism are emerging. But, in McCormick's sentence, "Party authorities closely monitor the press and Internet to make sure that their injunctions are followed." As he argues, it remains that state coercion is a major factor in keeping China as it is.

To echo this, Hamrin (Chapter 6) has observed a trend of the state's increasingly tight control over religions and this trend is more powerful than its willingness to adapt to the social transformation that has been allowing spiritual diversity. According to her, "The Soviet approach remains quite evident in the PRC's current outdated and unpopular framework of social policy towards non-communist groups, including religions." Various institutional and regulative mechanisms work in this line, including the United Front system that imposes indirect, hidden, but not less effective, nor less powerful, Party control over social organizations, and the bureaucratic regulations that aim to contain and re-shape religion to suit state purposes. By July 1999, with the regime's ban on Falun Gong and other cults, the state had become the primary arbiter of orthodoxy versus heterodoxy, with arbitrary application by most local officials.

The rise of social forces and the political dynamics of social transformation

One significant aftermath of the increasing social tension is its stimulation of citizens' collective actions of defending their various economic, social, and civic rights, and, accordingly, the emergence and crystallization of social forces in China's political life. Despite political restrictions, non-governmental organizations, most of them being internationalized, have emerged on the institutional landscape of authoritarian politics of China, while those social forces without clear or coherent organizational formats are equally powerful as movements influencing the country's state–society relations. They have been enlarging the social space of citizen engagement that had been banned or monopolized by the state and its affiliated associations. Moreover, they are often engaged, though spontaneously and loosely organized, in the fight against the willpower of government. Where violations of citizens' rights by the government–business coalition prevail, resistance arises in responses, as what we have discussed above concerning urban redevelopment eviction, rural land-seizure, environmental pollution, and the abuse of public power in making improper regulations. Most of the so-called "mass incidents" are actually more or less collective actions by citizens to defend their rights. *Weiquan*, or "defending rights", therefore, has become a new, popular word with a high frequency of usage.

This unleashing of new social forces speaks volumes about China's changing state–society relations and, accordingly, about the future political change of the nation. For the convenience of analysis, we may discuss the impact from several angles, including: the rise of civil society, its internationalization, and its politicization; the state's Janus-faced response to social forces and the limited effectiveness of such responses; and how mounting social pressure works to promote China's governance and further its political transformation. Generally speaking, state–society tensions arise to change the trajectory of China's transformation which during post-Mao years was once propelled by state–society collaboration. To quote Chen's sentences (Chapter 2), today's China is witnessing a situation that "has indeed raised the citizenship consciousness of ordinary citizens who have seen the failure of their expectation for redress of grievances through legal or political institutions", and the new set of state–society relations appears to be "developing into key factors that are challenging regime stability in the near future, and to a certain extent, are becoming primary incentives behind regime transformation".

On the side of society, citizenship consciousness has now risen to a degree that the PRC history had never seen before, which at least indicates the partial failure of the Party-state's strategy of combining economic buying and propagandized education for the purpose of maintaining its one-Party dictatorship. Though such a strategy is perhaps more successful among the younger generation in their twenties or even thirties, the elder citizens who have been educated by life still form the majority of the Chinese populace and will stay on the social stage for two to three decades – a span during which regime change is very likely to take place in China. Exposure to international opinion and practice, as observed by Hamrin, has fuelled a new rights consciousness among Chinese citizens. As the younger generations definitely have more opportunities of exposure to global society, the long-term future perhaps will be not so dim.

What deserves special attention is the cross-class nature of the phenomenon. This means that, first of all, the poor people, though more constrained by their disadvantageous material conditions, lack of organizational ability, and limited access into information and effective communication, are becoming aware of their rights. In this regard, Zou's contribution to this volume supports the findings by other scholars elsewhere such as O'Brien and Li, as Zou observes that the transition from appeals to rights protection movements has well indicated that the ordinary people no longer believe modern Bao Qing Tian. "Instead, they organize themselves to seek and safeguard their legitimate rights and interests prescribed under the law" (Chapter 8).

Second, social fabric with the potential of politicization has been developed, and will be further matured, during such a rise of social forces, which will help greatly to make a Chinese civil society that inclines to democratization. East Asian nations lack the tradition of liberal civil society; this is even true for those democratized polities like Taiwan and South Korea where scholars have found pro-authoritarian statist political attitudes prevailing among the middle classes, particularly the business groups, during the democratic transitions.[9] This seems truer in the China under the state-led market transition, as the middle classes are growing from none under Maoist politics to an emerging but state-dependent status.[10] Although China already has been away from Mao's era for three decades, until recently it was not able to escape the state–society dichotomy in which societal elements have to either attach themselves to the state or be content to be without political influence. The rise of social protests is seemingly changing this towards the direction of active citizen engagements with social support, though at this stage one has to be cautious in assessing its political power of influencing public policies.

Religious factors become prominent in this regard. As Hamrin notices (Chapter 6), religious beliefs and practices, Christianity in particular, continue to grow almost exponentially in China, as part of the underlying dynamic intrinsic to globalization. It has "penetrated all sectors and levels of society to include prominent business leaders, artists and entertainers, intellectuals, and even government officials who technically cannot embrace religion in their status as Communist Party members and thus practice their faith in private". With better equipment of autonomous organizations and global links, religious rights defenders are, to quote Hamrin, "becoming important to the negotiation of a new informal social contract and of new institutional relations between a society outgrowing socialism and a state experiencing a spillover effect from international economic and governance norms".

The ball thus comes into the regime's court. Sooner or later, a political transition away from existing institutions is inevitable. Though the direction of such a transition is uncertain, it probably will add more liberal and democratic elements to Chinese politics. The regime's attitude towards the arising of social forces can be a determining factor for the future path China takes for the political transition: if state–society cooperation occurs, regime transformation, as the scenario elaborated in Huntington's typology of democratization,[11] will be likely to take place with comparatively few social and economic costs. This may be desirable for many Chinese but so far, in the post-Tiananmen politics, there have been no such positive signs. On the contrary, the regime has drawn a lesson from the 1980s' toleration of social discontent that resulted in Tiananmen protests, and now defines them as "hostile" and takes a confrontational approach to independent social activities. As McCormick (Chapter 7) has observed, in the politically sensitive realm of mass communication, more journalists were detained in China than in any other country, and the vast majority of journalists have chosen to avoid doing anything that would cause trouble with the authorities. "The authorities have retained the ability to intervene at will almost anywhere in the media. They can and do suspend publications, dismiss journalists, and from time to time, arrest, slander, or beat those who challenge their authority." In general, there has been an overall effort by the Party-state to regain central authority over society, according to Hamrin, which has resulted in the weakening of the organizational capacity of all types of civic organizations.

The Party-state is no longer omni-powerful to do whatever it likes to do, however. McCormick is correct in saying that "Repression remains effective, but is more visible and open to public challenge than at any time since 1989." State repression can fail to achieve its goals, and this is what has often happened in today's China. Moreover, two interrelated factors, namely, state retreat and state impotence, make the state even more vulnerable while at the same time the factors powerfully generate the rise of social forces. As Xu has found, state retreat from providing social welfare makes a conundrum, to resolve which the Chinese government has to call on social forces to be involved in addressing social issues. Hamrin echoes this soundly, observing that the state can no longer afford to provide sufficient services for everyone, and is turning to non-state actors – domestic and foreign – to fill the growing gap. According to Hamrin, "This explains the growing awareness of governments of the usefulness of what are vaguely termed 'social forces,' even faith-based social service providers and religious charities."

This forms a vital pre-condition that shapes the political environment in which social pressure comes to work for promoting the quality of governance and the potentiality of political transformation. In general, Chen is right to conclude that "it is apparent that the alarming rise of mass protests over the past decade has provoked the government to pledge the building of a harmonious society". Specifically, we have many cases that have demonstrated how the protests of society pushed the state to remedy what it otherwise would choose to ignore. For rural–urban migrants, Wu shows us how public outrage culminated around the tragic fate of Sun Zhigang, a college-educated migrant in Guangdong province who was beaten to death in police custody after being detained on suspicion of vagrancy, gave impetus to the abolition of the Custody and Repatriation system. In Chapter 2, Chen also states how the national leadership became tolerant of and even encouraged the setting-up of trade unions in FDI enterprises for the purpose of empowering workers to defend their rights, as the deprivation of such rights often evokes popular opposition that threatens the regime's highest priority of maintaining social stability.

The regime works hard to defend its bottom line, of course, which is the single party's monopoly of political power. Changes that undermine this are not allowed. Further, various institutional and practical constraints exist, as we have discussed before, to curb the functions of new social forces such as trade unions. For example, only the worker unions affiliated with the state-led All China Federation of Trade Unions (ACFTU) are allowed, and this affiliation often reduces rather than strengthens the organizational capacity of grassroots trade unions to fight for workers' benefits, because the ACFTU has to closely follow the Party-state whose legitimacy depends on economic growth. Moreover, as Chen points out, as the effectiveness of worker organizations to enhance the workers' bargaining power with employers often depends on how the unions are run. Due to the absence of intra-democracy of such organizations in the Chinese reality, their organizational power in defence of workers' rights is weak. All it simply means is that China's new social forces will encounter tremendous political hindrance as they emerge, and that they must, first of all, struggle for their own survival and development while they struggle to improve social conditions. In any event, society–state interaction in China is becoming dynamic, and, therefore, direction of the nation's progress will not be solely determined by those who possess material wealth and political power.

Concluding remarks

After the investigations of the causes of social tensions that are spreading in today's China, we have found that the social problems are rooted in the Chinese pattern of economic development and the authoritarian political institutions that govern that development. We have also analysed the responses of the state to social tensions, particularly its policy adjustments and institutional adaptations in this regard, and have found that, the fundamental political restructuring being absent, such adjustments and adaptations cannot go beyond developmental and institutional constraints despite any effort the leadership may make. This suggests a portrait of China with either a lasting, parallel course ahead or, some may say, a race between rising social tensions and the state's ability to govern them, implying that in the foreseeable future neither one will be able to overwhelm the other. Social tensions will be growing despite the various strategies, effective or not, adopted by the state. In the short term, like five to ten years, the state will constantly strengthen its capacity, by every means it possesses, to maintain social stability, stability being defined as the absence of a great uprising of national chaos or regime change. Provided other factors, such as abrupt economic downturn or cross-Taiwan Strait crisis, do not occur, the state will continue as it currently proceeds.

This scenario means a China in dispersed, protracted, and, in terms of ignitable issues and political impacts, spasmodic social unrest for years to come, and a Party-state in a concentrated but nervous and insecure mood of making constant yet institutionally insubstantial efforts to deal with social discontent. Such state–society relations, in turn, imply an unfavourable climate for political reform from above, while the incentives to push such reforms from the bottom will not be strong enough to realize themselves while state repression still works. Social forces independent from the authoritarian state will grow, but remain far from becoming powerful enough to initiate national political change. They will mount greater and greater pressure on the regime, however, which will force the regime to struggle to improve its accountability. The tug-of-war between social progress and authoritarian stability will be a key to the comprehending of China.

Globalization provides resources and momentum for both sides, as we have said before, as a double-edged sword cutting into this Chinese framework of state–society relations. For its political purposes of enforcing state control, the authoritarian state is able to utilize the economic power it draws through the embracing of globalization, while it also learns, often successfully, to take some international norms and Western governance tactics to strengthen its ability to balance on the fine line between adapting to economic-social changes and resisting the fundamental restructuring of political institutions. Various social factors, on the other hand, are also able to draw strength from international norms and global links, taking advantage of the regime's ambiguous attitudes towards capitalist globalization. In other words, globalization and China's involvement in it do not yield a single-dimensional effect on China's social and political transformation. What kind of strategies China's social and political actors take to deal with globalization and what kind of international pressure that globalization puts on China's social and political structures are thus critical to the amount of weight behind those different parties in the state–society tug-of-war.

Notes

1 For a wider phenomenon of how the state increases its role in economic development of the developing world, see an update discussion in Atul Kohli, *State-Directed Development: Political Power and Industrialization in the Global Periphery*, New York: Cambridge University Press, 2004; and a comparative study in the East Asian context in Masahiko Aoki, Hyung-ki Kim, and Masahiro Okuno-Fujiwara (eds), *The Role of Government in East Asian Economic Development: Comparative Institutional Analysis*, Oxford: Clarendon Press, 1997. For the declining side of state power in Chinese citizens' daily life, see, for instance, Merle Goldman and Roderick MacFarquhar (eds), *The Paradox of China's Post-Mao Reforms*, Cambridge: Harvard University Press, 1999.

2 Kevin J. O'Brien and Lianjiang Li, *Rightful Resistance in Rural China*, New York: Cambridge University Press, 2006; Thomas P. Bernstein and Xiaobo Lu, *Taxation*

without Representation in Contemporary Rural China, New York: Cambridge University Press, 2003.

3 As following Tianjian Shi's defining of political participation in the Chinese context. See Tianjian Shi, *Political Participation in Beijing*, Cambridge: Harvard University Press, 1997.

4 For different, sometimes contradictory, interpretations and assessments of China's regime adaptation to a market society, see, for example, Andrew J. Nathan, "Authoritarian Resilience", *Journal of Democracy* 14:1, January 2003, pp. 6–17; Dali L. Yang, *Remaking the Chinese Leviathan: Market Transition and the Politics of Governance in China*, Stanford: Stanford University Press, 2004; Minxin Pei, *China's Trapped Transition: The Limits of Developmental Autocracy*, Cambridge: Harvard University Press, 2006; and Kellee Tsai, "Adaptive Informal Institutions and Endogenous Institutional Change in China", *World Politics* 59, October 2006, pp. 116–41.

5 There have been at least two major rounds of such proposals since China began its reform, as indicated in so-called "neo-authoritarianism" of the late 1980s and the fiscal centralization in the mid-1990s. For records of policy proposals and debates of the two rounds, see, for example, Liu Jun and Li Lin (eds), *Xin quanwei zhuyi* (Neo-Authoritarianism), Beijing: Beijing jingji xueyuan chubanshe, 1989 and Wang Shaoguang and Hu Angang, *Zhongguo guojia nengli baogao* (Report on China's State Capacity), Shenyang: Liaoning renmin chubanshe, 1993. This centralization impulse of reform is much more beyond the case of China and often across ideological spectrum. See, for example, Samuel P. Huntington, *Political Order in Changing Societies*, New Haven: Yale University Press, 1968 and Peter Evans, Dietrich Rueschemeyer, and Theda Skocpol (eds), *Bringing the State Back In*, New York: Cambridge University Press, 1985.

6 For an updated review of China's legal reform, see Keyuan Zou, *China's Legal Reform: Towards the Rule of Law*, Leiden: Martinus Nijhoff Publishers, 2006.

7 Stanley B. Lubman, *Bird in a Cage: Legal Reform in China After Mao*, Stanford: Stanford University Press, 1999.

8 See note 4, particularly Yang and Pei.

9 David Martin Jones, "Democratization, Civil Society, and Illiberal Middle Class Culture in Pacific Asia", *Comparative Politics* 30:2, January 1998, pp. 147–69.

10 Margaret Pearson, *China's New Business Elite: The Political Results of Economic Reform*, Berkeley: University of California Press, 1997; Bruce J. Dickson, *Red Capitalists in China: The Party, Private Entrepreneurs, and Prospects for Political Change*, New York: Cambridge University Press, 2003. Also, Victoria E. Bonnell and Thomas B. Gold (eds), *New Entrepreneurs of Europe and Asia: Russia, Eastern Europe and China*, Armonk: M. E. Sharpe, 2002.

11 Samuel P. Huntington, *The Third Wave: Democratization in the Late Twentieth Century*, Norman: University of Oklahoma Press, 1991, chapter 3.

Index